From the Lower Deck.

FROM
THE LOWER DECK

The Royal Navy

1780-1840

Henry Baynham

BARRE PUBLISHERS
BARRE, MASSACHUSETTS, 1970

First published in Great Britain 1969
First American edition 1970
Barre Publishers, Barre, Massachusetts, U.S.A.
Library of Congress Catalog Card No. 73–102005
S.B.N. 8271–7001–7
Copyright © 1969 by H. W. F. Baynham

Not for sale in the British Commonwealth or its territories

Printed in Great Britain

CONTENTS

**Dates are those of the seaman's service in the Royal Navy*

AUTHOR'S NOTE

This book is an attempt to tell briefly the story of the Royal Navy in the period 1780-1840 as far as possible in the words of the seamen who served on the fleet on the lower deck.

G. M. Trevelyan in the introduction to his *Social History of England* defines social history as history with the politics left out. This has always seemed to me a most inadequate definition. It is no more possible to write history leaving the politics out than it is to write a history of mankind leaving the men out, though this has been attempted. This book then is not simply a description of the conditions on the lower deck at the time as described by the men themselves. Certainly, wherever possible, I have let the men speak for themselves, but this is rather a history of the navy as viewed from the lower deck. Of course, conditions of service, punishments, the behaviour of the officers, all play a far greater part in this story than they would in an orthodox history of the navy, but equally the sailors' point of view must be examined against the background of the political history of the time, of the battles, and of the role that the navy was called upon to play.

The collection of sources was inevitably difficult and I am grateful first and foremost to the Headmaster and Governors of Canford School for allowing me a summer off to carry out these researches and to the Master and Fellows of Balliol College, Oxford, for awarding me a studentship at the College. I am also particularly grateful to the *Daily Express* for publishing an appeal for letters and papers which was most generously answered. All these cannot be acknowledged here but I would particularly like to thank Mr. Frederick Stokes for the loan of his forebear's journal. I received many more of a later period which I hope to include in another volume. Not least I am grateful to Mrs. Spooner of Wimborne for her help in typing the manuscript and to Christopher Sandy, Nicholas Willey and Peter Oakshett of Canford School for their help with the index and glossary, and to Professor Christopher Lloyd for reading the manuscript.

As copies of most of the memoirs that are quoted in this volume are extremely rare, it is worth while indicating where and when they were published. In addition, three further seamen's memoirs, not included here, should be mentioned. One of these, by John Bechervaise, though his career falls largely in this period, served for some time in the Arctic, and as Arctic exploration forms one of the major aspects of the period after 1840, I have not included his memoirs in this volume. A second, William Richardson, possibly could have been included here, especially as his services covered the period 1780–1817. He rose to the rank of Gunner and as a consequence his views are somewhat more favourable than those of his contemporaries, but though he was initially 'Pressganged' he does not strictly come 'From the Lower Deck'. His memoirs were edited by Colonel Spencer Childers and were published by John Murray in 1908. A third, Robert Wilson, I have not included as his memoirs are readily available in a volume of Journals, 1789–1817, edited by Rear Admiral H. G. Thursfield and published by the Naval Records Society in 1951. This volume also includes a number of letters from the lower deck which are of some interest.

Of the memoirs included here, only one has been reprinted in the last fifty years—those of John Nicol. These originally appeared in 1822, written down by John Howell who made Nicol's acquaintance when Nicol was an old and impoverished man and drew from the old seaman reminiscences of the navy. The book was published in Edinburgh by William Blackwood. In 1937 it was rediscovered by Alexander Laing and republished by Cassell.

Jack Nastyface's *Nautical Economy* first appeared in 1836. It was published by 'William Robinson' at 9 Staining Lane—the name of the publisher being one of the arguments for identifying Jack Nastyface with William Robinson. The book created quite a stir at the time, but has not been reprinted and is now very rare.

Samuel Leech's book had a more distinguished career. It was written for an American audience and was first published in Boston in 1843. It rapidly went through at least fifteen editions and clearly achieved considerable popularity. It was published in London in 1844 and there was another edition in 1851 and it appears to have been almost as popular in England. As a point of interest, the frontispiece in the American edition shows the dismasted *Macedonian* defeated by the *United States*, while the English edition has a ship in full sail! The book was republished in the U.S.A. in 1909 as an extra to the periodical, *The Magazine of History*.

The rarest of the printed memoirs are undoubtedly those of George Watson and there is not even a copy of them in the British Museum. The book was, unusually, published in Newcastle which was George Watson's home town. It has similarly not been republished. Charles M'Pherson published his *Life on Board a Man of War* in 1829 not long after the Battle of Navarino itself.

Of the printed memoirs to which brief reference has been made, Charles Pemberton's were published under the title of *Pel Verjudice* in London in 1853; Robert Hay's life was edited by his great grandson and this was published by Rupert Hart-Davis in 1953 to whom grateful acknowledgement is made for permission to quote. The account of the mutiny at Spithead comes from *Greenwich Hospital*, published in 1826, and the letter on Trafalgar from W. H. Long's *Naval Yarns*, published in 1899.

Of the manuscripts, that of Samuel Stokes was kindly lent by Frederick Stokes, and the letter from *H.M.S. Excellent* by Mrs D. M. Gosling.

The description of the masts, rigging and sails in Appendix Two comes from an anonymous autobiography *Ran away to Sea*, published by J. & C. Brown in 1854.

H.W.F.B

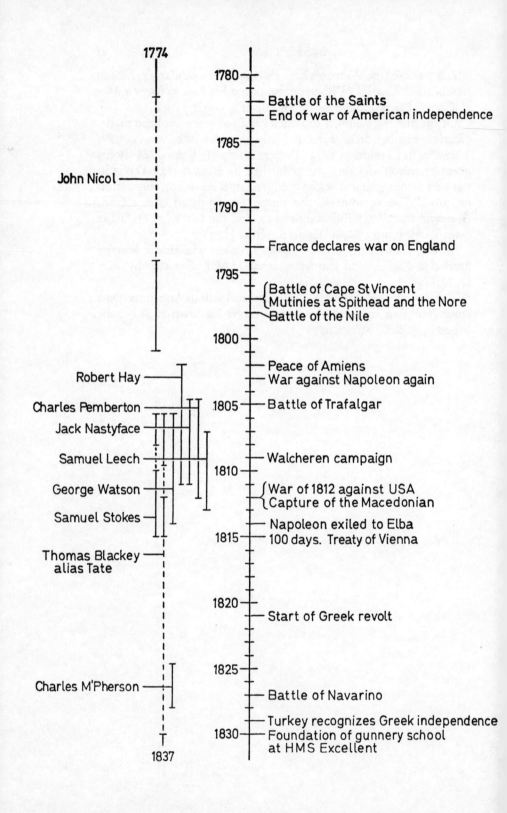

1774

1780 —
— Battle of the Saints
— End of war of American independence

1785 —

John Nicol ——

1790 —

— France declares war on England

1795 —
{ Battle of Cape St Vincent
{ Mutinies at Spithead and the Nore
— Battle of the Nile

1800 —

— Peace of Amiens
Robert Hay —— — War against Napoleon again

1805 — Battle of Trafalgar
Charles Pemberton ——
Jack Nastyface ——

Samuel Leech —— — Walcheren campaign
1810 —
{ War of 1812 against USA
George Watson —— { Capture of the Macedonian

Samuel Stokes —— — Napoleon exiled to Elba
1815 — 100 days. Treaty of Vienna
Thomas Blackey ——
alias Tate

1820 —
— Start of Greek revolt

1825 —
Charles M'Pherson ——
— Battle of Navarino

— Turkey recognizes Greek independence
1830 — Foundation of gunnery school
at HMS Excellent

1837

THE NAVY BEFORE NELSON

The Press Gang and the Mutinies of 1797

IN THE DOCKYARD at Portsmouth lies the last and the most famous of all the 'Ships of the Line', H.M.S. *Victory*, Nelson's flagship at Trafalgar. There she is, preserved as near as possible in the state she was when, in September 1805, she set sail from England carrying Nelson to his greatest victory and to his death. The rigging has been replaced and the rotten timbers in her hull renewed, and standing on the upper deck it is not difficult to imagine her, with canvas spread, setting out on her great mission. To recreate the scene below decks, however, requires more imagination. Broad stairways have replaced the rope ladders and, though there is an example of what a mess looked like, even in a Bank Holiday crowd it is almost impossible to conceive the crush of men on the lower deck by day. At night the whole area would have been solid with men (each man was only allowed from fourteen to sixteen inches in which to sling his hammock—'Like bats suspended by the heels to the roof of a cavern'), and it is certain that, with the wet and the stench, the impression obtained from a sight of conditions below decks would have little in common with the glamorous shore-side view of a majestic man-of-war dipping down the channel.

This unpleasant aspect of life on the lower deck in the time of Nelson is too often forgotten. The accepted image of the sailor is that presented by Marryat or even more sentimental authors; Jack is painted as a brave and fearless soul, generally contented with his conditions, caring only for the seafaring life and prepared to give his all in the service of his captain, his ship and his country. It would be over-emphasising the squalid aspects of life at sea if this was completely denied, and a letter supposedly written home by a seaman in the *Royal Sovereign* (Collingwood's flagship at the Battle of Trafalgar) is taken as a typical example of the attitude of a brave British sailor:

Honoured Father,

This comes to tell you that I am alive and hearty, except three fingers but that's not much, it might have been my head. I told my brother Tom that I should like to see a greadly battle and I have seen one, and we have peppered the Combined (fleet) rarely; and for matter of that they fought us pretty tightish for French and Spanish. Three of our mess are killed and four more of us winged. But to tell you the truth of it, when the game began I wished myself at Warnborough with my plough again, but when they had given us one duster, and I found myself snug and tight, I bid fear kiss my bottom and set to in good earnest and thought no more of being killed than if I were at Murrell Green Fair; and I was presently as busy and as black as a collier. How my fingers got knocked overboard I don't know, but off they are and I never missed them till I wanted them. You see by my writing, it was my left hand so I can write to you and fight for my King yet. We have taken a rare parcel of ships but the wind is so rough we cannot bring them home, else I should roll in money, so we are busy smashing them and blowing 'em up wholesale.

Our dear Admiral Nelson is killed, so we have paid pretty sharply for licking 'em. I never set eyes on him for which I am both sorry and glad; for, to be sure, I should have liked to have seen him—but then all the men in our ship who have seen him are such soft toads they have done nothing but blast their eyes and cry, ever since he was killed. God bless you! Chaps that fought like the Devil, sit down and cry like a wench. I am still in the *Royal Sovereign* but the Admiral has left her, for she is like a horse without a bridle, so he is in a frigate that he may be here and there and everywhere, for he's as cute a here and there one and as bold as a lion, for all he can cry! I saw his tears with my own eyes, when the boat hailed and said my Lord was dead. So no more at present from your dutiful son,

Sam

Unfortunately, it is not certain that this letter was in fact written by a sailor named Sam. It appears in a collection of yarns by W. H. Long who calls it a verbatim copy of a letter written by a sailor in H.M.S. *Royal Sovereign* to his father in Odiham but there is no direct evidence for its veracity. To the best of my knowledge no-one has seen the original of the letter. On the other hand, there were nine seamen named Samuel on board the *Royal Sovereign* at the time, but none of them came from Hampshire. More significant still, none of the nine appeared on the sick list following the battle, and one would have thought that the absence of three fingers would need an element of medical care, poor though that may have been at the time. All the other factual evidence, as opposed to the fictional stories, also implies that sailors simply did not behave as Sam suggests, though they may indeed have sat down and cried after the battle from sheer exhaustion.

This is not to say that the British sailors were cowards, quite the contrary. One of the major reasons for the British success against the French was the courage and skill of the British sailors. Nonetheless, they did not behave quite as Sam or even Captain Marryat suggest. The reasons why the British sailors fought so bravely are clearly given by John Nicol, a sailor of whom more will be said later. Describing the preparations for battle he writes: 'A serious cast was to be perceived on every face; but not a shade of doubt or fear. We rejoiced in a general action; not that we loved fighting; but we all wished to be free to return to our homes, and follow our own pursuits. We knew there was no other way of obtaining this than by defeating the enemy. "The hotter war, the sooner peace", was a saying with us.'

What is abundantly clear is that in Nelson's day few sailors were in the Royal Navy from choice. Many had to be forced to join by the Press Gang and many, if they got the chance, deserted. Of the sailors whose records are presented here, the majority initially volunteered, generally as boys, but nearly all at one point or an other made some attempt to avoid service. John Nicol, the one who probably least disliked the navy, did not actually desert but spent years avoiding the Press Gang and ruined his business in the process. Of the remainder, only one, George Watson, never deserted. All the others succeeded in getting away from the navy, at least for a period, though they were nearly all picked up again by the Press Gang.

It can be argued that the seamen here are not typical, and indeed, anyone on the lower deck who could read and write sufficiently well to write his memoirs could hardly be a typical representative of the sailors of Nelson's navy. John Nicol, though, could neither read nor write and his recollections were written down for him by an author named Howell who met him in Edinburgh as an old and impoverished man. Nicol can certainly be called a typical sailor, as can Thomas Blackey whom we know of from a petition he sent to the Admiralty many years later. It is possible that he could not read or write. Certainly he did not regard his petition as a memoir for posterity.

The others may be less typical, but nevertheless probably represent a fair cross-section. Three published their memoirs in their lifetime with the intention of attacking certain aspects of the naval service. Two others, whose memoirs were not published, disliked the navy almost as much. All these may give an unfavourable picture of the service but it is rather more convincing than the honeyed tales of Captain Marryat and other novelists.

The other seaman-author, George Watson, does give a more attractive picture, but then he was one of the lucky few who obtained a pension and a berth in the Naval Hospital at Greenwich. He might be supposed to have had a more romantic attitude to his time in His Majesty's Service. Yet even he, as we shall see, had no illusions about his fellow shipmates.

One could wish that it were possible in the same way to describe life on the Lower Deck before the end of the eighteenth century. The seamen who circumnavigated the globe with Drake could, no doubt, have told even more harrowing tales than their successors under Nelson. Unfortunately the first ordinary sailor of whose life and views we have any great detail is John Nicol, and only from his time, that of the war against the American colonies, can a continuous narrative be constructed.

Before presenting the seamen themselves it may be as well to add a few lines to give a general idea of some of the aspects of life on board at that time. Beginning with their respective methods of entry, these eight seamen are probably a fairly typical cross-section. Five volunteered when young: for one, Jack Nastyface—though he does not directly admit it—it was probably the glamour of the navy that attracted him; for Samuel Leech it was really a mistake—he joined expecting advancement from an influential patron which he never received, quite possibly a common occurrence. Of these five, though, three deserted—also probably an average proportion—and two of them were 'pressed' afterwards. Of the remainder, these were originally taken by the Press Gang and forced into the service, and during the wars almost certainly the majority of seamen on board had been taken in this way. The official number of pressed men in the navy was not overwhelming, but this was partly because after being taken by the gang there were certain advantages to be gained by 'volunteering', and appearing on the ship's books as a 'volunteer'.

The Press Gang itself had very considerable powers, though strictly it could only press seamen. In practice, the onus of proof lay on the pressed man, and the term 'seaman' could be widely defined. Farm labourers were generally free of the Press, as were gentlemen—though the latter had to dress as such to avoid the attention of the gang. A sum of money could always procure a release and it was not uncommon for the better-off seamen to carry a sum of money—something like £20—around their waist against the event of their falling into the gang's clutches. But for most seamen such a large sum of money was out of the question.

Hated though it was by all, the Press was the only means that existed of providing sufficient men for the Fleet. Officially it remained the only method of manning the Fleet in wartime until after the Crimean War and it is probably still legal today, if a magistrate could be found to sign the warrant. In practice no gangs went out again after 1815, with the result that at times it was difficult to man a ship at all—a ship might wait for some months after commissioning before a full complement of seamen could be found. Unpleasant and unpopular the gang certainly was, but it was essential for the safety of the country.

The popular picture of the gang roaming the streets of seaports and grabbing any young man they could find, or picking up the sweepings of the local hostelry, is only partly true. Certainly, at times of great emergency when there was a 'Hot Press', anyone they could find was taken, but under normal wartime conditions (the Press was only really necessary during wartime) it was largely seamen that were really needed and these were more often than not taken off homeward bound merchant vessels. Samuel Stokes gives a good description of a Hot Press and the full horror is recorded by George Watson. At these times the gangs were particularly concerned to obtain seamen who had deserted from the Royal Navy.

Jack Nastyface gives a graphic description of how he outwitted a gang and got them to chase him some way.

I landed at Gosport, and proceeded on my road to the boundary of the town, where the soldiers stopped me; but, after shewing them my liberty ticket, and having a little parley with them, I was allowed to go on. I bent my course forward until I reached Fareham, and being aware that a press gang was lurking about that neighbourhood, I felt very much inclined to give them a little trouble; I had gone nearly through the town unobserved by them, but at length the alarm was given that a sailor was making good his way in full sail to London; when two members of that worthless set of body snatchers set out in pursuit. I could, by keeping a good lookout, observe their movements and I walked sharply on; they commenced running. I did the same, and kept well on until I arrived at an inn by the road-side, when I thought proper to stop, and let them come up with me. I did not take any notice of them, nor show any appearance of alarm, but, supposing I was a prize, one of them grappled me on the starboard, and the other on the larboard side, by the collar of my jacket, demanding the name of the ship I belonged to; when on coolly showing them my liberty ticket, they showered a broadside of curses on me for giving them such a run, and quietly left me to pursue my journey. After this, however, I had to contend with the land sharks, for on my arrival at Alton, I was stopped by a party of soldiers, to whose inspection I had again to exhibit my ticket of leave, and thus for thirty miles from the sea port was a poor seaman hunted by this detestable set, who are constantly watching in the bye lanes and fields, to intercept any seaman who may be passing that way; the inducement held out to each of these men stealers is five pounds for each seaman they may capture; and thus many a poor fellow is hunted by these blood hounds, who chase them with greater eagerness than the hunter pursues the fox. After getting so far clear of those nests of vipers, I proceeded on to London, where I stayed with my friends until my liberty was out.

It was an expensive process and it was estimated that in 1795 each 'recruit' cost £6, and in 1803, when there was a very great demand for seamen, £20 a head.

Not all seamen were liable to be pressed, but in order to escape the gang's clutches, it was necessary to have a 'protection' signed by a Justice of the Peace. Masters and mates of all merchant ships, boatswains and carpenters of vessels over 50 tons could obtain these affidavits on oath, but these only applied on board, or on shore if on the ship's business, so even they had to tread warily if they left their vessel. Apprentices who had signed indentures to the Captain and had been to sea for less than two years were also exempt and some groups of seamen, for example the Thames Watermen, escaped the attentions of the gangs by purchasing immunity from the Press by a periodic levy of able-bodied men. Pilots were exempt, but not if they ran their ship aground.

Some cities were powerful enough to resist the press altogether —for example in Chester no magistrate would sign a press warrant, and the city was consequently free of gangs. At Leith the crowd at times took control, and prevented the gang from making arrests, but these were exceptions to the general rule.

The majority of pressed men, though, were taken at sea and the best recruiting ground was the area between the Nore and the Downs. All homeward bound ships were boarded (outward bound vessels were officially exempt) and any able-bodied sea-man without a 'Protection' was taken and his place filled if necessary by a member of the gang, by an old man, or a boy. Foreigners were not officially accepted—though many seamen claiming to be Americans were taken—and foreign ships were boarded in the same way as British ones, which was one of the major reasons for the war with America in which Samuel Leech fought. A particular problem was caused by the fact that many British seamen attempted to pass themselves off as United States citizens. A certain Paddy Riley in New York created American citizens at the rate of a dozen a day so that the sailors had ex-emption papers from the Press, though these papers were fre-quently ignored by the gangs. False American papers were also forged in England.

On board, without papers, it was difficult to escape. Ashore there were more opportunities. There are numerous stories of seamen escaping by jumping out of a window, or successfully hiding from the gang in the most unlikely places. Sailors were also occasionally helped by the crowd (the example of Leith has already been mentioned), but generally the gang was too strong for them. However, it was the sailor's enjoyment of strong drink that most frequently proved his undoing; 'very much in liquor' or 'snugly moored in Sot's Bay' he was an easy victim. Informers were paid 20 shillings for information leading to an arrest and most men's hands were against the fugitive sailor, especially 'big-bellied placemen', but there were some opponents to the Press. For example, at Poole, the magistrates would not always back the warrants and the Poole gangs were very rough. One sailor, William Trim, was knocked senseless resisting a gang, his sister was assaulted and his father stabbed and this was reported as being 'nothing more than what usually happened on such occasions in the town of Poole'. In general, though, the gangs and the magistrates worked together. Certain groups were excused, the gangs were given full assistance by the magistrates and in return 'Vagabonds' were taken by the gang and even criminals—'some who preferred to swing in a hammock at sea rather than on the gallows at home'.

Resistance to the gang was not uncommon but only rarely successful. The Leith mob did succeed at times, as did the crowd at Greenock which was always ready to defend the coopers, carpenters, riggers and caulkers wanted by the Navy, but on whose labours the prosperity of the town largely depended. If as a result of a struggle with the gang, a man was killed, it was better for the gang if the 'accident' occurred afloat rather than ashore. On shore there was a trial by jury and quite possibly a verdict of manslaughter; at sea the 'inquiry' would almost certainly exonerate the gang. Tenders, ships used to collect and hold pressed men before being sent to the fleet, were generally safe from the anger of the mob, but the rendezvous, the headquarters of a shore-based gang, was not infrequently successfully stormed by a hostile crowd, again emphasising the advantages of the seaborne activities over shore-based ones.

With such a 'recruiting' organisation, it is hardly surprising that there were numerous complaints about the calibre of the 'recruits' obtained. The following list, though not exhaustive, gives some of the comments made on the characters of the pressed men: 'blackguards'; 'sorry poor creatures that don't earn half the victuals they eat'; 'sad thievish creatures'; 'not a rag left, but which was of such nature as had to be destroyed'; 'a hundred and fifty on board, the greatest part of them sorry fellows'; 'poor ragged souls, and very small'; 'miserable creatures, not a seaman amongst them and the fleet in the same condition'; 'unfit for service and a nuisance to the ship'; 'never so ill manned a ship since I have been at sea'; 'the worst sot I ever saw'; 'twenty-six poor souls but three of them seamen, ragged and half dead'; 'landsmen, boys, incurables and cripples, and wretches the general part of them are'; 'more fit for a hospital than the sea'; 'all the ragg-tagg that can be picked up'.

After such a catalogue it is necessary to state again that not all the seamen on the lower deck were pressed men; indeed, if they had been, England would never have won the war, and even the pressed men themselves were not all the 'ragg-tagg' described above. Nevertheless, pay was totally inadequate; an Able Seaman received twenty-two shillings a month and an Ordinary Seaman nineteen shillings. This was the same as it had been in the time of Cromwell. Even the ordinary soldier received a shilling a day by this time. Leave was almost non-existent, partly because of the exigencies of the service, but primarily because most captains believed that if leave were granted practically none of the sailors would ever voluntarily return on board—a supposition that was proved to be not entirely correct by the few captains who actually granted leave to their ships' companies.

Administratively, the hire and discharge system, whereby even volunteers only signed on for the duration of the commission of a ship—sometimes as little as three years—resulted in total lack of continuity, and made the Press Gang essential. This system, though, did not apply to the Marines upon whom the discipline of the ship largely depended and who even acted as sentries in harbour to prevent the sailors from deserting. They were marched on board from barracks at the beginning of the commission and marched back again at the end. Without them it is difficult to see how the navy could have survived, but even they could not stem the rising flood of discontent. Brutality was regarded as being essential for discipline, and in the circumstances it almost certainly was. Though a few captains avoided the worst excesses, the men were largely held by the rattan and the rope's end. Nelson was one of the few who showed a real concern for his ships' companies and this, of course, accounts for a good deal of his popularity. Nevertheless, the early years of the Revolutionary War was marked by an ominous restlessness in the Fleet which culminated in the nearly completely disastrous mutinies of 1797. Though they lasted for two months, the French took no advantage from the immobility of the British Fleet and the concessions wrung from a reluctant authority did something to mollify the British seamen. Indeed, the year 1797 probably marks the great divide in the pattern of conditions of life on the lower deck. This is not to say that previously no captain treated his crew well, or that conditions on every ship were automatically improved as a consequence of the mutiny. As a result though, conditions did improve and in the long run it also played a part in the disappearance of the Press Gang.

None of the sailors included here was present at either the mutiny at Spithead, or at the one of the Nore but a description of the mutiny at Spithead written by an 'Old Sailor' from Greenwich Hospital gives a fair picture of some of the events even if the author was not an 'Old Sailor'.

At first the fleet laid their complaints before Lord Howe; but somehow or other the old genman didn't think 'em worth notice and consequently they were wholly unattended to. Well, d'ye see the barge's crews used to assemble at the Sallyport, after landing their Captains; and then *we*—that is the crews, but you kown what I mean—would overhaul accounts and haul over the Admiral; and that began the communication with the delicates (delegates). At last, finding that our grievances were disregarded, the fleet determined as a last resource, not to go to sea 'till all was settled. I remember as if it was but yesterday, the signal was made by old Bridport in the *Royal George* to prepare for sailing. It was Easter Sunday, seven and twenty years ago. Up went number 154 to the mast head, and up went the ships' crews into the rigging and along the gangways to give 'em three cheers. The *Queen Charlotte's* began first, indeed they were always first in the fray; but poor fellows, most of 'em perished a year or two afterward when the ship was burnt up in the Mediterranean. The *Queen Charlotte's*, as I said, began first, and the rest of the fleet soon followed the example. There wasn't so many let onto the secret of the mutiny as was at first imagined; but then they were chiefly Petty Officers and able seamen who possessed a strong influence over all hands, fore and aft. Many of the men, when they first heard the cheering came running on deck and asked what was the matter. After it broke out, it was a curious sight to watch the looks of the seamen and notice the conduct of the officers. Yet those who had exercised mercy, were mercifully and generously treated. Some of the men would stand with their arms folded, rummaging upon what they had done, with countenances 'more in sorrow than anger', seeming to think their fate was sealed, yet feeling more for their messmates than themselves. Others, with bold frounts, would brave the consequences and dare the worst, though you might frequently catch their eye taking a broadside glance at the yard-rope, with the hangman's noose at the end. On the main deck might be seen two or three eyeing a group of talkers with the utmost suspicion and stealing by degrees to catch hold of their discourse. But the forecastle was the principal resort, and all the various working of the mind might be traced—from undaunted recklessness to sickness of heart and here the hardy boatswain's mate vociferated his oaths, turned his quid and cracked his joke, insensible to danger; there, the more placid, yet not less firm quarter-master, leaned over the nettings, looking towards the shore in all the distraction of thought:—wife, children, honour, life, seemed hanging by a breath. Thus it continued for several days, till all hands found they were tarred with the same brush and sure to live or die together.

As soon as the news reached the Admiralty there was all confusion, and they eagerly made so many offers that we doubted their sincerity. Bill Pitt* at first affected to turn up his nose, but he soon altered and tried to smooth us down: howsomeever, we had laid out anchor to windward and couldn't be easily persuaded to weigh it again till redress and damnification (indemnification) were spliced to the buoy-rope. About a week afterwards, several of the admirals assembled on board the *Queen Charlotte*; and Sir Allan G—— (Gardner) indulged in such invectives and threats that it only exasperated the people and made 'em stick closer to one another. I was alongside, waiting for the Delicates of the ——, and old Sir Allan spun into his boat like a cockchafer, glad to escape from the anger of the men. What, though we were mutineers, we warn't traitors: if they enemy had put to sea, we were ready to go out and fight for our king and country to the last gasp; and there warn't a man in the whole fleet but what would have cheerfully nailed the colours to the mast and gone down with them flying; but we were oppressed, and everybody knew it. Howsomeever, the differences were tolerably clinched and, in the beginning of May, Bridport again hoisted 154. But still doubts remained among the men that Billy Pitt would be down on 'em before long, and the promises were only a pretence to get them to sea; so, one and all refused to obey till they had called a convention on board the London, 98: Sir John C—— (Colpys) had his flag in the fore in her, and he resolved to prevent their meeting by resistance; so he drew up the marines and pointed two of the quarter-dock carronades down below. The men,

*William Pitt the younger, the Prime Minister.

however, persisted; the guns were fired, and several killed; but the admiral and officers were compelled to surrender. A council of war was called and the delicates met in the great cabin; the platform was rigged out on the forecastle, the yard-rope rove, and the signal made for all boats to attend execution. In about half-an-hour the —— was brought (This was Lieutenant Peter Bover who had played a leading part in the struggle on deck and had apparently shot one of the men), and the noose put over his head; a death-like stillness prevailed; the Boats laid upon their oars; and an agonising suspense was visible upon the agitated face of the seamen; the gangways and ports of the fleet were crowded but not a voice was heard; at last an indistinct murmur arose as the —— kneeled down to bid farewell to time, and make his peace with heaven; the spirits of those who had just suffered death had already flown to the presence of their maker, and now his was about to confrount them before that judge from whose decisions there is no appeal. The bitterness of nature struggling with its fond affection was apparent on the —— face; but in a few moments all was un-daunted serenity and calm resignation. The murmur rose higher and many a furrowed countenance—many a sun-burnt cheek—was moistened with the rich drops of generous sympathy.

Several minutes elapsed when Joyce*, of the *Royal George* called the delicates aft into the cabin and begged them to sup-press their passions. Shipmates, said he, this has gone too far; what can we promise ourselves by the destruction of an old man? what advantage shall we obtain by it? Believe me, it will be a mark of disgrace upon a blue jacket as long as it shall continue to be worn. No, let us rather send 'em ashore and wash our hands from blood. He obeyed his instructions and has only done his duty. Accordingly they proceeded to the forecastle, and communicated their decision to the. . . . He heard the commencement, that his life was spared, and then dropped down like a stone; but he recovered in an instant, and shortly afterwards went ashore. The men that were killed were also landed, and a grand and mournful sight it was; never was such a scene exhibited in Portsmouth before nor since: the ships' companies went in procession with the colours hung with black crepe, and saw the bodies laid in the ground in

*Valentine Joyce, 26, a quarter-master's mate and one of the most impor-tant and influential of the delegates.

Kingston Church where a monument was afterwards erected over them. It was a sight that would have drawn tears from the most obdurate heart.

Well, Lord Howe at last settled the business and came round the fleet attended by his lady and some great gentlemen, and when they landed, the delicates hoisted his Lordship upon their shoulders, and carried him up to the house, where they dined with the admiral and a large party. Up went 154; again the anchors were weighed, and the fleet sailed under Bridport to cruise for the enemy.

Little more need be said about the mutiny at Spithead, but it is interesting to compare the 'Old Sailor's' account of the incident aboard the London with a description given by Sir John Colpoys himself in a letter to Lady Louisa Lennox:

When forward on the fore castle, pleading with the people not to execute Bover, the fourth lieutenant, who had only acted agreeable to orders received from me, and of course that myself only was guilty at this time, surrounded by hundreds who had all manner of weapons lifted up against me in order to destroy, at the instant Bover was to be run up to the yard arm, one of the men called me a scoundrel, and a blood-thirsty one, which immediately gave a turn to affairs, the massive weapons which had been uplifted against me were immediately dropped and the offender called to. . . 'How dare you speak to the Admiral in that manner'. You may imagine I availed myself of such an unlooked for calm, called up all my powers of rhetoric, and in a few moments, both Bover and myself were marched aft to our cabins.

Which of these two is the more accurate account is not certain. What is clear though, is the emphasis which the Admiral places upon the loyalty of the sailors to him in particular, and by implication to naval officers in general. In his version, it is the inate discipline of the men that saves the day; to the 'Old Sailor' on the other hand, it is the men's humanity and their pride that prevents the execution. Taking into consideration the Press Gang and the cat-o'-nine tails, the latter's seems a more plausible explanation.

In general then, the mutiny at Spithead did improve the situation for the sailors without entirely alienating the officers. The fleet put to sea again from Spithead as, if anything, a more rather than a less efficient fighting unit. This was not true of the mutiny at the Nore. There the mutiny began just as the mutiny at Spithead was being settled. The mutineers claim that they were not convinced that the terms of the settlement applied to them seemed hardly adequate when they were directly offered the same terms, but declined to accept. The mutiny itself was markedly more violent and lawless. At Spithead the frigates were compelled to go to sea to continue scouting against the French; at the Nore, the mutineers attacked the neighbouring town, looted merchant ships and practically blockaded London, actions which alienated the general public who had been sympathetic to the demands made at Spithead and ensured the eventual defeat of the mutineers. Again, at Spithead, the mutineers tabled precise demands, primarily about pay which had been the substance of the grievances sent to Lord Howe. The mutineers at the Nore did not know what they were after. They made further demands, which did not lack justification, but the Admiralty had already gone as far as it could at Spithead and could give way no further. There may have been some political agitation involved, and certainly some of the mutineers escaped to France, but there was no evidence of a widespread 'Jacobin Plot' and the leader of the mutiny, Richard Parker, was simply a malcontent. He had started life as an officer, but had been dismissed for insubordination. He then became a school-master but fell into debt, was imprisoned, and drafted to the navy. He was incapable of controlling the situation; one by one the ships fell away, the mutiny fizzled out and Parker paid for it with his life—not a particularly edifying story. Nevertheless at Spithead the possibilities of combination had been successfully demonstrated and as a consequence the men, if not well treated, were at least better treated. The mutiny at the Nore, on the other hand, was completely unsuccessful but perhaps both in its pointlessness and in its inevitable failure it demonstrated more completely the attitude of the seamen on the lower deck towards the Navy.

A statistical end-piece concerning the first eight sailors: between them they fell into the clutches of the Press Gang seven times and deserted eight times.

After this brief introduction we now turn to examine the lives and attitudes of the individual seamen.

2

JOHN NICOL

1774-1783 and 1794-1801
His service in King's Ships in War and Peace

THE EARLIEST DETAILED personal narrative from the lower deck to have survived is that of John Nicol. It is true that something is known of the opinions of some of his contemporaries—especially John Adams who sailed in the *Bounty* under Bligh and took part in the famous mutiny. Many years later when Adams was the sole survivor of the mutineers on Pitcairn Island some notes were taken of his recollections of life on the *Bounty*, but they are disjointed and even contradictory. Bligh, by all accounts, treated his sailors extremely harshly—though other captains behave in a similar way without suffering the indignity of being cast adrift to cross two thousand miles of ocean in an open boat.

The story of the mutiny is well known; a number of the crew led by Lieutenant Christian seized the captain and placed him in an open boat with those other members of his crew who would not join the mutiny and cast them adrift and, through a remarkable navigational feat by Captain Bligh, they finally reached safety. The *Bounty* was sailed to Tahiti where some of the mutineers remained, while the others with Tahitian wives settled on an uninhabited island where the survivors were many years later discovered and where their descendants live to this day.

The mutiny, though, was exceptional; it could not have occurred if the seamen had not had a supporter among the officers —Lieutenant Christian—who was prepared to go to any lengths in his opposition to the Captain. The mutiny was at least partly the direct consequence of Bligh's extreme, though not unequalled, severity and his conduct achieved such notoriety that it is hardly possible to regard life on the *Bounty* as being typical of conditions on the lower deck in the latter part of the eighteenth century though it was probably more typical than is generally supposed.

The ships John Nicol served in formed a fairer cross-section of the navy, and the fact that he could not write his memoirs down himself serves to show still further how typical he was. He served in the Navy only in wartime, returning to the merchant service in time of peace; and in this he was also no exception. He fought in two wars—against the Americans in the War of Independence and against the French in the Revolutionary War—but like most sailors from the lower deck he knew little of the wider issues involved. This is hardly surprising. Because of illiteracy, information was passed by word of mouth. The ships' boats rapidly carried any news round the fleet; but the lower deck tended to adopt a very personal attitude to the war. Not that they were disinterested in the outcome—far from it, as is shown in the passage from John Nicol already quoted, 'We rejoiced in a general action; not that we love fighting but we all wished to be free to return to our homes and follow our own pursuits'. Everyone was most anxious for the war to end. They were primarily concerned, though, with what was going on in the immediate vicinity. The lower deck did not envisage the tactics of the engagement in which they were involved but saw only the smoke, blood, sweat and corpses by which they were surrounded.

For John Nicol this is particularly true of the first of the two wars in which he was involved—that of American Independence. He took no part in any of the major engagements not even in the final great victory—the Battle of the Saints. He spent most of the war on the eastern seaboard of the colonies or in the West Indies. He was also briefly in the Channel between two transatlantic convoys and his comments on this period emphasise the weakness of the British position in home waters. He was on board the *Surprise*, a 28 gun frigate at the time.

We came to England with convoys, and were docked; then had a cruise in the Channel, where we took the *Duke de Chartres*, 18 gun ship, and were ourselves chased into Monts Bay, on the coast of Cornwall, by a French sixty-four. We ran close in shore, and were covered by the old fort, which I believe had not fired a ball since the time of Oliver Cromwell, but it did its duty nobly, all night the Frenchman keeping up her fire, the fort and *Surprise* returning it. When day dawned he sheered off, and we only suffered a little in our rigging. The only blood that was shed on our side was an old fogie of the fort, who was shot by his own gun.

Twenty years later it was the French who scuttled under the guns of their forts and the English who were sometimes bold enough to sail in and 'cut them out', taking them as prizes. To be sure, even under Nelson a 28 gun frigate would not attempt to challenge a French ship of the line, but then the Frenchman would hardly dare to sail down the Channel alone and a frigate would soon be supported by an English Ship of the Line. During the American War, though, the French made little use of their superiority. For once, invasion could have been undertaken in the knowledge that the troops could be safely transported across the Channel but no serious attempt was made.

On the other side of the Atlantic, the British position was, for most of the time, better, largely because of the incompetence of the French admirals, who rarely attempted a conjunction of their fleets. On one crucial occasion, though, de Grasse, the French Admiral, stole a march on the British and brought his whole fleet into North American water, cutting the British army off from its supplies and forcing them to surrender at Yorktown, thus virtually deciding the war. British naval supremacy was re-established at the Battle of the Saints but the war had been lost.

Nichol makes no mention of any of these engagements since he himself did not take part in any of them. For him, the war was a humdrum affair, largely composed of endless convoy duties, sailing forwards and backwards across the Atlantic in a manner strikingly reminiscent of the Second World War.

We took convoy for St. John's, Newfoundland. On this voyage we had very severe weather; our foremast was carried way, and we arrived off St. John's in a shattered state, weary, and spent with fatigue. To add to our misfortunes, we were lying three weeks before the harbour, and could not make it, on account of an island of ice that blocked up its mouth. During these three tedious weeks, we never saw the sun or sky, the fogs were so dense. Had it not been for the incessant blowing of the fishermen's horns, to warn each other, and prevent their being run down, we might as well have been in the middle of the ocean in a winter night. The bows of the *Proteus* could not be seen from her quarter deck; we received supplies and intelligence from the harbour by the fishermen. At length this tedious fog cleared up, and we entered the harbour.

Shades of the 'Cruel Sea:' the 'dangers of the sea' were as much to be feared as the 'violence of the enemy'.

Nichol's first ship was the *Proteus*. Here is how he describes his experiences on board:

I was sent on board the *Proteus*, 20 gun ship, commanded by Captain Robinson, bound for New York. We sailed from Portsmouth with ordnance stores and one hundred men, to man the floating batteries upon Lake Champlain. I was appointed cooper which was a great relief to my mind, as I messed with the steward in his room. I was thus away from the crew. I had been much annoyed, and rendered very uncomfortable, until now, from the swearing and loose talking of the men in the Tender. I had all my life been used to the strictest conversation, prayers night and morning; now I was in a situation where family worship was unknown; and, to add to the disagreeable situation I was in, the troops were very unhealthy. We threw overboard every morning a soldier or a sheep. At first I said my prayers and read my Bible in private; but truth makes me confess I gradually became more and more remiss, and, before long, I was a sailor like the rest: but my mind felt very uneasy and I made many weak attempts to amend.

We sailed with our convoy direct for Quebec. Upon our arrival, the men, having been so long on salt provisions, made too free with the river water, and were almost all seized with flux. The *Proteus* was upon this account laid up for six weeks, during which time the men were in hospital.

After having done the ship's work, Captain Robinson was so kind as to allow me to work on shore where I found employment from a Frenchman who gave me excellent encouragement. I worked on shore all day and slept on board at night.

After one more crossing of the Atlantic to St. John's, Newfoundland, (the one already referred to) the *Proteus* was in such a state of dilapidation that it was not possible to repair her, so she was turned into a prison-ship and the crew dispersed. Nicol was employed on shore, brewing for the fleet, spruce, a drink made from sugar or treacle and the green tops of spruce. He spent a year and a half doing this and became, as he puts it, 'a man of some

consequence even with the inhabitants, as I could make a present
of a bottle of essence to them: they made presents of rum to me.
I thus live very happily and on good terms with them.' After this
he was drafted into the *Surprise*, a frigate commanded by Captain
Reeves and he was involved shortly afterwards in his one serious
action of the war—the duel with an American privateer, the *Jason*.

After a short but severe action, we took the *Jason* of Boston,
commanded by the famous Captain Manly who had been
taken prisoner and broke his parole. When Captain Reeves
hailed him to strike he returned for answer, 'Fire away I
have as many guns as you.' He had heavier metal, but fewer
men than the *Surprise*. He fought us for a long time. I was
serving powder as busy as I could, the shot and splinters
flying in all directions; when I heard the Irishmen call from
one of the guns (they fought like devils and the captain was
fond of them upon that account,) 'Halloo, Bungs, where are
you?' I looked to their gun, and saw the horns of my study
[anvil] across its mouth; the next moment it was through the
Jason's side. The rogues thus disposed of my study which I
had been using just before the action commenced, and had
placed in a secure place, as I thought, our of their reach.
'Bungs for ever!' they shouted when they saw the dreadful hole
it made in the Jason's side. Bungs was the name they always
gave the cooper. When Captain Manly came on board the
Surprise to deliver his sword to Captain Reeves, the half of
the rim of his hat was shot off. Our Captain returned his
sword to him again, saying, 'You have had a narrow escape,
Manly.'—'I wish to God it had been my head,' he replied.

This is the only engagement of the war which Nicol records in
any detail. Sometimes he simply notes that a number of American
privateers were taken. Often they would surrender without a
fight.

Soon after this we hailed an American privateer, commanded
by a Captain Revel and she struck. He was a different character
from the gallant Manly. The weather was so foul, and the sea
ran so high, we could not send our boat on board, neither
could theirs come on board of us. Captain Reeves ordered her
under our quarter. As he sailed alongside, the weather still
very stormy, and night coming on, we were hailed by voices
calling to us, scarcely to be distinguished in the rattling of

our rigging and the howling of the blast. At length we made out with difficulty that the American Captain was going to make some prisoners he had walk overboard. Captain Reeves, in great anger ordered the privateer to place a light on her maintop instead of which he placed one on a float and cast it adrift. The voices again hailed and let us know what had been done. Captain Reeves called to the American that he would sink her in a moment if he did not do as he desired and come close under our lee. Towards morning the weather moderated and we brought Revel and his prisoners on board the *Surprise*. He was a coarse ill-looking fellow; his treatment of the prisoners made his own treatment worse: while Manly dined every day at the Captain's table, Revel messed by himself, or where he chose with the prisoners.

On another occasion an armed transport dealt with one of the privateers.

We again took convoy for St. John's. In the fleet was a vessel called the *Ark*, commanded by Captain Noah. She was an armed transport. This we called Noah's Ark. In our voyage out, an American privateer, equal in weight of metal, but having forty-five men, the Ark only sixteen, bore down upon her. The gallant Noah in his Ark gave battle, we looking on; and, after a sharp contest, took the American, and brought her alongside, her captain lying dead upon her deck. Captain Reeves with consent of the crew, gave the prize to Noah, who carried her in triumph to Halifax and sold her.

This convoy duty backwards and forwards across the Atlantic with an occasional diversion to the West Indies, was hardly exciting and Nicol ends his account of the war.

Quite weary of the monotonous convoy duty, and having seen all I could see, I often sighed for the verdant banks of the Forth. At length my wishes were gratified, by the return of peace. The *Surprise* was paid off in the month of March 1783. When Captain Reeves came ashore he completely loaded the long-boat with flags he had taken from the enemy. When one of the officers enquired what he would do with them, he said, laughing 'I will hang one upon every tree in my father's garden'.

The other war in which Nicol served, the Revolutionary War against France, was both longer and considerably more successful. Nicol took part in several of the major engagements yet the picture he gives is not much clearer than of the American War.

A good deal of the success of the navy in this latter war was undoubtedly due to the high state of preparedness of the fleet, the result of all the untiring efforts of Lord Barham. John Nicol is, of course, entirely unaware of such factors. Equally the reforms in naval signalling that were introduced at this time find no mention. This is certainly not surprising. Even today it is doubtful whether the ordinary sailor is much of a judge of the relative advantages of expenditure in the defence budget on submarines, or aircraft carriers. Nonetheless this is a matter that receives considerable discussion on the lower deck. Not so in John Nicol's time. Even the battles themselves receive but scant attention.

After the first battle of the war—the Glorious First of June—the French abandoned any hope of winning control of the sea and though for a time with the Spanish joining France, the British evacuated the Mediterranean, the victories in 1797 off Cape St. Vincent, at which Nicol himself was present, and at Camperdown, saved Britain in spite of the mutinies that summer. The following year Nelson won the famous battle in Aboukir Bay, generally known as the Battle of the Nile, which cut off Napoleon's fleet from France and virtually determined its fate. At this battle, too, John Nicol was present though at the last great battle of the war—Copenhagen—he was not. With the British Fleet in the ascendency everywhere—though Napoleon had virtual control of the continent—a peace which proved to be merely a truce, was signed at Amiens.

Nicol's view of the war was very different from this. As a cooper he had little opportunity to witness the actual progress of the battle though neither did the seamen working at the guns and like them 'Any information we got was from the women and boys who carried the powder' and suprisingly enough there was a fair number of women on board.

For this war John Nicol did not volunteer. Between the wars he had served in a number of different merchant ships. He had sailed round the world, had been whale fishing, had even served on a convict ship transporting female prisoners to Australia. On return to England from China, however, the Press Gang came aboard and he was taken to the *Venerable* whose boats made a clean sweep of his ship, the *Nottingham*, which then had to be taken up river by 'ticket-porters and old Greenwich men.'

c

From there, on June 11th 1794, he was turned over to the *Edgar*, a 74 gun ship and was lucky to be under a good Captain—Sir Charles Henry Knowles. Undoubtedly Nicol was a useful sailor. When they were at Leith the captain was even prepared to allow Nicol ashore but 'Lieutenant Collis prevented it saying, 'It is not safe to allow a pressed man to go on shore at his native place.' Had I been allowed, I did not intend to leave the *Edgar*. I would not have run away for any money, upon my kind captain's account. My uncle came on board and saw me before we sailed; and I was visited by my other friends, which made me quite happy.'

While they were at Leith an unfortunate incident occured in another ship there which emphasises how lucky Nicol was with his Captain.

While we lay in Leith Roads, a mutiny broke out in the *Defiance*, 74: the cause was, their captain gave them five-water grog; now the common thing is three-waters. The weather was cold; the spirit thus reduced was, as the mutineers called it, as thin as muslin, and quite unfit to keep out the cold. No seaman could endure this in cold climates. Had they been in hot latitudes, they would have been happy to get it thus, for the sake of the water; but then they would not have got it. The *Edgar* was ordered alongside the *Defiance* to engage her, if necessary, to bring her to order. We were saved this dreadful alternative by their returning to duty. She was manned principally by fishermen, stout resolute dogs. When bearing down upon her, my heart felt so sad and heavy, not that I feared death or wounds, but to fight my brother, as it were. I do not believe the *Edgar's* crew would have manned the guns. They thought the *Defiance* men were in the right; and had they engaged us heartily, as we would have done a French 74, we could have done no good, only blown each other out of the water, for the ships were of equal force; and if there was any odds the *Defiance* had it in point of crew. Had I received my discharge, and one hundred guineas, I could not have felt my heart lighter than I did, when we returned to our anchorage; and the gloom immediately vanished from every face in the ship.

In spite of the work of Lord Barham all the ships were not as fully prepared as might have been wished. In particular the *Edgar* was clearly not yet ready for sea. She was only newly in commission and the timbers and rigging had not been properly seasoned with the result that when in that October they ran into a severe gale there was considerable danger of the ship's foundering and Nicol considered that it was the greatest danger he was ever in.

We in a few hours carried away our bowsprit and foremast in this dreadful night; then our mizen and main-top-mast. With great difficulty we cut them clear. Soon after our main-mast loosened in the step, and we every moment expected it to go through her bottom. Then no exertion could have saved us from destruction. The carpenter, by good fortune, got it secured. We lost all our anchors and cables in our attempts to bring her to, save one. At length it moderated a little, when we rigged jury masts, and made for the Humber, where we brought to with our only remaining anchor, when the *Inflexible*, Captain Savage, hove in sight, and took us in tow. When in this situation, the coasters, as they passed, called to the *Inflexible*, 'What prize have you got in tow?' A fresh gale sprung up and the *Inflexible* was forced to cast us off. The weather moderated again, and we proceeded up the Swain the best way we could into Blackstakes, Chatham. My berth, during the storm, as one of the gunner's crew, was in charge of the powder on deck we used in firing our guns of distress. The ship rolled so much we were often upon our beam ends, and rolled a number of guns overboard. We were forced to start all our beer and water to lighten the ship, but we rode it out, contrary to our expectation.

The *Edgar* required a complete refit after this and the Captain and the entire crew were turned over to the *Goliah*, another 74, and sailed to join Sir John Jarvis in the blockade of Toulon. This Nicol enjoyed:

I was constantly on shore, when any service was to be done in destroying stores, spiking guns, blowing up batteries, and enjoyed it much. We carried off all the brass guns, and those metal ones that were near the edge of the rocks we threw into the sea. This was excellent sport to us, but we were forced to leave it, and sail to Gibraltar for water and provisions, but could obtain no supplies, and sailed for Lisbon where we got plenty having been on short allowance for some time before.

Nicol passes this period off very briefly. They spent two years either off Toulon or Corsica which must have been a fairly monotonous time, but in Febrary 1797 he took part in one of the greatest victories of the war. The British Fleet was even more heavily outnumbered than he records. Twenty-seven Spanish ships to fifteen British. The Spanish fleet had been ordered to Brest from the Mediterranean and Jarvis intercepted them off Cape St. Vincent. This battle marked the turning point of Nelson's career for without orders he left the line of battle to keep open the gap carved by the British ships in the Spanish line. His ship the *Captain* alone engaged seven Spanish ships and more than held her own taking two of them, boarding one from the deck of her already captured prize. The battle ended at nightfall with the Spanish Fleet severely crippled and unable to reach Brest, thus assuring the control of the Channel to Britain. However this was not the battle that John Nicol saw.

While we lay at Lisbon we got private intelligence overland that the Spanish Fleet was at sea. We with all dispatch set sail in pursuit of them. We were so fortunate as come in sight of them by break of day, on the 14th Febrary, off Cape St. Vincent. They consisted of twenty-five sail, mostly three-deckers. We were only eighteen; but we were English and we gave them their Valentines in style. Soon as we came in sight, a bustle commenced, not to be conceived or described. To do it justice, while every man was as busy as he could be, the greatest order prevailed. A serious cast was to be perceived on every face; but not a shade of doubt or fear. We rejoiced in a general action; not that we loved fighting; but we all wished to be free to return to our homes, and follow our own pursuits. We knew there was no other way of obtaining this than by defeating the enemy. 'The hotter the war the sooner peace,' was a saying with us. When everything was cleared, the ports open the matches lighted, and guns run out, then we gave them three such cheers as are only to be heard in a British man-of-war. This intimidates the enemy more than a broadside, as they have often declared to me. It shows them all is right; and the men in the true spirit baying to be at them. During the action, my situation was not one of danger, but most wounding to my feelings, and trying to my patience. I was stationed in the after magazine, serving powder from the screen, and could see nothing, but I could feel every shot that struck the *Goliah*, and the cries and groans of the wounded were most distressing as there was only the thickness of the blankets of the screen between me and them. Busy as I was the time hung upon me with a dreary weight. Not a soul spoke to me but the master-at-arms, as he went his rounds to inquire if all was safe. No sick person ever longed more for his physician than I for the voice of the master-at-arms. The surgeon's mate, at the commencement of the action, spoke a little, but his hands were soon too full of his own affairs. Those who were carrying ran like wild creatures, and scarce opened their lips. I would far rather have been on the decks, amid the bustle, for there the time flew on eagle's wings. The *Goliah* was sore beset; for some time she had two three-deckers upon her. The men stood to their guns as cool as if they had been exercising. The Admiral ordered the *Britannia* to our assistance. 'Ironsides,' with her forty-twos, soon made them sheer off. Towards the close of the action, the men were very weary. One lad put his head out of the port-hole, saying, 'D——n them, are they not going to strike yet?' For us to strike was out of the question.

At length the roar of the guns ceased, and I came on deck to see the effects of a great sea engagement; but such a scene of blood and desolation I want words to express. I had been in a great number of actions with single ships in the *Proteus* and *Surprise*, during the seven years I was in them. This was my first action in a fleet, and I had only a small share in it. We had destroyed a great number, and secured four three-deckers. One, they had the impiety to called the Holy Ghost, we wished much to get; but they towed her off. The Fleet was in such a shattered situation, we lay twenty-four hours in sight of them, repairing out rigging. It is after the action the disagreeable part commences; the crews are wrought to the utmost of their strength; for days they have no remission of their toil; repairing the rigging, and other parts injured in the action; their spirits are broke by fatigue: they have no leisure to talk of the battle; and, when the usual round of duty returns, we do not choose to revert to a disagreeable subject. Who can speak of what he did, when all did their utmost? One of my messmates had the heel of his shoe shot off; the skin was not broke, yet his whole leg swelled and became black. He was lame for a long time.

After the battle they returned to Lisbon but they ran into a severe gale and one of the ships—the *Bombay Castle*—was lost. Captain Knowles was tried for failing to lend assistance but was acquitted and his popularity in the ship was shown by the incident which occured after the Court Martial.

Collis, our first lieutenant, told us not to cheer when he came on board; but we loved our captain too well to be restrained. We had agreed upon a signal with the coxswain, if he was, as he ought to be, honourably acquitted. The signal was given and in vain Collis forbade. We manned the yards, and gave three hearty cheers. Not a man on board but would have bled for Sir C. H. Knowles. To our regret we lost him to our ship at this very time. He was as good a captain as I ever sailed with. He was made admiral, and went home in the *Britannia*.

Knowles was succeeded by Captain Foley and after a brief period of blockading Cadiz, thirteen of the fleet, including the *Goliah*—which Nicol claimed was the fastest sailing ship in the fleet—were 'picked' by Admiral Nelson to chase the French.

We did not stay to water; but got a supply from the ships that were to remain, and away we set under a press of sail, not knowing where. We came to anchor in the Straits of Messina. There was an American man-of-war at anchor; Captain Foley ordered him to unmoor, that the *Goliah* might get her station, as it was a good one, near the shore; but Jonathan would not budge, but made answer. 'I will let you know I belong to the United States of America, and will not give way to any nation under the sun, but in a good cause.' So we came to an anchor where we could. We remained here but a short time, when we got intelligence, that the French Fleet were up in the Straits. We then made sail for Egypt, but missed them, and came back to Syracuse, and watered in twenty-four hours. I was up all night filling water. The day after we left Syracuse we fell in with a French brig, who had just left the fleet. Admiral Nelson took her in tow, and she conducted us to where they lay at anchor in Aboukir Bay.

There followed the Battle of the Nile which, by destroying the French fleet, left the Mediterranean virtually a British sea. Nicol's description of the battle is no more complete than that of Cape St. Vincent. The French fleet were anchored in what their

Admiral imagined was a safe position, so near the rocks and shoal water off Aboukir Point that he thought nothing could pass between them and the shore. The decision to sail between the French line and the shore was taken by Captain Foley who led the line. The idea was not, as Nicol supposes, to cut the enemy off from the shore, but by placing a British ship on either side of the French ships it left the French in a hopeless position. Only two of the thirteen escaped. Here is Nicol's description.

We had our anchors out at our stern port, with a spring upon them, and the cable carried along the ship's side, so that the anchors were at our bows, as if there was no change in the arrangement. This was to prevent the ships from swinging round, as every ship was to be brought to by her stern. We ran in between the French fleet and the shore, to prevent any communication between the enemy and the shore. Soon as they were in sight, a signal was made from the Admiral's ship for every vessel, as she came up, to make the best of her way, firing upon the French ships as she passed and 'every man to take his bird,' as we joking called it. The *Goliah* led the van. There was a French frigate right in our way. Captain Foley cried, 'Sink that brute, what does he there?' In a moment she went to the bottom, and her crew were seen running into her rigging. The sun was just setting as we went into the bay, and a red and fiery sun it was. I would, if I had my choice, have been on the deck, there I would have seen what was passing, and the time would not have hung so heavy; but every man does his duty with spirit, whether his station be in the slaughter-house or the magazine.

I saw as little of this action as I did of the one of the 14th February off Cape St. Vincent. My station was in the powder magazine with the gunner. As we entered the bay, we stripped to our trowsers, opened our ports, cleared and every ship we passed gave them a broad-side and three cheers. Any information we got was from the boys and women who carried the powder. The women behaved as well as the men, and got a present for their bravery from the Grand Signior. When the French Admiral's ship blew up, the *Goliah* got such a shake, we thought the afterpart of her had blown up until the boys told us what it was. They brought us every now and then the cheering news of another French ship having struck, and we answered the cheers on deck with heart-felt joy. In the heat of the action, a shot came right into the magazine, but did no harm, as the carpenters plugged it up and stopped the water that was rushing in. I was much indebted to the gunner's wife, who gave her husband and me a drink of wine every now and then which lessened our fatigue much. There were some of the women wounded and one woman belonging to Leith died of her wounds, and was buried on a small island in the bay. One woman bore a son in the heat of the action; she belonged to Edinburgh. When we ceased firing, I went on deck to view the state of the fleets, and an awful sight it was. The whole bay was covered with dead bodies, mangled, wounded and scorched, not a bit of clothes on them except their trowsers. There were a number of French, belonging to the French Admiral's ship, the *L'Orient*, who had swam to the *Goliah* and were cowering under her forecastle. Poor fellows, they were brought on board, and Captain Foley ordered them down to the steward's room, to get provisions and clothing. One thing I observed in these Frenchmen quite different from anything I had ever before observed. In the American war, when we took a French ship, the *Duke de Chartres*, the prisoners were as merry as if they had taken us, only saying, 'Fortune de guerre,'—you take me today, I take you tomorrow. Those we now had on board were thankful for our kindness, but were sullen and as downcast as if each had lost a ship of his own. The only incidents I heard of are two. One lad who was stationed by a salt-box on which he sat to give out cartridges and keep the lid close— it is a trying berth—when asked for a cartridge, he gave none, yet he sat upright; his eyes were open. One of the men gave him a push; he fell all his length on the deck. There was not a blemish on his body, yet he was quite dead, and was thrown overboard. The other, a lad who had the match in his hand to fire his gun. In the act of applying it a shot took off his arm; it hung by a small piece of skin. The match fell to the deck. He looked to his arm, and seeing what had happened seized the match in his left hand and fired off the gun before he went to the cockpit to have it dressed. They were in our mess, or I might never have heard of it. Two of the mess were killed and I knew not of it until the day after. Thus terminated the glorious first of August, the busiest night in my life.

Industry and Oeconomy by Henry Singleton. A young man signing on to go to sea. So must Samuel Stokes have looked when he first joined.

OVERLEAF   *Nelson boarding the 'San Nicolas'*. An incident in the Battle of Cape St. Vincent. Nelson is in the centre pointing to his left with sword and hand.

Sailors in a Storm by Thomas Stothard. A dramatic reconstruction of a
group of sailors cutting away the damaged rigging.

In the last two years of the war Nicol was only engaged in one further significant action. He was for a brief period drafted to the *Ramillies* and from there shortly afterwards to the *Ajax*. In the latter he took part in the landings at Alexandria following which the French were finally drawn out of Egypt.

We sailed for Ferrol, and attempted to cut out some vessels, but did not succeed, then stood for Algiers to water, having a fleet of transports with troops on board under convoy. The troops were commanded by Sir Ralph Abercromby. Having watered we sailed with the army to Mamarice Bay, and the troops were encamped upon a fine piece of ground, with a rivulet running through the centre. The French had just left the place, having first done all the mischief in their power.

I belonged to one of the boats; Captain A. F. Cochrane was beach-master, and had the ordering of the troops in the landing. We began to leave the ships about twelve o'clock, and reached the shore about sunrise in the morning. We rowed very slow with our oars muffled. It was a pleasant night; the water was very still; and all was silent as death. No one spoke, but each cast an anxious look to the shore; then at each other, impatient to land. Each boat carried about one hundred men, and did not draw nine inches of water. The French cavalry were ready to receive us; but we soon forced them back, and landed eight thousand men the first morning. We had good sport at landing the troops, as the Frenchmen made a stout resistance. We brought back the wounded men to the ships.

For some time we supplied the troops on shore with provisions and water. After the advance of the troops into the country, I was with the seamen on shore, assisting at the siege of Alexandria, and working like a labourer in cutting off the branch of the Nile that supplied the city with water. One of the *Ajax's* boats, at Sir Ralph Abercromby's request, carried him after receiving his wound on board the hospital ship.

After this they sailed for Malta but Nicol became blinded with opthalmia for six weeks.

My sufferings were most acute. I could not lie down for a moment, for the scalding water that continually flowed from my eyes, filled them, and put me to exquisite torture. I sat constantly on my chest with a vessel of cold water bathing them.

If I slept I awoke in an agony of pain. All the time the flux was most severe upon me, and the surgeon would not dry it up, as it, he said, relieved my eyes. When we came to Malta a French surgeon cured me by touching the balls of my eyes with tincture of opium; but the pain of the application was very severe.

They then returned to England and, as peace had been concluded, they were all paid off and John Nicol did not go to sea again.

What, then, did Nicol think of the service? Possibly this is best answered in his own words. Before being taken by the Press in the *Nottingham* he had avoided being arrested by arriving aboard a Portuguese brig with a 'Protection' from the British court at Lisbon, but

When we arrived at Gravesend a man-of-war's boat came on board to press any Englishmen there might be on board. William and I did not choose to trust to our protections, now that we were in the river. So we stowed ourselves away among some bags of cotton, where we were almost smothered, but could hear every word that was said. The Captain told the Lieutenant he had not more hands than he saw, and they were all Portuguese. The Lieutenant was not very particular and left the Brig without making much search. When the boat left the vessel we crept from our hiding hole, and not long after a custom-house officer came on board. When we cast anchor, as I had a suit of long clothes in my chest, that I had provided should I have been so fortunate as have found Sarah at Fort Jackson, to dash away with her a bit on shore. I put them on immediately, and gave the custom-house-officer half a guinea for the loan of his cocked hat and powdered wig; the long gilt-headed cane was included in the bargain. I got a waterman to put me on shore. I am confident my own father, had he been alive, could not have known me with my cane in my hand, cocked hat, and bushy wig. I inquired of the waterman the way to the inn where the coach set out for London; I at the same time knew as well as him. I passed for a passenger. At the inn, I called for a pint of wine, pens and ink, and was busy writing any nonsense that came in my head until the coach set off. All those precautions were necessary. Had the waterman suspected me to be a sailor, he would have informed the press-gang in one minute. The waiters at the inn would have done the same.

He certainly regarded himself as fortunate not to be pressed on this occasion which is in itself an indication of his dislike of serving His Majesty. More direct still are his comments on his arrival in England in the *Nottingham*:

> Nothing uncommon happened until we reached the Downs. I had allowed my beard to grow long, and myself to be very dirty, to be as unlikely as possible, when the man-of-war boats came on board to press the crew. As we expected, they came. I was in the hold, sorting among the water casks, and escaped. They took every hand that would answer. I rejoiced in my escape, but my joy was of short duration. One of the men they had taken had a sore leg, the boat brought him back, and I had the bad luck to be taken, and he was left. Thus were all my schemes blown into the air. I found myself in a situation I could not leave, a bondage that had been imposed upon me against my will, and no hopes of relief until the end of the war—not that I disliked it, but I had now become weary of wandering for a time, and longed to see Scotland again. My heart always pointed to my native land. Remonstrance and complaint were equally vain. I therefore made up my mind to it and was as happy as a man in blasted prospects can be.

In one respect, though, Nicol was undoubtedly fortunate; all his captains were both humane and efficient. He never suffered the intolerable indignity of continual beatings which occurred in other ships. The details of punishments used in the navy at this time are best described by another sailor Jack Nastyface, but one incident described by John Nicol is worth recording here. Captain Bligh of the *Bounty* may have been extremely brutal, but 'flogging captains' as they were called were not uncommon in the navy. Flogging 'at the gangway' as ordered by the Captain, though, was mild to flogging 'through the fleet' which John Nicol describes:

> One of our men was whipped through the fleet for stealing some dollars from a merchant ship he was assisting to bring into port. It was a dreadful sight; the unfortunate sufferer tied down on the boat and rowed from ship to ship, getting an equal number of lashes at the side of the vessel from a fresh

man. The poor wretch, to deaden his suffering, had drunk a whole bottle of rum a little before the time of punishment. When he had only two portions to get of his punishment the captain of the ship perceived he was tipsy, and immediately ordered the rest of the punishment to be delayed until he was sober. He was rowed back to the *Surprise*, his back swelled like a pillow, black and blue; some sheets of thick blue paper were steeped in vinegar and laid to his back. Before he seemed insensible, now his shrieks rent the air. When better he was sent to the ship, where his tortures were stopped, and again renewed.

On being paid off in 1801 Nicol was free for the first time for seven years.

I was once more my own master and felt so happy. I was like one bewildered. Did those on shore only experience half the sensations of a sailor at perfect liberty, after being seven years on board ship without a will of his own, they would not blame his eccentricities, but wonder he was not more foolish. After a few days, my cooler reason began to resume its power, and I began to think what should be my after pursuits.

After briefly searching in vain for an old flame whom he had first met as a convict in the prison ship he had served in, he returned to Scotland, married and set up his own business as a cooper, but shortly afterwards war broke out again and the Press Gang came in search of him. He could not remain in Edinburgh and avoid the gang, and his wife was utterly distracted at the thought of his returning to the Navy. He therefore had to sell off his business and move but he could not continue to follow his trade as it could only be carried on in a sea-port or large town where he was in danger from the Press Gang. He settled in Cousland, some nine miles from Edinburgh, doing manual work in a quarry and looking forward to the end of the war:

'I hoped that every month would put a period to the war, and I would be allowed to return to Edinburgh. But peace still seemed to recede from Britain. Year after year I looked for it in vain. When the weather was good, night after night have I sat, after my day's labour, by the old windmill in Bartholomew's field, first gazing upon Edinburgh, that I dared not reside in then upon the vessels that glided along the Forth. A sigh would escape me at my present lot.

Even then he was not secure. A neighbour was impressed and though he got off Nicol became apprehensive at every stranger. He suffered bitter attacks from his work mates:

One would ask what I thought of British freedom; another, if I could defend a government which did such things? I was at no loss for my answer. I told them, 'Necessity had no law.' Could the government make perfect seamen as easily as they could soldiers, there would be no such thing as pressing of seamen, and that I was happy to be of more value than them all put together, for they would not impress any of them they were of so little value compared with me.

But he had his moment of triumph:

When the news of the victory of Trafalgar arrived, I had my triumph over them in return. None but an old tar can feel the joy I felt. I wrought none the next day, but walked about enjoying the feeling of triumph. Every now and then I felt the greatest desire to hurra aloud, and many a hurra my heart gave that my mouth uttered not.

By 1813 he was too old to be taken but too old also to work in the quarry. He returned to Edinburgh, but times were hard.

I could not get constant employment for myself. I therefore wrought for any of the other masters who were throng; but the cooper business is so very poor. I have been oftener out of employment than at work. Few of them keep journeymen. They, like myself, do all their work with their own hands.

In 1820 his wife died and he was left virtually penniless. He had no children and having been forced to sell all the rest of his property, he was left with only a small room and a cellar.

Doctor Davidson visits me in his ministerial capacity. These, I may say, are the only glimpses of sunshine that ever visit my humble dwelling. Mr. Mackenzie, my elder, is very attentive in giving me tickets of admission to the sermons that are preached in the school-house on the Castle Hill. In one of Doctor Davidson's visits, he made me a present of a few shillings; it was a great gift from God. I had not one penny at the time in the house.

Even his attempt to obtain a pension failed. He was lent

money by a cousin to visit London but his old Captain, Portlock, was dead and he could find no one to help him. The Clerk at the Admiralty Office told him he had been too late in applying; the Governor of Greenwich was in Scotland and Captain Gore, whose son's life he had saved, was not at home. After four weeks he was forced to return to Scotland without anything.

At one time, after I came home, I little thought I should ever require to apply for a pension; and, therefore, made no application until I really stood in need of it. I eke out my subsistence in the best manner I can. Coffee made from the raspings of bread, (which I obtain from the bakers), twice a day, is my chief diet. A few potatoes, or anything I can obtain with a few pence, constitute my dinner. My only luxury is tobacco, which I have used these forty-five years. To beg I never will submit. Could I have obtained a small pension for my past services, I should then have reached my utmost earthly wish, and the approach of utter helplessness would not haunt me as it at present does in my solitary home. Should I be forced to sell it, all I would obtain could not keep me, and pay for lodgings for one year; then I must go to the poor's house, which God in his mercy forbid, I can look to my death bed with resignation; but to the poor's house I cannot look with composure. I have been a wanderer and the child of chance, all my days; and now only look for the time when I shall enter my last ship, and be anchored with a green turf upon my breast; and I care not how soon the command is given.

3

JACK NASTYFACE

(1805-1811)

Extracts from ' Nautical Economy of Forecastle
Recollections of Events during the last war',
including a description of the Battle of Trafalgar

JOHN NICOL could only rejoice in Scotland over the great
victory of Trafalgar, but the next seaman author, Jack Nastyface,
was present in person and in 'Nautical Economy' has left a very
graphic description of the battle. For John Nicol the first war
against the French, the Revolutionary War, marked the end of his
service; in the second, the Napoleonic War, he did not serve.
Yet, the clear division comes after the great Battle of Trafalgar.

In 1803 Napoleon had not yet accepted maritime defeat. He
still believed he could control the English Channel for a sufficient
time to make an invasion of England possible, and Villeneuve
was entrusted with the task. He first attempted to lure the British
fleet to the West Indies, and then with the Spanish, and further
French ships from Brest, form an overwhelming concentration in
the Channel. This failed, as Nelson chased him round the West
Indies, and Admiral Calder prevented the planned junction of the
French and Spanish fleets at Ferrol. Left with virtually no news
from Napoleon, Villeneuve, in order to save his reputation with
Napoleon, determined on the desperate gamble of a full-scale
battle. He managed to unite with the Spaniards and the combined
fleet met the British off Cape Trafalgar.

Jack Nastyface's description of the events leading up to this
battle is certainly more accurate and knowledgeable than the
accounts by John Nicol of the Nile though he was certainly
wrong about the French intentions. Nastyface was serving at the
time in the *Revenge* which played an important, though not outstanding role, in the battle.

After beating about the Channel for some time, we were ordered to proceed along the Spanish coast to look after the combined fleet of France and Spain. Having heard that Sir Robert Calder had fallen in with them a few days previous, we pursued our course, looking in at Ferrol and other ports, until we arrived off Cadiz, where we found they had got safe in. Here we continued to blockade them, until Nelson joined us with five sail of the line. In order to decoy the enemy out, stratagem was resorted to, and five sail were sent to Gibraltar to victual and water, whilst Nelson with his five sail kept out of sight of the enemy, and thus they thought we were only twenty-two sail of the line, whilst their fleet consisted of thirty-three sail. With this superior force they put to sea, with the intention, as we afterwards learned, of taking our fleet; and if they had succeeded, possessed of so great a force they were to occupy the Channel, and assist in the invasion of England by the troops then encamped along the French coast, with an immense number of flat bottomed boats, with which the French ports swarmed. But here, as in many other instances, they reckoned without their host. British valour and seamanship frustrated their design and destroyed their hopes; for on the memorable 21st of October 1805, as the day began to dawn, a man at the topmost head called out 'A sail on the starboard bow', and in two or three minutes more he gave another call, that there was more than one sail, for indeed they looked like a forest of masts rising from the ocean, and as morning got light we could plainly discern them from the deck, and were satisfied it was the enemy, for the Admiral began to telegraph to that effect. They saw us and would gladly have got away when they discovered we counted 27 sail of the line, but it was too late and situated as they were hemmed in by Cape Trafalgar on the one side and not being able to get back to Cadiz on the other.

As the enemy was thus driven to risk a battle, he exhibited a specimen of their naval tactics by forming themselves into a cresent, or half-moon, waiting for our approach, which did not take place until ten minutes of twelve o'clock, so that there was nearly six hours to prepare for battle; while we glided down to them under the influence of a gentle breeze, cheering to every seaman's heart, that Providence took us in tow, and from a signal made by Lord Nelson, our ships were soon formed into two lines, weather and lee.

During this time each ship was making the usual preparations such as breaking away the Captain's and officer's cabins, and sending all the lumber below—the doctors, parson, purser and loblolly men, were also busy getting the medicine chests and bandages out, and sails prepared for the wounded to be placed on, that they might be dressed in rotation as they were taken down to the aft-cockpit. In such a bustling and, it may be said, trying as well as serious time, it is curious to notice the different dispositions of the British Sailor. Some would be offering a guinea for a glass of grog, whilst others were making a kind of mutual verbal will, such as: 'If one of Johnny Crapeau's shots (a term given to the French) knocks my head off, you will take all my effects, and if you are killed and I am not, why, I will have yours and this is generally agreed to.' During this momentous preparation the human mind had ample time for meditation and conjecture, for it was evident that the fate of England rested on this battle; therefore well might Lord Nelson make the signal 'England expects each man will do his duty'. Here, if I may be indulged the observation, I will say that could England but have seen her sons about to attack the inhabitants of Spain with an inferior force, our number of men being not quite twenty thousand whilst theirs was upwards of thirty thousand; from the zeal which animated every man in the fleet, the bosom of every inhabitant of England would have glowed with indescribable patriotic pride; for such a number of line-of-battle ships have never met together and engaged, either before or since. As we drew near, we discovered the enemy line was formed with a Spanish ship between two French ones nearly all through their line, as I suppose, to make them fight better; and it must be admitted that the Dons fought as well as the French in that battle; and, if praise was due for seamanship and valour, they were well entitled to an equal share. We now began to hear the enemy's cannon opening on the *Royal Sovereign*, commanded by Lord Collingwood, who commenced the action, and a signal being made by the Admiral to some of our senior captains to break the enemy's line at different points, it fell to our lot to cut off the five stern-most ships; and, while we were running down to them, of course we were favoured with several shots and some of our men were wounded. Upon being thus pressed, many of our men thought it hard that the firing should all be on one side and became im-

D

patient to return the compliment; but our captain had given
orders not to fire until we got close in with them, so that all our
shot might tell;—indeed these were his words: 'We shall want
all our shot when we get close in. Never mind their firing:
when I fire a carronade from the quarter deck, that will be the
signal for you to begin, and I know you will do your duty as
Englishmen.' In a few minutes the gun was fired and our ship
bore in and broke the line, but we paid dear for our temerity,
as those ships we had thrown into disorder turned round and
made an attempt to board. A Spanish three-decker ran her
bowsprit over our poop, with a number of her crew in it, and,
in her fore rigging, two or three hundred men were ready to
follow; but they caught a Tartar, for their design was discovered and our marines with their small arms, and carronades
on the poop, loaded with canister shot, swept them off so fast,
some into the water and some on the decks, that they were glad
to sheer off. While this was going on aft, we were engaged with
a French two-deck ship on our starboard side, and on our
larboard bow, another, so that many of their shots must have
struck their own ships, and done severe execution. After
being engaged about an hour, two other ships fortunately
came up, received some of the fire intended for us and we
were now enabled to get at some of the shot-holes between
wind and water and plug them up. This is a duty performed
by the carpenter and his crew. We were now unable to work the
ship, our yards, sails, and masts being disabled, and the braces
completely shot away. In this condition we lay by the side of the
enemy, firing away, and now and then we received a good
raking from them passing under our stern. This was a busy
time with us for we had not only to endeavour to repair our
damage, but also to keep to our duty. Often during the battle
we could not see for the smoke whether we were firing at a foe
or a friend, and as to hearing, the noise of the guns had so
completely made us deaf, that we were obliged to look only to
the motions that were made. In this manner we continued the
battle till near five o'clock when it ceased.

It was shortly made known by one of our boat's crew that
Lord Nelson had received a fatal shot; had this news been
communicated through the fleet before the conflict was over,
what effect it might have had on the hearts of our seamen I
know not, for he was adored, and in fighting under him,

every man thought himself sure of success; a momentary but naturally melancholy pause among the survivors of our brave crew ensued.

We were now called to clear the decks, and here might be witnessed an awful and interesting scene, for as each officer and seaman would meet (oh! what an opportunity for the Christian and man of feeling to meditate on the casualty of fate in this life) they were inquiring for their mess mates. Orders were now given to fetch the dead bodies from the after cockpit and throw them overboard; these were the bodies of men who were taken down to the doctor during the battle, badly wounded and who, by the time the engagement was ended, were dead. Some of these perhaps could not have recovered while others might, had timely assistance been rendered which was impossible, for the rule is as to order is requisite, that every person shall be dressed in rotation as they are brought down wounded and in many instances some have bled to death.

The next call was 'all hands to splice the main brace', which is the giving out a gill of rum to each man, and indeed they much needed it, for they had not ate or drank from breakfast time. We had now a good night's work before us; all our yards, masts, and sails were sadly cut, indeed the whole of the sails were obliged to be unbent, being rendered completely useless, and by the next morning we were partly jury-rigged. We now began to look for our prizes, as it was coming on to blow hard on the land, and Admiral Collingwood made signals for each ship that was able to take a prize in tow, to prevent them drifting into their own harbour as they were complete wrecks and unmanageable.

We took an eighty gun Spanish ship in tow for a day and night, but were obliged to cast her off, it blew so hard, and our ship being so very much disabled; indeed, we were obliged to scuttle a few of them. Some we contrived to take into Gibraltar; some were wrecked near Cadiz harbour, and others drifted into the harbour from whence they had only come two days before. It was a mortifying sight to witness the ships we had fought so hard for and had taken as prizes, driven by the elements from our possession, with some of our own men on board as prize masters, and it was a great blight to our victorious success; but, in justice to the enemy, it may with truth be recorded that however contrary to the Spanish character as

an enemy generally, yet, upon this occasion, they used our men
well.

In order to show the crippled state in which our ships must
have been in, it will be requisite to mention that, in preparing to
engage the enemy closely and protect ourselves as much as
possible, the seamen's hammocks with the bedding and
blankets were lashed to the shrouds which served much to
save our rigging, as was very evident from examination on the
second night after the battle; for when our men got their
hammocks down many were found to have received a great
deal of damage being very much cut with the large shot, and
some were found to have had grape or canister shot lodged in
them. The most destructive shot to us appeared to be the 32
pound double-headed; two of these deafeners we observed to be
sticking in our main-mast, which miraculously and fortunately
for us, was not carried away.

There is little doubt that Nelson's 'stratagem', if it was even
that, was not at all responsible for the French and Spanish fleet
coming out, and, of course, Jack Nastyface sees the battle as a
confused scramble. He says that they cut off the five sternmost
ships, though they actually sailed between the second and third
from the end of the line. He gives no indication as to why the
English ships sailed towards the combined fleet in two columns,
or the considerable effect that this had on the final outcome of
the battle as it enabled the English ships to form on both sides of
the combined fleet and also to concentrate on the rear section. The
French army had already left the Channel coast and there were not
enough flat bottomed barges for an invasion. Nonetheless his
description of the events is a most graphic one and his account of
the news of Nelson's death, and his attitude towards the great
Admiral seems more acceptable than the 'soft toads' of the young
seamen in the Royal Sovereign mentioned in the first chapter.

It was in the events that followed the battle that almost the
greatest tragedy occurred for the sailors themselves. One great
hope they had was to capture a rich prize as this would augment
their pitiful wages possibly to a considerable extent. Of course,
the prize had to be taken to a friendly port and after the battle a
severe gale blew up, and with the shattered state of the ships,
it was all but impossible to bring them in and indeed only one
prize reached Gibraltar in a servicable condition.

Some of our men were sent on board of the Spanish ship before alluded to, in order to assist at the pumps, for she was much shattered in the hull between wind and water. The slaughter and havoc our guns had made, rendered the scene of carnage horrid to behold; there were a number of dead bodies piled up in the hold; many, in a wounded or mutilated state, were found lying amongst them, and those who were so fortunate as to escape our shot were so dejected and crest-fallen that they could not, or would not, work at the pumps, and of course the ship was in a sinking state.

The gale at this time was increasing so rapidly that manning the pumps was of no use, and we were obliged to abandon our prize, taking away with us all our men and as many prisoners as we could. On the last boat's load leaving the ship, the Spaniards who were left on board appeared on the gangway and ship's side, displaying their bags of dollars and doubloons and eagerly offering them as a reward for saving them from the expected and unavoidable wreck, but however well inclined we were, it was not in our power to rescue them, or it would have been effected without the proffered bribe.

Here, a very distressing and affecting scene took place; it was a struggle between inclination and duty. On quitting the ship, our boats were overloaded in endeavouring to save all the lives we could, that it is a miracle they were not upset. A father and his son came down the ship's side to get on board one of our boats; the father had already seated himself, but the men in the boat thinking from the load and boisterous weather that all their lives would be in peril, could not think of taking the boy; as the boat put off, the lad, as though determined not to quit his father, sprang from the ship into the water, and caught hold of the gunwale of the boat; but his attempt was resisted as it risked all their lives, and some of the men resorted to their cutlasses to cut his fingers off, in order to disengage the boat from his grasp; at the same time, the feelings of the father were so worked upon, that he was about to leap overboard and perish with his son. Britons could face an enemy, but could not witness such a scene of self-devotion; as it were, a simultaneous thought burst forth from the crew, which said 'Let us save both the father and son, or die in the attempt'. The Almighty aided them in their design; they succeeded, and brought father and son safe on board our ship where they remained until with other prisoners, they were exchanged at Gibraltar.

Two other aspects of the aftermath mentioned by Jack Nasty-face can be added here. First, the pride of the sailors in the ships that suffered most:

Whilst we were at this place, patching our shattered hulk to make us sea worthy for returning home, some of the crews of the different ships in the fleet would occasionally meet on shore, and one would say to another tauntingly, on enquiring to what ship he belonged, 'Oh! you belong to one of the ships that did not come up till the battle was nearly over!' Others would be heard to say 'Oh! you belong to one of the Boxing Twelves; come and have some black strap and Malaga wine,' at the same time giving them a hearty shake by the hand. This was signi-fying that the heat of the battle was borne by the twelve ships which first engaged and broke the line; and though in a great measure this was true; yet no fault or blame could be attributed either to the officers or men belonging to the ships, as it was the tremendous firing from the ships first engaged, which so be-calmed the water and lulled the winds, that a few of our largest ships could only come up in time to receive a straggling shot or two, and take possession of some of the prizes.

There were not many persons, perhaps, who would believe that the firing of cannon could have such an effect on the air and water; but a little reflection will convince of its truth, when they learn the notorious fact that one gun will have power to burst a raging waterspout; and then it may be imagined what effect must be produced from a thousand cannons, heavily charged, every minute, for some hours.

(This effect is well attested elsewhere.)

Second, the warm welcome they received in returning home and the granting of leave—a rare privilege.

Our ship being made sea worthy, we set sail for Old England, and arrived safe at Spithead. The next day we weighed anchor for Portsmouth and on our way into the harbour mouth we were loudly cheered and welcomed home by an immense number of persons who came to greet us on the occasion. The ship being put into dock to repair, the crew were sent on board of a hulk, from which many of them obtained a temporary leave of absence, and, among the rest, I had a six days liberty ticket, with which, and two shilling and ninepence in my pocket, I was resolved to go to London.

This description of the battle is one of the few sections in the 'Nautical Economy' in which Jack Nastyface has much good to say of the navy. Unfortuately we know very little of him, aside from his book 'Nautical Economy or Forecastle Recollections of Events during the Last War', dedicated to the Brave Tars of Old England by a sailor politely called by the officers of the navy 'Jack Nastyface'. Even the ship he served in is not entirely certain as he nowhere names it, though the *Revenge* is the only really possible one. His proper name is also uncertain though he was probably William Robinson who entered the service on 9th May 1805 and deserted at Portsmouth on 30th April 1811, but in his own words at the end of his book he writes 'We prepared for our return to England and arrived at Portsmouth in the latter end of the year, when I quitted, and took my leave of the naval service,' which does not seem like April. All we can tell for certain about him is what he reveals in his book. His father, as he himself puts it, was an honest tradesman but in humble circumstances as a shoe-maker. At an early age Jack was put to business but 'his roving mind would not suffer him to pursue it.' With the war against Napoleon reaching a climax, he decided to join the Navy. Although he does not explicitly say so, it seems probable that it was the glamour of a sailor's life that attracted him. He went to the Rendezvous—the naval recruiting centre—on Tower Hill, on 9th May 1805 and offered his services to His Majesty. Because he was wearing an apron it was supposed that he was a runaway apprentice, but when he had persuaded them that he was not, he was sent on board the receiving ship then laying off the Tower. Here he was soon undeceived about the glamour of the navy. The receiving ships received not only volunteers but also the scum of the London streets, swept up by the Press Gang, for this was a time of the 'Hot Press'.

Whatever may be said about the boasted land of liberty, whenever a youth resorts to a receiving ship for shelter and hos-pitality, he, from that moment must take leave of the liberty to *speak* or to act; he may *think*, but he must confine his thoughts to the hatchway of utterance.

On being sent on board the receiving ship, it was for the first time I began to repent of the rash step I had taken, but it was of no avail, submission to the events of fate was my only alternative; murmuring or remonstrating, I soon found would be folly. After having been examined by the doctor and reported sea-worthy, I was ordered down the hold, where I remained all night (9th May 1805) with my companions in wretchedness and the rats running over us in numbers. When released, we were ordered into the admiralty tender which was to convey us to the Nore. Here we were called over by name, nearly two hundred, including a number of Lord Mayor's men, a term given to those who are sent on board by any of the City Magistrates for a street frolic or night charge. These poor fellows have a sad time of it, as they are the derision of the old and more experienced and hardened sailors who generally cut the tails from their coats and otherwise abuse and ridicule them. Upon getting on board this vessel we were ordered down in the hold and the gratings put over us as well as a guard of Marines placed round the hatchway with their muskets loaded and fixed bayonets, as though we had been culprits of the first degree, or capital convicts. In this place we spent the day and the following night huddled together for there was not room to sit or stand separate. Indeed we were in a pitiable plight, for numbers of them were sea-sick, some retching, others were smoking whilst many were so overcome by the stench that they fainted for want of air. As soon as the officer on deck understood that the men below were overcome with foul air, he ordered the hatches to be taken off, when day light broke in upon us; and a wretched appearance we cut, for scarcely any of us were free from filth and vermin. We had by this time arrived at the Nore and were all ordered on deck, where boats from the receiving ship were alongside to take us away from the tender and place us on board those ships, where we were supplied with slops, the price of which is stopped from our pay by the purser, and in due time we were transferred and distributed among the different ships, where we awaited an order for a supply of men and boys to complete each ship's complement.

I must here state a regular system of plunder observed on board these ships on the *birds of passage* as we were called, more than was agreeable, partly, perhaps, from what may be termed larking, but principally from a wicked design. Some lost their shoes in open day while others had their blankets taken from them as they lay on deck at night; they would disappear instantly, as if by magic. The mode resorted to, I learned, was by using fish-hooks and a line, which were contrived so dextrously, that, aided by its being dark between decks, it was almost impossible to detect them.

Jack Nastyface was from here drafted to a ship of the line, almost certainly the *Revenge*, which was fitting out to join Lord Nelson, and this he liked no better.

Here we began to feel discipline with all its horrors. Our crew was divided into two watches, starboard and larboard. When one was on deck the other was below; for instance the starboard watch would come on at eight o'clock at night which is eight bells; at half-past is called one bell and so on; every half hour is a bell, as the hour glass is turned and the messenger sent to strike the bell which is generally affixed near the forehatchway. It now became the duty of the officer on deck to see that the log line is run out, to ascertain how many knots the ship goes an hour, which is entered in the log book with any other occurances which may take place during the watch. At 12 o'clock or eight bells in the first watch the boatswain's mate calls out lustily 'Larboard watch a-hoy'. This is called the middle watch and when on deck, the other watch go below to their hammocks till eight bells which is 4 o'clock in the morning. They then come on deck again, pull off their shoes and stockings, turn up their trousers to above their knees and commence holy-stoning the deck, as it is termed (for Jack is sometimes a little impious in the way of his sayings)—Here the men suffer from being obliged to kneel down on the wetted deck and a gravelly sort of sand strewed over it. To perform this work is very injurious. In this manner the watch continues till about four bells or 6 o'clock; they then begin to wash and scrub the decks till seven bells, and at eight bells the boatswain's mate pipes to breakfast. This meal usually consists of burgoo made of coarse oatmeal and water; others will have scotch coffee which is burnt bread boiled in some water and sweetened with sugar. This is generally cooked in a hook-pot in the galley where there is a range. Nearly all the crew have one of these pots, a spoon and a knife; for these are things indispensable. There are also basons, plates, etc. which are kept in each mess, which generally consists of eight persons who berth in between two of the guns on the lower deck, where there is a board placed which swings with the rolling of the ship and answers for a table. It sometimes happens that a lurch will dash all the crockery to pieces; they are then obliged to eat out of wooden or tin utensils, until they come into harbour, where they can get another supply. At half past eight o'clock, or one bell in the forenoon watch, the larboard goes on deck, and the starboard remains below. Here again the *holy-stones* or *hand-bibles* as they are called by the crew are used and sometimes iron scrapers. After the lower deck has been wetted with swabs, these scrapers are used to take the rough dirt off. Whilst this is going on the cooks from each mess are employed in cleaning the utensils and preparing for dinner; at the same time the watch are working the ship and doing what is wanted to be done on deck.

About eleven o'clock or six bells, when any of the men are in irons, or on the black list, the boatswain's mates are ordered to call all hands; the culprits are then brought forward by the Master-at-Arms, who is a Warrant Officer and acts the part of Jack Ketch, when required. He likewise has the prisoners in his custody until they are put in irons under any charge. All hands being now mustered, the Captain orders the man to strip: he is then seized (i.e. lashed) to a grating by the wrists and knees; his crime is then mentioned and the prisoner may plead but in nineteen cases out of twenty he is flogged for the most trifling offence or neglect, such as not hearing the watch called at night, not doing anything properly on deck or aloft, which he might happen to be sent to do, when, perhaps, he has been doing the best he could and at the same time ignorant of having done wrong, until he is pounced on, and put in irons. So much for the legal process.

After punishment the boatswain's mate pipes to dinner, it being eight bells or twelve o'clock; and this is the pleasantest part of the day, as at one bell the fifer is called to play 'Nancy Dawson' or some other lively tune, a well known signal that the grog is ready to be served out. It is the duty of the cook from each mess to fetch and serve it out to his messmates, of which every man and boy is allowed a pint, that is one gill of rum and three of water, to which is added lemon acid sweetened with sugar. Here I must remark that the cook comes in for the perquisites of office by reserving to himself an extra portion of grog, which is called the over-plus and generally comes to the double of a man's allowance. Thus the cook can take upon himself to be the man of consequence, for he has the opportunity of inviting a friend to partake of a glass, or of paying any little debt he may have contracted. It may not be known to everyone that it is grog which pays debts and not money in a man-of-war. Notwithstanding the cook's apparently pre-eminent situation, yet on some occasions he is subject to censure or punishment by his mess mates, for not attending to the dinner properly, or suffering the utensils of his department to be in a dirty condition. Justice in these cases is awarded by picking a jury of cooks from different messes, for it falls to the lot of each man in a mess to act as cook in his turn. The mode or precept by which this jury is summoned is by hoisting a mess swab or beating a tin dish between decks forward, which serves as a proclamation to call the court together, when the case is fully heard and decided upon.

At two bells in the afternoon, or one o'clock, the starboard watch goes on deck and remains working ship, pointing the ropes or doing any duty that may be required until the eight-bells strike when the boatswain's mate pipes to supper. This consists of half a pint of wine or a pint of grog to each man with biscuit, and cheese, or butter. At the one bell or half-past four which is called one bell in the *first dog watch*, the larboard watch comes on duty and remains until six o'clock when it is relieved by the starboard watch which is called the *second dog watch*, which lasts till eight o'clock. To explain this, it must be observed that these four hours, four to eight o'clock are divided in two watches with a view of making the other watches come regular and alternate and are called the *first and second dog watches*. By this regular system of duty. I became inured to the roughness and hardship of a sailor's life. I had made up my mind to be obedient, however irksome to my feelings, and our ship being on the Channel station, I soon began to pick up a knowledge of seamanship.

Shortly after this, they sailed to Spain, and fought in the Battle of Trafalgar as has already been told. This marked the turning point in the war as far as the navy was concerned. Napoleon no longer even played with the idea of invading England and determined to destroy Britain through cutting off her trade by means of the Continental System. England, as Napoleon is supposed to have said, is a nation of shopkeepers and by banning all trade between the Continent and England, he hoped to bring England to submission. How near this scheme came to success is not often realised, but the task of the Royal Navy was to prevent any enemy, or even neutral ships if they carried contraband, from entering or leaving enemy ports, which at one time or other including the entire continent. This blockade became the monotonous task of the navy for the rest of the war.

> After refitting, we sailed to join the blockading squadron off Cadiz, and remained there about eighteen months, during which time we were tacking or wearing ship continually, as the blockading service required us to keep as near the harbour's mouth as possible, and consequently, when the wind was blowing on the land, we were obliged to beat off, and when it was blowing off the land, then to beat up to the harbour's mouth as near as we could, to prevent the escape of the enemy.

Or again, a little nearer home:

> Our Captain having left us, we were joined by another, and the ship put to sea, and we soon found we had become *Channel Gropers*, a term given to the Channel fleet in wartime, which is destined to hover about Brest when the wind is fair, for the French fleet to come out, as we were blockading this; and when the wind blows strong into the harbour, so that they could not well get out; in those cases our fleet would sometimes put in at Cowsand or Torbay, and might be what sailors call a *fresh beef station*, but it is such as few seamen like, for they say it is neither being abroad nor at home. One reason why they have a dislike of it is that they are open to the ridicule of seamen who may be coming from foreign stations, as well as by the girls and people in the sea-port towns, by cantingly telling them they would never have the scurvy or that they might as well be by their mother's fireside and tied to the apron-strings, as merely running in and out of harbour; and nothing hurts Jack's feelings more than being taunted of anything unmanly or inferior.

There were occasional incidents to relieve the monotony. Off Cadiz, for example:

> ... we sometimes fired at, and brought to, some of the Spanish fishing boats, and by these means, a fresh meal for the crew was

often obtained; for they not only had fish on board but some would have grapes, whilst others would have fowls and eggs, and our Captain was always anxious to get fresh provisions for the ship's company.

There were also occasional clashes with the enemy.

Whilst on the look-out, we happened to discover the enemy one morning loose their sails, and this we thought was merely to dry them, but it turned out to be otherwise. A Russian Fleet of nine sail of the line had just come down the Gut of Gibraltar, and wanted to enter Cadiz harbour; we were now in a somewhat awkward predicament, not being certain whether that nation had declared war with England or not; but at all events we prepared for action. Our Admiral sent his boat with an officer to the Russian admiral to inform him that he could not go in, and, if he attempted, that we must dispute the point with him. Our force being nine sail of the line made us but equal, yet we were in a awkward position, for on the other side of us were ten or eleven sail of French and Spanish ships of the line, ready to come out, and no doubt would give their assistance to cripple us. The Russians, however, shaped their course to Lisbon where I believe they were afterwards captured by one of our squadrons.

The navy was engaged in other activities besides the blockade, but the two in which Jack Nastyface was involved were both most unfortunate. The first was an incident in the Basque Roads following which the leading frigate Captain involved, Lord Cochrane, demanded a Court Martial for the Commander-in-Chief, Sir James Gambier, though almost inevitably the latter was honourably acquitted. The full facts of the matter are still somewhat in dispute, and Admiral Harvey of whom Jack Nastyface makes much, had his faults, but there is no doubt that the whole incident was extremely badly managed by the Commander-in-Chief. Here is Jack Nastyface's description of the events:

We were joined by some other ships, amongst which was the Caledonian, with Lord Gambier as Commander-in-Chief. We now anchored in their outer roads, or as the French call it, the Basque Roads, and Lord Gambier thought it would be very advisable that some fire-ships should be employed to destroy the enemy at their anchorage, instead of our going in to engage

50 From*From the Lower Deck*

them, but Admiral Harvey was of the opinion that it might have been effected by the fleet we then had with us; and such was the idea entertained by nineteen out of twenty composing the fleet. Admiral Harvey suggested to Lord Gambier the propriety of engaging the enemy directly, rather than give them time to escape to their inner harbour, where we could not by any means get at them on account of the batteries. Admiral Harvey's plan was to form our Fleet in two division: the one to attack and take the Isle d'Aix, which commands the harbour by its strong batteries, and the other was to engage the French shipping and amuse it until the island surrendered, and then this division to join and give its assistance, and with aid from the batteries, their whole fleet would inevitably have fallen into our possession; but the suggestion, however reasonable, yet it was not approved of the Commander-in-Chief, notwithstanding so sanguine was Admiral Harvey of its success, and being second in command, offered to lead either division to the enterprise. The plea of the Commander-in-Chief was that it would be a great risk of men's lives: and yet, he could prepare to adopt the mode of destroying them by fire-ships; and if that idea had been carried into effect to the full extent of its object, we should not only have burnt their shipping, but also the crews in them must have become sacrificed; and though it was an enemy, yet the thought is shuddering, that nearly ten thousand men, whilst they were harmlessly asleep in their cots and hammocks, might be roasted to death and perhaps without a moment's time to say 'Lord have mercy on me!' and how the Commander-in-Chief could express himself as to the fear of taking away life, with this murderous plot on his brain, is inconceivable, and a strange reason for not agreeing to the proposition which had been made to him.

Admiral Harvey having been one of the Nelson school and seeing the enemy within our reach, happened to express himself rather too warmly, at not being allowed to engaged them. This gave great umbrage to the Commander-in-Chief, and for which he was sent home and tried and broke, but re-instated at the bottom of the list of admirals. This must have been no very comfortable reflection for one who had often signalised himself, and on one occasion so gallantly repulsed the enemy, when boarded on each side of him, and whose ship suffered more than any other of the fleet at the Battle of Trafalgar, and who felt as an Englishman

and an officer and was well satisfied that he possessed the means
to capture the French fleet, without recourse to the hazardous,
expensive, and doubtful expedient of fire-ships. However,
orders were given, and fire-ships were to be the mode of warfare. Having several merchant vessels with us, from two to
three hundred tons burthen, each man-of-war was to fit out one
of these as a fire-ship, and we had also one much larger, which
was the *Mediator*, store-ship, which was successful in breaking
the bar placed across the entrance to prevent our ships getting
in. After they were all prepared and made ready, the wind being
fair, the signal was made to weigh anchor and proceed to the
work of destruction. Notwithstanding all these preparation,
as the cruel substitute for a manly engagement, it did not
exactly answer the helm of the Admiral's expectations, for not
one of the fire-ships went near enough to catch hold of the
enemy's rigging with the grapplings; it certainly frightened,
for they cut their cables and ran up to the inner harbour, with
the exception of four line-of-battle ships that got aground;
but to affright them was not the object; it was not
conquest.

Here was exhibited a grand display of fire-works at the
expense of John Bull; no gala night at Ranelagh or Vauxhall
could be compared to it. Our Fleet was lying quite composedly
at a distance, with the crews in and about the rigging for the
greater part of the night, witnessing the effect of the Congreve
rockets, as well as the explosion of each fire-ship which
illuminated the air, one after the other. However dangerous the
service, yet there are never wanting British seamen to embark
in it, and on this occasion a boat's crew from each ship of the
line volunteered their services to take those fire-ships in; it is a
sort of forlorn hope adventure, for every man taken on such an
expedition by the enemy, is liable to be delt with in a similar
manner as a spy, and put to death. It is a mode of warfare
dreadful to resort to and should not be practised by a civilised
nation. Those who are so fortunate as to return safe, were
generally, at least in most cases, promoted.

On daylight appearing in the morning of the 12th of April,
we discovered the four French ships aground, and two frigates
and a bomb vessel were sent in, under the command of Lord
Cochrane, to destroy them, or to ascertain the means by which
it could be effected. This was a task which just suited his lord-

ship's taste, and that he was well calculated to carry into execution, for he commenced raking and firing away directly he got in, but the contest was a very unequal one; his Lordship should have had a greater force with him. The Captains and officers of the different ships were much hurt on this occasion, and might be seen to walk the decks, biting their lips with regret at not being allowed to go and assist the frigates. At length our ship asked permission to afford them our aid, and the admiral gave his consent that ourselves and another line-of-battle ship got to his Lordship's assistance. Our anchor in a second kissed the bows, was stowed, and the ship in full sail in the twinkling of an eye; in fact, never was seen such dispatch, so great was the anxiety of all hands to be busy. In a very short time, we anchored in the harbour, between the batteries and the shipping and commenced pouring our broadsides so rapidly into the French ships aground, that they became an easy conquest. Two of them struck to us, and the other two to the frigates.

Our ship having touched the ground, we were forced to lie under their batteries all night and had they been skillful marksmen, they must have cut us to pieces. Their shots were whistling over us, some a-head, some a-stern, and a great many fell short; there was not one in fifty that hit us, but those that did effected great execution. Amongst them was a very distressing and mischevious one, which knocked a man's head completely from his shoulders and struck a Lieutenant on the breast. The Lieutenant was knocked down by the force of the head striking him: he was of course, taken down to the cockpit as a wounded man from his being very much be-smeared with the blood from the man's head. The Doctor immediately enquired of him whereabouts he was hurt and he pointed to his breast; but when the doctor unbuttoned his waistcoat and examined, there was not the least symptom of his having been wounded; indeed, he was more frightened than hurt, but certainly it was enough to alarm any man. He was requested to sit down and compose himself, and to state the truth, it was some time before that fit of composure went off, for he very prudently had no notion of going on deck again while men's heads were flying about and doing so much mischief. Nearly twenty of our men were killed and wounded and among these was a steady seaman, with the calves of both his legs shot away. It became necessary to amputate one of the legs immediately, and during the operation he did not utter a syllable; and shortly after, on the doctor examining the other leg, that was also doomed to undergo a similar fate. Upon being told this, the poor fellow pleaded very hard that it might be left him, and very cooly observed that he should like one leg left to wear his shoes out, but the doctor was obliged to take off the other leg, the symptoms of mortification being very apparent. Like a brave fellow, he bore his sufferings with great fortitude, and to the surprise of everyone present at the finish of the second amputation, he exclaimed 'Now to the devil with all shoe-makers; I have done with them.' This man was progressively doing well, and his wounds were healing fast; but, from lying in one position for such a length of time, his back mortified and he breathed his last, much regretted by all his shipmates.

I will now return to the four French ships we had possessed ourselves of; the prisoners were taken out and we set fire to them on the night of the 13th of April and they gradually burnt, until the fire reached the magazines, when they blew up with a tremendous shock, but it was awefully grand. After the destruction of the four ships, we were ordered home to repair our damage and re-fit.

Whatever may be said for Gambier, and indeed he could argue, as Jellicoe did after Jutland, that his duty was to keep his fleet intact, a chance was missed of inflicting a further shattering blow on Napoleon. Gambier had been a brave and capable officer in a subordinate capacity, but faced with the supreme command he lacked the inspiration and resolution that had brought overwhelming victories to St. Vincent and Nelson. Certainly the sailors themselves were aware of these weaknesses though they failed to realise their causes. Admiral Harvey was held up as 'one of the Nelson school' and this was the supreme compliment that could be paid to him, but Jack Nastyface simply blames the failure of the navy to achieve any outstanding success after Trafalgar on the officers:

In the first, a radical reform in her officers is the only means to effect it (the improvement of the navy), for did these men but think a little more of *natural honour* and a little less of *self importance* there would be less difference between the belly and the members. A seaman will as soon risk his life for his kind and

E

good captain, as he would defend his country's honour; but among the many who have had command in the British Navy how few there are who are spoken well of by those who have served with them.

Inevitably this was reflected, in the sailors' eyes, more in their captain than their admiral, but pride in having served under Nelson and hatred of a bullying captain are both evident in this description of the changes effected by a new commanding officer— the Honourable Sir Charles Paget.

On returning to Portsmouth, I learned that our Captain had left, and another had taken the command; I also found that a vast number of our men had run in consequence of our new captain having the character of being a tyrannical officer. This self important nautical demagogue very soon set about not a reform, but a revolution in the ship. It had been a favourite mode with Lord Nelson to paint the side of all ships under his command in chequers, which made them to be distinguished with greater certainty in case of falling in with an enemy; and became a well known and general term in a squadron or fleet, so much so that, when speaking of any other ship, it was usual to say, 'Oh! she's one of Nelson's chequer-players,' signifying thereby that she had been one of the fighting ships. The seamen liked the distinction, and took great pride in being considered a chequer player and could not wish to part with the name; but no sooner had this self-sufficient blusterer come on board and possessed himself of the reins of government, then he changed the paint of the ship's side from that of a chequer to a single stripe. The character which came on board with him was quite sufficient to create dissatisfaction in the ship's company, but this single act caused so much disgust, that nothing was heard but execrations on his head; for it seemed as though he had studiously intended to blot out or rob them of what they considered as the badge of their glory. 'Ah', many might be heard to say, 'that fellow never liked the smell of powder, I'm sure, for it's a damned cowardly act and the greater the tyrant, the greater the coward; and if the signal was made now for him to engage an enemy, he'd lag astern. No! he'll never be a chequer-player, let him command for fifty years to come.' This worthy, whose name was a terror to every ship's company he commanded, and was cursed from stem to stern in the British navy, now shines forth as an M.P. and is always to be found at his post; and whenever the subject of impressment or flogging in the navy or army is brought forward in the House of Commons, he is ever ready with his Nero heart and famed for his skill in the support of this diabolical system.'

Further, Jack Nastyface blames Admiralty promotion itself for following the incident in the Basque Roads where Paget had not been in command.

On arriving in England, our great swell and M.P. Captain took the command again, and the man who had so gallantly fought our ship was turned adrift; he was a noble fellow, although of no high family or titled connections; but valour, without these appendages is not always sure of meeting its reward, at least in this instance it did not, for Admiralty promotion is a difficult canvas.

Shortly after this the *Revenge* was involved in a second and even more disastrous adventure—the Walcheren Expedition. Here Jack Nastyface's account is extremely accurate. The expedition was intended to relieve the Austrians who had again revolted against Napoleon and unlike many previous expeditions it was handsomely equipped. Largely because of the lack of co-operation between the navy and the army no immediate action was taken in the early stages, allowing the French time to bring up reinforcements and prevent the capture of Antwerp—one of the main objectives of the expedition. As it was, disease soon spread among the troops—malaria 'Polder Fever' and dysentry—though not caused simply as Jack Nastyface suggests by eating too many apples. The expedition then returned home having achieved nothing of any significance.

After refitting at length we sailed, and Walcheren was our destination. Had we been a fleet of Lilliputians going to attack Gulliver, we were numerous enough to have killed and eaten him, and to have towed the island home afterwards. Our force was near forty sail-of-the line, besides frigates, sloops and gun-brigs, making altogether upwards of one hundred and thirty ships of war besides gun-boats and transports full a thousand in number, and the military force consisted of forty thousand men.

Having arrived at Walcheren, we commenced disembarking

the troops at about five o'clock in the morning, previously serving every man with three days provisions, or rations, as the soldiers called them. On reaching land some of the horses' and men's feet were unexpectedly cut with iron spikes which had been ingeniously placed in the grass and cow fields for that purpose by the enemy.

Having completed our disembarkation, the ships of war anchored at a distance from the island, and remained inactive for nearly a fortnight; the small-arms men from different ships-of-the-line were sent ashore to assist the troops, and also to be employed in throwing up fortifications and erecting barriers. Whilst this was going on, the military and some of the naval officers were regaling themselves at Middleburgh, which is an inland town and is the capital. Sir William Curtis having just arrived in his yacht, and had brought plenty of turtles with him, it is easy to imagine that there was no lack of feasting, lounging and parading about; some of the military were at this hour employed in driving the enemy's sharp-shooters from the thickets and bushes, and here they had a fine opportunity of gathering plenty of apples as they were growing spontaneously and in abundance on different parts of the island. Many of our people, by eating too freely of this fruit were apt to drink to an excess of the hollands, and would incautiously lay down to sleep on the earth, when from the dampness of the atmosphere, the island lying low and interspersed with a number of canals, it caused an ague and a number of lives were lost, who fell victims to their imprudence.

Our newly erected batteries now being completed, a summons was sent in for the town of Flushing to surrender. To this the commandant sent in a negative, unless compelled by the force of arms; a second message was then sent, requesting that the women and children might be sent away, as the intention was to bombard the town and it was desirable that their lives should not become thus sacrificed. The commandant's reply was that he would not allow any person to leave the town.

The time given having expired, we commenced an attack upon the town, and during the bombardment, one of our batteries had unfortunately an explosion of powder which killed and wounded several of our men. I will here remark, that on one of these sallies made by the enemy out of the gates of the town, the soldiers and small-arms men from the ships were employed in engaging them and the small-arms men being seamen with an impetuosity not to be controlled, they rushed on the enemy with such rapidity that they actually drove the enemy within the gates of the town with the loss of a very few lives, at the same time vociferating that the soldiers should not go before them to battle. Several times during the conflict the soldiers would have fired on the enemy, but could not, for fear of killing our seamen.

After destroying a great portion of the town by shots, shell and rockets, it surrendered, and on our taking possession, the sight was melancholy to behold. There was scarcely a street, but which the greater part of the houses were knocked down, with women and children buried under their ruins. Some were dug out scarcely alive and much mutilated, whilst others found a ready grave amidst the devastation. One third of the town was completely destroyed, and other parts were much damaged; even the church did not escape; it received much injury by catching fire.

The roaring of cannon having subsided, and the din of war, with all its horrors, being heard no more, the Commander-in-Chief and his colleagues, together with the naval officers, enjoyed a little leisure, and made a grand display in the town; nothing was to be seen but red coats and blue coats, epaulettes and feathers; there were, however, a few of the naval officers who could not join in these lounges, as they were employed to superintend the taking to pieces of one ship and the launching another to be sent to England. It fell to our lot to be ordered home with near seven hundred prisoners; these were some of all nations—French, Dutch, Russian, Prussian, Austrians, Danes, Swedes and a sprinkling of Spaniards.

There was with one of the Spaniards the curious circumstance of a musket ball that had struck him, and was lodged between the lower lip and chin; it must have been what is termed 'a spent ball', or it would have shattered his face to pieces. It had not injured the jaw bone, and the skin had healed over it. He had received it, he said, whilst fighting in Spain, and did not seem to feel any inconvenience from it. He observed that many medical men had been very anxious, and had offered their kind services to relieve him of what he called his *chap-fallen* companion, and to make a sound cure; for though not attended with pain, it was working down to the under part of the chin; but he said it was an honourable badge, and, as a trophy, he would carry it to his grave.

Having landed our prisoners in England, we were ordered again to Flushing and there remained until the English evacuated the place, which was near the Christmas of 1809. Previous to our coming away, we did all the mischief we could; we set fire to everything in the dockyard and filled up the entrance of the different canals with stones and rubbish. This obtained for us no good name, for on leaving, we were much ridiculed and jeered by the Dutchmen, who exclaimed that we had brought a large force there, and had done nothing worthy of war, but to knock down their houses, and distress the poor inhabitants, and this was partly true. It was certainly a great error that the naval force was not allowed to make the attack until the army could act with it, for we could have taken very nearly all the Dutch shipping then lying about Flushing, together with the town, without aid either from the army transports or flat bottomed boats, the ships of war and men being so numerous. Instead of which, the enemy were allowed to run up river to Antwerp, cooly, and at their pleasure; whilst we were obliged to come away without having obtained our object. To be sure some hundreds of men's lives were sacrificed, and, as we were told on our arrival in England, that nearly twenty millions of money had been expended on that expedition.

If anything can lower the spirits of the British sailor, it is that of not being able to speak triumphantly of any enterprise he may have been upon; and certainly on our return from this formidably prepared undertaking, we had nothing to reflect on that could gladden the heart, or be the cause of exultation; but, on the contrary, disappointment was seen to hang upon every man's visage and he was ashamed to own whither he had been. When accosted and talked to, they would generally try to waive or elude the subject; they were sneered at, and saluted with the sarcastic title of 'The grand secret expedition men,—yes? they'll let us into the secret too by and by, in the way of a side wind of heavy taxation.' This sort of ungenerous taunting did not help to dispel the cloud in which their minds would be enveloped; they were compelled to bear it, but with regret.

This was the last incident of importance in which Jack Nasty-face was engaged. For a time the *Revenge* became a 'Channel

Groper' again; then she was involved in transporting troops to Lisbon to join Lord Wellington and it was on the completion of this trip that he deserted.

Having safely landed our freight and bearing no orders to go on any particular service, we prepared for our return to England and arrived at Portsmouth in the latter end of the year, when I quitted, and took my leave of the naval service.

This is all we know of him though presumably he was still alive when the book was published in 1835. It is clear, though, that the author had considerable knowledge of the events he describes. His account of the Walcheren Expedition includes most of the important incidents and could have been written many years later relying at best on second-hand information. Indeed much of it may not have been actually written by a sailor at all, though in general this seems unlikely. It has been suggested that if Jack Nastyface was William Robinson, then he had a particular dislike of the service because he remained a 'landsman' throughout his service and unlike the rest of his contemporaries was not even promoted to ordinary seaman. This would also account for his remarks about the bandsmen being rated as Able Seamen or Petty Officers, not doing the work of the ship which the 'landsmen' did. There is no doubt, though, of his intense hatred of the officers and the attitudes adopted by most of the other seamen mentioned here seem to imply that the view was common. At all events, Jack Nastyface's experiences were such that it is hardly surprising that he felt as he did. In particular one Midshipman who was killed at Trafalgar, he remembers as follows:

If an officer is of a tyrannical disposition on board a ship, whatever accident may happen to him, he will never receive pity or commiseration from any of the ship's crew—as for instance—We had a Midshipman on board our ship of a wickedly mischievious disposition, whose sole delight was to insult the feelings of the seamen and furnish pretexts to get them punished. His conduct made every man's life miserable that happened to be under his orders. He was a youth not more than twelve or thirteen years of age; I have often seen him get on the carriage of a gun, call a man to him, and kick him about the thighs and body, and with his feet would beat him about the head; and these, although prime seamen, at the same time dared not murmur. It was ordained, however, by Providence, that his reign of terror and severity should not last; for during the engagement, he was killed on the quarter-deck by a grape-shot, his body greatly mutilated, his entrails being driven and scattered against the larboard side; nor were there any lamenta-taions for his fate! No! for when it was known that he was killed, the general exclamation was, '*Thank God we are rid of the young tyrant!*' His death was hailed as the triumph over an enemy.

It must be added that a number of his complaints against officers are typical lower-deck grumbles.

On board the different ships, there were numerous packages, which had been shipped at Flushing, and no doubt but they were intended to be smuggled into England from the secret manner, and the different stratagems used, in the getting of them afterwards on shore. The bread-room of our ship was crowded with them, directed for different officers holding high rank, both in army and navy, and may have been intended as presents or for their own use, but they did not pay the duty. These packages consisted of sets of Hamburg china, and table services, down for beds, spirits and various other articles of foreign produce. Not being able to land all these goods at once without detection, we contrived it at different intervals, safely thus got rid of some of them by different conveyances and then we became ' Channel Gropers' again, and whilst on duty we landed the balance of our secret cargo, at Weymouth and Plymouth, as we were frequently running into these ports. Whilst on the Cherbourg blockade station, it often occurred that we were in chase of vessels supposing them to be smugg-lers, and at the same time, we were meditating how to get rid of the bulk of our bread-room stowage which did not intend to pay any duty, for we had His Majesty's pendant which no custom-house officer searches so strictly. Contrast this with a seaman's bringing home the most trifling article, as a present to a relation or friend: the poor fellow is pounced upon im-mediately and compelled to submit to the laws of his country, whilst others, holding His Majesty's commission, by the aid of his Lieutenant, and his boat's crews, commits a flagrant act of smuggling with impunity: but the poor seaman, if taken, is sure to suffer.

It would savour more of propriety if the revenue officers were a little more vigilant, and kept an eye on those who are paid to prevent infractions, instead of being the first violators of our laws.

Grumbles such as these are still heard today about the officer who smuggles a bottle of duty-free gin ashore.

Undoubtedly the Captain's almost unlimited right to punish accounted for a good deal of the hostility and Jack Nastyface had the misfortune to serve under at least one 'flogging captain', the Honourable Sir Charles Paget . . .

He was an M.P., of high birth and had great influence at head quarters and was fond of being placed near home. He was constantly taking a trip to London, whenever he pleased, leaving the command of the ship in the hands of the first lieutenant, who was a tyrant on board, and was sure to be supported by this (M.P.) captain who flogged every man that was reported to him by the aforesaid Lieutenant without enquiring into the complaint, for that would have been beneath his dignity as a man and an officer. This sort of conduct had nearly brought the ship into a state of mutiny, and indeed, many of our men ran away. He was so much the lofty high-spirited gentleman, that he would not condescend to command the ship when he was on board, but would leave it in the hands of the Lieutenant, so that, as to the discharge of duty as an officer, he might as well have been on shore. He was so independent and so much the man of pleasure, that he had never been through the ship to examine the state of it, or the crew. He had his band on board, to the amount of upwards of twenty performers, sending as many prime seamen away and having this musical junto in their stead, and thus weakening our force; for these worthies were excused from ship's duty; they were rated as petty officers or able seamen and received pay as such, whilst the men who were actually doing the ship's duty were some rated as landsmen, and others as ordinary seamen. As a band, these gentlemen were kept fully employed, for whilst he was indulging himself in the cabin with the importance of a great bashaw, they would be playing at the door; for the band and his dog drew all his attention, and seemed to be his sole delight. He was pompous, proud, imperious, unfeeling, and, of course, detested.

It was probably the extent and the brutality of these punishments that affected him most strongly. At least the long description of punishments which he gives, seems to imply this:

Any person who has been on board a ship of war must be aware that discipline and subordination is necessary, but the extent to which cruelty was carried on under the name of discipline, on board many ships during the late war, is not generally known, nor will a British public believe that any body of men would submit to such marks of degredation as they were compelled to undergo. It was partially known at Somerset House by the different ships' logs, but the real crime, if any, was not, it is believed, therein set down; for there it came under the head of '*disobedience*' or under a peculiar article of war which run as follows: 'All crimes not capital shall be punished according to the customs and manners used at sea.' This article shelters the captains in the navy in resorting to almost any mode of punishment they may think proper.

Flogging through the fleet

Whilst lying at Spithead in the year 1809 or 1810, four impressed seamen attempted to make their escape from a frigate then lying there; one of their shipmates, a Dutchman, to whom they had entrusted their secret, betrayed their intention and informed the commanding officer of their designs. They were tried by a court-martial and sentenced to receive three hundred lashes each through the fleet. On the first day after the trial that the weather was moderate enough to permit, the signal was made for a boat from each ship, with a guard of marines, to attend the punishment. The man is placed in a launch (i.e. the largest ship's boat) under the care of the master-at-arms and a doctor. Then a capstan bar is rigged fore and aft, to which the poor fellow is lashed by his wrists and for fear of hurting him—humane creatures—there is a stocking put over each, to prevent him from tearing the flesh off in his agonies. When all is ready, the prisoner is stripped and seized to the capstan bar. Punishment commences by the officer, after reading the sentence of the court martial, ordering the boatswains' mates to do their duty. The cat-of-nine tails is applied to the bare back, and at about every six lashes, a fresh boatswain's mate is ordered to relieve the executioner of his duty, until the prisoner has received perhaps twenty-five lashes. He is then cast loose, and allowed to sit down with a blanket rolled round him and is conveyed to the next ship, escorted by the vast number of armed boats, accompanied by the dreadful music 'the Rogues' March.' In this manner he is conveyed from ship to ship, receiving alongside of each a similar number of stripes with the cat, until the sentence is completed. It often, may generally happens, that nature is unable to sustain it, and the poor fellow faints and sinks under it, although every kind of method is made use of to enable him to bear it by pouring wine down his throat. The doctor will then feel his pulse, and often pronounces that the man is unable to bear more. He is then taken, most usually insensible, to what is termed the *sick bay*, and, if he recovers, he is told he will have to receive the remainder of his punishment. When there are many ships in the fleet at the time of the court martial, this ceremony, if the prisoner can sustain it, will last nearly half the day.

On the blanket being taken from his back, and he supported or lifted to be lashed to the capstan-bar, after he has been alongside of several ships, his back resembles so much petrified liver, and everystroke of the cat brings away congealed blood and the boatswain's mates are looked at with the eye of a hawk to see they do their duty and clear the cat's tails after every stroke, the blood at the time streaming through their fingers. In this manner are men in the navy punished for different offences, more particularly impressed men, who attempt to make their escape. The court that awards this punishment is composed of naval captains or commanders; the judge is a naval officer, and the accuser is a naval officer. One of those men after the trial, when addressed by one of his messmates with, 'I was sorry to hear you were found guilty; I was in hopes you would have been acquitted.' 'So I should have been,' was the reply, 'had I been tried by a jury of seamen; indeed I am sure I cannot go through with this torture; I would rather have been sentenced to be shot or hung at the yardarm; aye, and for my only attempting to escape after having been impressed.'

Running the Gauntlet

This is a punishment inflicted for any petty theft. The criminal himself is placed with his naked back in a large tub, wherein a seat has been fixed, and his hands lashed down to the sides. This tub is secured to a grating, and is drawn round the deck by the boys, the master-at-arms with his drawn sword pointing to the prisoner's breast. The cavalcade starts from the break of the quarter deck, after the boatswain has given the prisoner a dozen lashes, and the ship's crew are ranged round the decks in two rows, so that the prisoner passes between them, and each man is provided with a three yarn nettle; that is, three rope yarns tightly laid together and knotted. With this, each man must cut him, or be thought to be implicated in the theft. Six boatswain's mates give him half a dozen each, as he passes round the deck, so that he receives four dozen lashes from the boatswain and his mates with a cat-o'-nine-tails and six hundred cuts with the three yarn nettles from the crew of a line-of-battle ship, that being the average number of men before the mast in war time. The punishment is inflicted by the Captain's orders, without the formal inquiry by a court martial.

Flogging at the gangway or on the quarter deck

The Captain orders this punishment for anything that himself or any of his officers may consider as a crime. The prisoner is made to strip to the waist; he is then seized by his wrists and knees to a grating or ladder; the boatswain's mate is then ordered to cut him with the cat-o'-nine-tails; and after six or twelve lashes are given, another boatswain's mate is called to continue the exercise; and so they go on until the captain gives the word to stop. From one to five dozen lashes are given according to the captain's whim, but the general number is three dozen; and this number the Captain has power to give every day, if he has any bad feeling for an individual, and a tyrant of a Captain will frequently tell the boatswain's mate to lay it on harder, or that he should be flogged next himself.

This punishment is also inflicted without trial by court-martial, at the discretion of the Captain. It is not so in the army.

Starting

This may be carried to a great extent of torture, as every boatswain's mate carries a rope's-end in his pocket; and it is part of their equipment. When ordered to start the man by any of the officers, they must not be found wanting of that appendage. The man is ordered to pull off his jacket and sometimes his waistcoat if he has one on at the time. The boatswain's mate then commences beating him and continues to do so until he is ordered to stop, or unless his arm is tired and then another boatswain's mate is called to go on with the ceremony. Some of these men's backs have often been so bad from the effects of the *starting system* that they have not been able to bear their jackets on for several days. As the punishment is inflicted without tying the man up, he will naturally endeavour to ward off or escape as many blows as possible, and in doing so, frequently gets a serious cut in the face or on the head. This punishment is so common that no mention is made of it even in the log book, and but few men in wartime can escape the above mode of punishment, particularly in those ships where the Captain gives that power to his inferior officers.

Gagging

This punishment is inflicted at the time of the offence being committed, which is generally for a seaman's daring to make a reply to his superior. The man is placed in a sitting position, with both legs put in irons, and his hands secured behind him. His mouth is then forced open, and an iron bolt put across, well secured behind his head. A sentinel is placed over him with his drawn bayonet, and in this situation he remains until the Captain thinks proper to release him, or until he is nearly exhausted.

And his final comments on punishments are even more outspoken.

To go through all the different modes of punishment resorted to in the British Navy would be impossible, as almost every captain when appointed to a fresh ship adopts new customs, with different ways to punish, and I have heard the Captain say, when a man has been brought to the gangway to be flogged, and he has pleaded hard, by honestly stating that he did not know he was doing wrong, as it had been the customary order of the former Captain: and what was the reply of the furious and unreasonable officer? It was this: '*It was not my order, and I will flog every man of you, but I will break you in to my ways*'. And he nearly kept his word, for within a short period of time upward of three hundred men had been flogged or started and this too, whilst we were blockading an enemy's port. It is generally supposed that no man could be punished without having been guilty of some serious offence, but that is not always the case, for nineteen out of twenty men that are punished, suffer without being conscious that they have violated any law; and in many instances they are the most expert and able seamen. For instance, the fore, main, and mizzen-top men are selected from the crew as the most sprightly and attentive to their duty; and yet these men are more frequently punished and are always in dread when aloft that they should be found fault with for not being quick enough, for punishment is sure to follow, and sure enough, their conjectures are generally too true, for they are not only flogged but their grog is stopped, or compelled to drink six or eight water grog for a certain length of time. How many of the valuable seamen perished during the late war when aloft and trembling from fear? How many have actually fallen from the yards and lost their lives, either on deck or overboard? How many hundreds have run away and by disguising themselves have got over to America, leaving behind perhaps two or three years hard earned pay and prize money? In this manner, together with those killed in battle, our ship was three times manned in a little less than seven years for our complement of men was upwards of six hundred, and we had on our ship's books within that period twenty one hundred. Many of these seamen had fictitious names, to avoid detection in case they saw an opportunity to run away; and in most of these cases their pay went to the droits of the Admiralty as their relatives could not recover under a false name.

It is only fair to add that with the exception of flogging all the punishments which he describes here had been abolished by the time he wrote in 1836.

His other particular object of attack was the system of impressment and he gives accounts of two particularly high-handed actions.

The first was that whilst we lay at Flushing in the year 1809. One day when the Captain was on shore, the Master hailed a transport and not receiving a quick reply, he sent one of our boats alongside to press the *fellow* he hailed, and who was not ready enough to answer. When they had got on board, they found the crew had hid themselves in different parts of the ship on seeing a man-of-war's boat approach. The boats crew were ordered to probe with their cutlasses in searching the ship, until they found him, and said they would take the whole crew unless he was forthcoming. Upon this they all made their appearance, with the exception of this great offender. They each denied that they had answered the hail, but on searching, they found him who had. They brought him on board and he was compelled to serve for thirty-two shillings per month whereas he was receiving five pounds ten shillings in the vessel he was pressed from. We had our full complement and did not want a man; the reader therefore will pronounce what judgment he may think proper on such an outrageous act under the mask of authority.

The next that I shall relate is, that when we were convoying an East Indian fleet from England to the Tropic, one of them happened to have an excellent band on board. Our Captain took a fancy into his head that he would have some of them: so, before he took leave of his convoy, he very kindly sent a lieutenant and boat's crew to press the two best musicians which they did and brought them on board, to increase our band for the Captain's amusement, and not to strengthen our force to engage any enemy.

He does not quite view all life on board as being unbearable, though beside the grog which has already been mentioned most of the other pleasures seem somewhat undesirable. Some of their diet we might regard as edible if not particularly appetising.

. . . This was a fine opportunity for our seamen to feast themselves on bullock's liver, or Torbay goose as they call it, for this, fried with salt pork, makes not only a relishing, but a delicious meal for a mess; indeed it has frequently occurred that our captain would, when we were killing a bullock at sea, send orders to the butcher for his cook to be supplied with a plate of the liver, to be fried for his table. At Torquay, a town in Torbay, it has been usual in wartime to kill for a supply of beef to the channel fleet, and then we often partook of this very excellent dish, as the livers were plentiful.

He also enjoyed the women.

After having moored our ship, swarms of boats came round us; some were what we generally termed bomb-boats, but are really nothing but floating chandler's shops; and a great many of them were freighted with cargoes of ladies, a sight that was truly gratifying, and a grand treat; for our crew, consisting of six hundred and upwards, nearly all young men, had seen but one woman on board for eighteen months and that was the daughter of one of the Spanish chiefs, who made no stay on board, but went on shore again immediately.

So soon as the boats were allowed to come alongside, the seamen flocked down pretty quick, one after the other, and brought their choice up, so that in the course of the afternoon, we had about four hundred and fifty on board.

Of all the human race, these poor young creatures are the most pitiable; the ill usage and the degredation they are driven to submit to, are indescribable, but from habit they become callous, indifferent as to the delicacy of speech and behaviour, and so totally lost to all sense of shame, that they seem to retain no quality which properly belongs to woman but the shape and name. When we reflect that these unfortunately deluded victims to our passions, might at one time have been destined to be the valuable companions and comforts of man but now so fallen; in these cooler moments of meditation, what a charge is raised against ourselves; we cannot reproach them for their abject condition, lest this startling question should be asked of us, 'Who made us so?'.

On the arrival of any man-of-war in port, these girls flock down to the shore, where boats are always ready; and here may be witnessed a scene, somewhat similar to the trafficking for slaves in the West Indies. As they approached a boat, old Charon, with painter in hand, before they step in board, surveys them from stem to stern, with the eyes of a bargaining Jew; and carefully *culls* out the best looking and the most dashingly dressed; and in making up his complement for a load, it often happens that he refuses to take some of them observing (very politely) and usually with some vulgar oath, to one that she is *too old*; to another that she is too ugly; and that he shall not be able *to sell them*; and he'll be damned if he has any notion of having his trouble for nothing. The only apology that can be made for the savage conduct of these unfeeling brutes is, that they run a chance of not being permitted to carry a cargo alongside unless it makes a good show-off; for it has been often known that, on approaching a ship, the officer in command has so far forgot himself as to order the waterman to push off—that he should not bring such a cargo of damned ugly ducks on board, and that he would not allow any of the men to have them. At this ungentlemanly rebuff, the waterman lays upon his oars a-while, hangs his lip, musing on his mishap; and in his heart no doubt cursing and doubly cursing the quarter-deck fool, and gradually pulls round to the shore again and the girls are not sparing of their epithets on the occasion. Here the waterman is a loser, for he takes them conditionally: that is, if they are made a choice of, or what he calls *sold*, he receives three shillings each, and, if not, then no pay—he has his labour for his pains; at least these were the terms in Portsmouth and Plymouth in war time at these great naval depots. A boat usually carries about ten of these poor creatures at a time, and will often bring off three cargoes of these ladies in a day; so that if he is fortunate in his *sales*, as he calls them, he will make nearly five pounds by his three trips. Thus these poor unfortunates are taken to market like cattle, and whilst this system is observed, it cannot with truth be said that the slave-trade is abolished in England.

About the men's pay he says:

Our ship having been in dock, she was prepared and got ready for sea again. A day or two previous to our sailing, the ship's crew were paid agreeably to an Admiralty order, and, to picture the scene which at this time occured, is a task almost impossible. In the early part of the day, the Commissioners came on board bringing the money which is paid the ship's crew, with the exception of six months pay, which it is the rule of the government to hold back from each man. The mode of paying is, as the names are, by rotation, on the books. Every man when called, is asked for his hat, which is returned to him with his wages in it and the amount chalked on the rim. There is not perhaps one in twenty who actually knows what he is going to receive, nor does the particular amount seem to be of a matter of much concern; for, when paid, they hurry down to their respective berths, redeem their honour with their several ladies and bomb-boat men and then they turn their thoughts to the Jew pedlars, who are ranged round the decks and in the hatchway gratings, in fact the ship is crowded with them. They are furnished with every article which will rig out a sailor,

F

never omitting in their parkains, a fine large watch and appendages, all warranted, and with which many an honest tar has been taken in: they can supply them likewise with fashionable rings and trinkets for their ladies, of *pure gold*, oh! nothing could be purer! Yet with all Mordecai's asservations, its purity may be doubted.

With such conditions and attitudes it is hardly surprising that Jack Nastyface deserted, or that he should feel so strongly against the officers. It is almost more surprising that he found anything good to say at all, but his postscript shows him to have been something more than a malcontent.

In contemplating the varied scene of so motley a profession as that of a sailor, there is much to be thought on with pleasure and much with a bitter anguish and disgust. To the youth possessing anything of a roving disposition it is attractive, nay, it is seducing, for it has its allurements, and when steadily pursued and with success, it enobles the mind, and the seaman feels himself a man. There is, indeed, no profession that can vie with it, and a British seaman has a right to be proud, for he is incomparable when placed alongside those of any other nation. Great Britain can truly boast of her hearts of oak, the floating sinews of her existence, and the high station she holds in the political world; and if she could but once rub out those stains of wanton and torturing punishments, so often unnecessarily resorted to, and abandon the unnatural and uncivilised custom of impressment, then, and not till then, can her navy be said to have got to the truck of perfection.

4

SAMUEL LEECH
(1808-1813)

Extracts from 'A Voice from the Main Deck' with an account of the War of 1812

HOWEVER MUCH Jack Nastyface may have disliked the Royal Navy, and certainly he disliked it enough to desert, he had no doubt of the overwhelming superiority of the British Tar, whatever he thought of the officers. The same is not true of Samuel Leech though this was the result of circumstance. Against France, the Royal Navy was overwhelmingly successful; as the British seamen cleared away the guns they were certain of victory—'For us to strike was out of the question'. The same was equally true of their attitude to the Americans before the War of 1812. This war was the almost inevitable result of the opposing maritime interests of the British and the United States. Samuel Leech, writing as a United States citizen some years after it, put the American view strongly:

Cause of War

Many of our hands were in the service against their will; some of them were Americans, wrongfully impressed, and inwardly hoping for defeat; while nearly every man in our ship sympathised with the great principle for which the American nation so nobly contended in the war of 1812. What that was, I suppose all my readers understand. The British at war with France, had denied the Americans the right to trade thither. She had impressed American seamen, and forcibly compelled their service in her navy; she had violated the American flag by insolently searching their vessels for her runaway seamen. Free trade and sailors' rights, therefore, were the objects contended for by the Americans. With their objects our men could but sympathise, whatever our officers might do.

This is not an entirely fair account of the causes of the war, though the fact that the British did impress American seamen and compel them to serve in British ships, is undoubtedly true. As Leech himself states:

Being in want of men, we resorted to the Press Gang which was made up of our most loyal men, armed to the teeth, by their aid we obtained our full numbers. Among them were a few Americans; they were taken without respect to their protection which were often taken from them and destroyed. Some were released through the influence of the American consul; others less fortuate, were carried to sea to their no small chagrin.

And even after the outbreak of war:

We had several Americans in our crew, most of whom were pressed men. These men, had they been certain that war had broken out, would have given themselves up as prisoners of war, and claimed exemption from that unjust service which compelled them to act with the enemies of their country. This was a privilege which the magnanimity of our officers ought to have offered them. They had already perpetuated a grievous wrong upon them in impressing them; it was adding cruelty to compel their service in a war against their own nation.

There was, though, a British point of view which Leech fails to mention. In the struggle with France the weapon of blockade was an essential element for success. If the Americans traded freely with France this weapon became ineffective. Equally Britain was desperately short of seamen. Wages on board American ship were high and conditions were not particularly severe. British seamen, therefore, entered the American merchant marine in their thousands. The easy naturalisation laws were even more easily circumvented and any trained British seamen had little difficulty in obtaining naturalisation papers as an American. Small wonder that Americans' 'Protections' received scant attention from British captains whose word was law in this, as in so many other respects. One of the common incidents of the time was for an American merchantmen to be left helpless on the high seas, unable to reach her port of destination because the majority of her crew had been taken off by some British man-of-war though the British were not always quite so unreasonable.

One incident, related by Leech, will be sufficient to illustrate the growing hostility between the two countries:

It was at this port (Norfolk) that the difficulty between the British ship *Leopard* and the American frigate *Chesapeake* took place. Several American seamen, having escaped from the former, took refuge on board the latter. The captain of the *Leopard* demanded their restoration; the captain of the *Chesapeake* refused submission to the demand. The *Leopard* fired into the frigate, which, being of inferior force, stuck to her opponent. As it was a time of peace, the *Chesapeake* was not kept as a prize; the claimed men were taken from her, and she was restored. This was among the circumstances which led up to the war of 1812.

When America eventually declared war, as has already been suggested, the British Navy was entirely confident of its ability to defeat the former colonists. In practice this was by no means the case, as the first year of the war was to show. Samuel Leech, then on board the *Macedonian* describes one of the engagements. It should be added that, though this account of the battle was written down many years later, at the time of the battle itself, Samuel Leech was only fourteen years old and there were a number of other boys on board considerably younger.

We had scarecely finished breakfast, before the man at the mast head shouted, 'Sail ho!'.
The Captain rushed upon deck, exclaiming, 'Masthead there!'
'Sir!'
'Where away is the sail?'
The precise answer to the question I do not recollect but the Captain proceeded to ask, 'What does she look like?'
'A square-rigged vessel, sir,' was the reply of the lookout.
After a few minutes the Captain shouted again, 'Masthead there!'
'Sir!'
'What does she look like?'
'A large ship, sir, standing towards us!'
'By this time most of the crew were on deck, eagerly straining their eyes to obtain a glimpse of the approaching ship, and murmuring their opinions to each other on her probable character. Then came the voice of the Captain, shouting,

'Keep silence, fore and aft!' Silence being secured, he hailed the lookout, who, to his question of 'What does she look like?' replied, 'A large frigate, bearing down upon us, sir!

A whisper ran along the crew that the strange ship was a Yankee frigate. The thought was confirmed by the command of 'All hands clear the ship for action, ahoy!' The drum and fife beat to quarters: bulkheads were knocked away: the guns were released from their confinement: the whole dread paraphernalia of battle was produced: and after the lapse of a few minutes of hurry and confusion, every man and boy was at his post, ready to do his best service for his country, except the band, who, claiming exemption from the affray, safely stowed themselves away in the cable tier. We had only one sick man on the list, and he, at the cry of battle, hurried from his cot, feeble as he was, to take his part of danger. A few of the junior midshipmen were stationed below, on the berth deck, with orders given in our hearing, to shoot any man who attempted to run from his quarters.

Our men were all in good spirits; though they did not scruple to express the wish that the coming foe was a Frenchman rather than a Yankee. We had been told, by the Americans on board, that Frigates in the American service carried more and heavier metal than ours. This, together with our consciousness of superiority over the French at sea, led us to a preference for a French antagonist.

The Americans among our number felt quite disconcerted at the necessity which compelled them to fight against their own countrymen. One of them, named John Card, as brave a seaman as ever trod a plank, ventured to present himself to the captain as a prisoner, frankly declaring his objection to fight. That officer, very ungenerously, ordered him to his quarters, threatening to shoot him if he made the request again. Poor fellow; He obeyed the unjust command, and was killed by a shot from his own countrymen. This fact is more disgraceful to the captain of the *Macedonian*, than even the loss of his ship. It was a gross and palpable violation of the rights of man.

As the approaching ship showed American colours all doubt of her character was at an end. 'We must fight her,' was the conviction of every breast. Every possible arrangement that could ensure success was accordingly made. The guns were shotted; the matches lighted, for although our guns were all furnished with first-rate locks, they were also provided with matches, attached by lanyards, in case the lock should miss fire. A Lieutenant then passed through the ship, directing the mariner and boarders who were furnished with pikes, cutlasses and pistols, how to proceed if it should be necessary to board the enemy. He was followed by the captain who exhorted the men to fidelity and courage, urging upon their consideration the well-known motto of the brave Nelson, 'England expects every man to do his duty.' In addition to all these preparations in deck some men were stationed in the tops with small arms, whose duty it was to attend to trimming the sails, and to use their muskets, provided we came to close action. There were others also below, called sail trimmers to assist in working the ship, should it be necessary to shift her position during the battle.

My station was at the fifth gun on the main deck. It was my duty to supply my gun with powder, a boy being appointed to each gun in the ship on the side we engaged for this purpose. A wooden screen was placed before the entrance to the magazine, with a hole in it, through which the cartridges were passed to the boys; we received them there, and covering them with our jackets, hurried to our respective guns. These precautions are observed to prevent the powder taking fire before it reaches the gun.

Thus we all stood awaiting orders in motionless suspense. At last we fired three guns from the larboard side of the main deck; this was followed by the command, 'Cease firing: you are throwing away your shot!'

Then came the order to 'wear ship', and prepare to attack the enemy with our starboard guns. Soon after this I heard firing from some other quarter which I at first supposed to be a discharge from our quarter deck guns: though it proved to be the roar of the enemy's cannon.

A strange noise, such as I had never heard before, next arrested my attention; it sounded like the tearing of sails, just over our heads. This I soon ascertained to be the wind of the enemy's shot. The firing after a few minutes cessation, recommenced. The roaring of cannon could now be heard from all parts of our trembling ship, and mingling as it did with that of our foes, it made a most hideous noise. By-and-by I heard the shot strike the sides of our ship; the whole scene grew indescribably confused and horrible; it was like some awfully tremendous thunderstorm whose deafening roar is attended by incessant streaks of lightening, carrying death in every flash, and strewing the ground with the victims of the wrath; only, in our case, the scene was rendered more horrible than that by the presence of torrents of blood which dyed our decks.

Though the recital may be painful, yet, as it will reveal the horrors of war, and show at what a frightful price a victory is won or lost I will present the reader with things as they met my eye during the progress of this dreadful fight. I was busily supplying my gun with powder when I saw blood suddenly fly from the arm of a man stationed at our gun. I saw nothing strike him, the effect alone was visible; in an instant the Third lieutenant tied his handkerchief round the wounded arm, and sent the groaning wretch below to the surgeon.

The cries of the wounded now rang through all parts of the ship. These were carried to the cockpit as fast as they fell, while those more fortuate men who were killed outright were immediately thrown overboard. As I was stationed but a short distance from the main hatchway, I could catch a glance at all who were carried below. A glance was all I could indulge in, for the boys belonging to the guns next to mine were wounded in the early part of the action, and I had to spring with all my might to keep three or four guns supplied with cartridges. I saw two of these lads fall nearly together. One of them was struck in the leg by a large shot; he had to suffer amputation above the wound. The other had a grape canister shot sent through his ankle. A stout Yorkshireman lifted him in his arms, and hurried him to the cockpit. He had his foot cut off, and was thus made lame for life. Two of the boys stationed in the quarter deck were killed. They were both Portugese. A man who saw one of them killed, afterwards told me that his powder caught fire and burnt the flesh almost off his face. In this pitiable situation, the agonised boy lifted up both hands, as if imploring relief, when a passing shot instantly cut him in two.

I was an eye witness to a sight equally revolting. A man named Aldrich had one of his hands cut off by a shot, and almost at the same moment received another shot, which tore open his bowels in a terrible manner. As he fell two or three men caught him in their arms and, as he could not live, threw him overboard.

One of the officers in my division also fell in my sight. He was a noble-hearted fellow named Nan Kivell. A grape or canister shot struck him near the heart; exclaiming, 'Oh! my God'! he fell and was carried below where he shortly after died.

Mr. Hope, our first Lieutenant, was also slightly wounded by a grummet or small iron ring, probably torn from a hammock clew by a shot. He went below, shouting to the men to fight on. Having had his wound dressed he came up again, shouting to us at the top of his voice and bidding us fight with all our might. There was not a man in the ship but would have rejoiced had he been in the place of our master's mate, the unfortunate Nan Kivell.

The battle went on. Our men kept cheering with all their might. I cheered with them though I confess I scarcely knew for what. Certainly there was nothing very inspiring in the aspect of things where I was stationed. So terrible had been the work of destruction round us, it was termed the slaughter-house. Not only had we had several boys and men killed or wounded, but several of the guns were disabled. The one I belonged to had a piece of the muzzle knocked out; and when the ship rolled it struck a beam of the upper deck with such force as to become jammed and fixed in that position. A twenty-four pound shot had also passed through the screen of the magazine, immediately over the orifice through which we passed our powder. The schoolmaster received a death wound. The brave boatswain, who came from the sick bay to the din of battle, was fastening a stopper on a back-stay, which had been shot away, when his head was smashed to pieces by a cannon ball; another man going to complete the unfinished task was also struck down. Another of our midshipmen also received a severe wound. The unfortunate ward-room steward was killed. A fellow named John, who, for some petty offence, had been sent on board as a punishment was carried past me, wounded. I distinctly heard the large blood-drops fall pat, pat, pat, on the deck; his wounds were mortal. Even a poor goat, kept by the officers for her milk, did not escape the general carnage; her hindquarters were shot off, and poor Nan was thrown overboard.

Such was the terrible scene amid which we kept on our shouting and firing. Our men fought like tigers. Some of them pulled off their jackets others their jackets and vests; while some, still more determined, had taken off their shirts, and, with nothing but a hankerchief tied round the waistbands of their trousers fought like heroes. Jack Sadler was one of these. I also observed a boy, named Cooper, stationed at a gun some distance from the magazine. He came to and fro on the full run, and appeared to be as 'merry as a cricket'. The third Lieutenant cheered him always, occasionally by saying, 'Well done, my boy, you are worth your weight in gold.'

I have often been asked what were my feelings during this fight. I felt pretty much as I suppose everyone does at such a time. That men are without thought when they stand among the dead and the dying is too absurd an idea to be entertained a moment. We all appeared cheerful, but I know many a serious thought ran through my mind: still, what could we do but keep up a semblance, at least, of animation? To run from our quarters would have been certain death from the hands of our own officers; to give way to gloom, or to show fear, would do no good, and might brand us with the name of cowards, and ensure certain defeat. Our only true philosophy therefore, was to make the best of a situation, by fighting bravely and cheerfully. I thought a great deal, however, of the other world; every groan, every falling man, told me that the next instant I might be before the Judge of all the earth. For this, I felt unprepared; but being without any particular knowledge of religious truth, I satisfied myself by repeating again and again the Lord's Prayer, and promising that if spared, I would be more attentive to religious duties than ever before. This promise I had no doubt, at the time, of keeping; but I have learned since that it is easier to make promises amidst the roar of the battle's thunder or in the horrors of shipwreck than to keep them when danger is absent, and safety smiles upon our path. While these thoughts secretly agitated my bosom, the din of battle continued. Grape and canister shot were pouring through our port-holes like leaden rain, carrying death in their trail. The large shot came against the ship's side like iron hail, shaking her to the very keel, or passing through her timbers and scattering terrific splinters, which did a more appalling work than even their own death-giving blows. The reader may form an idea of the effect of grape and canister when he is told that grape shot is formed by seven or eight balls confined to an iron and tied in cloth. These balls are scattered by the explosion of the powder. Canister shot is made by filling a powder canister with balls, each as large as two or three musket balls; these also scatter with direful effect when discharged. What then with splinters, cannon balls, grape and canister poured incessantly upon us, the reader may be assured that the work of death went on in a manner which must have been satisfying even to the King of Terrors himself.

Suddenly, the rattling of the iron hail ceased. We were ordered to cease firing. A profound silence ensued, broken only by the stifled groans of the brave sufferers below. It was soon ascertained that the enemy had shot ahead to repair damages, for she was not so disabled but she could sail without difficulty; while we were cut up that we lay utterly helpless. Our head bracer was shot away; the fore and main top masts were gone; the mizzen mast hung over the stern having carried several men over in its fall; we were in a state of complete wreck.

A council was now held among the officers on the quarter deck. Our condition was perilous in the extreme. Victory or escape was alike hopeless. Our ship was disabled; many of our men were killed and many more wounded. The enemy would without doubt bear down upon us in a few moments, and, as she could now choose her own position, would without doubt rake us fore and aft. Any further resistance was therefore folly. So, in spite of the hot-brained Lieutenant, Mr. Hope, who advised them not to strike, but to sail alongside, it was determined to strike our bunting. This was done by the hands of a brave fellow named Watson, whose saddened brow told how severely it pained his lion heart to do it. To me it was a pleasing sight, for I had seen fighting enough for one Sabbath; more than I wished to see again on a weekday. His Britannic Majesty's frigate *Macedonian* was now the prize of the American Frigate *United States*.

I now went below to see how matters appeared there. The first object I met was a man bearing a limb which had just been detached from some suffering wretch. Pursuing my way to the wardroom, I necessarily passed through the steerage which was strewed with the wounded; it was a sad spectacle, made more appalling by the groans and cries which rent the air. Some were groaning, others were swearing most bitterly, a few were praying, while these last arrived were begging most piteously to have their wounds dressed next. The surgeon and his mate were smeared with blood from head to foot; they looked more like butchers than doctors. Having so many patients, they had

once shifted their quarters from the cockpit to the steerage; they
now removed to the wardroom, and the long table, round
which officers had sat over many a merry feast, was soon
covered with the bleeding forms of maimed and mutilated
seamen.

While looking round the wardroom, I heard a noise above,
occasioned by the arrival of the boats from the conquering
frigate. Very soon a lieutenant, I think his name was Nicholson,
came into the ward-room and said to the busy surgeon, 'How
do you do, Doctor?'

'I have enough to do,' replied he, shaking his head thought-
fully; 'You have made wretched work for us.' These officers
were not strangers to each other, for the commander and
officers of these two frigates, had exchanged visits when we
were lying at Norfolk, some months before.

I now set to work to render all aid in my power to the sufferers. Our carpenter, named Reed, had his leg cut off. I helped to
carry him to the after wardroom; but he soon breathed out his
life there, and then I assisted in throwing his mangled remains
overboard. We got the cots as fast as possible; for most of them
were stretched out on the gory deck. One poor fellow who lay
with a broken thigh, begged me to give him water. I gave him
some. He looked with unutterable gratitude, drank, and died.
It was with exceeding difficulty that I moved through the steerage,
it was so covered with mangled men, and so slippery with
streams of blood. There was a poor boy there crying as if his
heart would break. He had been servant to the bold boatswain,
whose head was dashed to pieces. Poor boy! He felt that he had
lost a friend. I tried to comfort him by reminding him that he
ought to be thankful for having escaped death himself.

Here, also, I met one of my messmates, who showed the utmost joy at seeing me alive, for, he said, he had heard that I
was killed. He was looking up his messmates, which, he said,
was always done by sailors. We found two of our mess wounded.
One was the Swede, Logholm, who fell over board, as mentioned in a former chapter, and was nearly lost. We held him
while the surgeon cut off his leg above the knee. The task was
most painful to behold, the surgeon using his knife and saw on
human flesh and bones as freely as the butcher at the shambles
does on the carcass of the beast! Our other messmate suffered
still more than the Swede; he was sadly mutilated about the

legs and thighs with splinters. Such excess of suffering as I
saw in that wardroom I hope never to witness again. Could
the civilised world behold them as they were, and as they are,
infinitely worse than on that occasion, it seems to me that they
would forever put down the barbarous practices of war, by
universal consent.

Most of our officers and men were taken on board the
victor ship. I was left with a few others to take care of the
wounded. My master, the sailing master, was also among the
officers who continued in their ship. Most of the men who remained were unfit for any service, having broken into the
spirit-room and made themselves drunk. Some of them broke
into the purser's room and helped themselves to clothing;
while others, by previous agreement, took possession of their
dead messmates' property. For my own part I was content to
help myself to a little of the officers' provisions which did me a
great deal more good than could be obtained from rum. What
was worse than all, however, was the folly of the sailors in
giving spirit to their wounded messmates, since it only served
to aggravate their distress.

Among the wounded was a brave fellow named Wells. After
the surgeon had amputated and dressed his arm, he walked
about in fine spirits, as if he had received only a slight injury.
Indeed, while under the operation, he manifested a similar
heroism—observing to the surgeon, 'I have lost my arm in the
service of my country, but I don't mind it, doctor, it's the
fortune of war.' Cheerful and gay as he was, he soon died. His
companions gave him rum; he was attacked by fever and died.
Thus his messmates actually killed him with kindness.

We had all sorts of dispositions and temperaments among our
crew. To me it was a matter of great interest to watch their
various manifestations. Some who had lost their messmates
appeared to care nothing about it, while others were grieving
with all the tenderness of women. Of these, was the survivor
of two seamen who had formerly been soldiers in the same
regiment; he bemoaned the loss of his comrade with expressions
of profound grief. There were, also, two boatswain's mates,
named Adams and Brown, who had been messmates for
several years in the same ship. Brown was killed, or so wounded
that he died soon after the battle. It was really a touching
spectacle to see the rough, hardy features of the brave old

sailor, streaming with tears, as he picked out the dead body of
his friend from among the wounded and gently carried it to the
ship's side, saying to the inanimate form he bore, 'O Bill, we
have sailed together in a number of ships, we have been in
many gales and some battles, but this is the worst day I have
seen! We must now part!' Here he dropped the body into the
deep, then a great torrent of tears streaming over his weather-
beaten face he added, 'I can do no more for you. Farewell!
God be with you!' Here was an instance of genuine friendship,
worth more than the heartless profession of thousands, who,
in the fancied superiority of their elevated position in the social
circle, will deign nothing but a silly sneer at this record of a
sailor's grief.

The great number of the wounded kept our surgeon and his
mate heavily employed at their horrid work until late at night;
and it was a long time before they had much leisure. I remember
passing round the ship the day after the battle. Coming to a
hammock I found someone in it apparently asleep. I spoke;
he made no answer. I looked into the hammock; he was dead.
My messmates coming up, we threw the corpse overboard,
there was no time for useless ceremony. The man had probably
crawled to his hammock the day before, and not being perceived
in the general distress, bled to death! O War! who can reveal
thy miseries.

The war was not entirely disastrous for Britain. The *Macedonian* was neither the first nor the last British ship to be taken by
an American in single combat. In the year 1812 alone five British
men-of-war hauled down their colours to American conquerors.
Nevertheless in what was probably the most famous engagement
of the war *H.M.S. Shannon* forced the *U.S.S. Chesapeake* to haul
down her colours, both sides suffering appalling losses.

Before the end of the war, the British succeeded in more or less
blockading the East coast, though in the battles on the Great
Lakes, the Americans undoubtedly held the advantage. The
treaty left matters between the two countries where they had
been before the war began, though the Americans could well be
satisfied that they had inflicted such severe losses on the British
Navy. The reason that Samuel Leech gives for American victory
cannot be fully accepted.

The crew of our opponent (*The United States*) had all shipped *voluntarily* for the term of two years only; (most of our men were shipped for life). What wonder then that victory adorned the brows of the American commander?'

There is little doubt that the difference in skill in gunnery was the major factor and this will be discussed in a later chapter.

Samuel Leech's father, who had been a valet to Lord William Fitzroy, son of the Duke of Grafton, had died when Samuel was only three; and two years later, as his mother became 'an inmate of the family of Lady Francis Spencer' he went to live with his aunt in a family of twenty sons and two daughters.

my three years residence among these 'sailors bold' decided the nature of my future calling; it captivated my imagination and begat a curiosity, which ultimately led me to make my 'home upon the boundless deep'.

He then moved to the house of a widowed aunt at Wanstead who treated him less kindly.

For aught that now occurs to me, but for this unkindness, my early predilection for the sea would have died within me, while, as it was, I panted to enjoy the freedom my fancy painted in its pictures of sailor life. Several incidents occurred during my abode here, which tended to increase my growing desire. A smart active sailor, over six feet in height and well-proportioned, one day presented himself at my aunt's door. He told us he had been to America, where he had seen a young man named George Turner, who was her nephew and my cousin. He proceeded to tell her many stories about him and at last inquired if she should not like to see him and if she should know him.

'I don't know as I should,' said my aunt, 'he has been away so long'.

'Well then,' replied he, 'I am George Turner!'

'This fine bold seaman then was my own cousin, son to my Aunt Turner; he had been eleven years at sea, and, after visiting his parents, took this method of surprising his aunt. Most likely he had made this adventure the subject of many a forecastle yarn since then. While he remained he was so jolly, so liberal and so full of pleasant stories, that I began to feel sure that sailors were noble fellows.

We were also favoured with a visit from an uncle, then

visiting Europe from the West Indies. He was one of two brothers who was educated at Greenwich for the navy. One of them had entered the British navy and by dint of merit and hard service rose to the possession of a commission in the service but ultimately perished at sea. This one had chosen the merchant service but afterwards settled at Antigua. He took me with him to London and carried me over the West Indian docks; he being well acquainted with many of the captains; they treated me with playful attention, inquiring if I did not wish to be a cabin boy, and the like. When I returned to Wanstead, it was with a stronger desire than ever to be a sailor.'

Shortly after this his mother married again, a carpenter employed by the Duke of Marlborough, and was again in a position to have her son to live with her.

But I was now about to leave Wanstead, and, although delighted to be rid of the surveillance of a cross old relation, there were some things which threw an air of sadness occasionally over my mind. There were many pleasant associations connected with the place; its beautiful park, with herds of timid deer grazing under its tall oaks, upon whose green old heads the sun had shone for centuries; the venerable mansion, seated like a queen amid the sylvan scene; the old parish church, with its gorgeously painted windows to which I had often walked on the Sabbath with my fellow scholars in the Sabbath school, and beside whose deep toned organ I had sat listening to the learned priest; the annual hunt at East in which I had often joined the crew of idle lads that gave chase to the distracted deer, and the pleasant walks, made cheerful by the songs of innumerable birds, in Epping Forest, were all to be left—perhaps for ever. This thought made me somewhat sad, but it was swallowed up in the joy I felt when my mother appeared to conduct me to Bladon.

On the journey:

We had another source of relief in the antics of a wild hairbrained sailor. From spinning yarns, which looked amazingly like new inventions, he would take to dancing on the roof of the coach; at the foot of a hill he would leap off, and then spring up again with the agility of a monkey, to the no small amusement of the passengers. The more I saw of this reckless

The R——*l Speech*, a cartoon by Shortshank. The cartoon refers to the
Royal Speech to Parliament in January 1828 in which the Duke of
Wellington, the new prime minister—'The marine at the helm of old
England'—called the Battle of Navarino an 'untoward event'.

ABOVE *Exporting Cattle not for Insurance*. A caricature by W. Elmes of a group of 'ladies' being rowed out to the fleet. Similar incidents are described by several of the seamen. (See Samuel Leech p. 94.)

BELOW *Sailors carousing*, a caricature by Cruikshank. A not untypical scene of sailors on shore in a local hosteltry.

thoughtless tar, the more I became enamoured with the idea of a sea life; and thus this journey to my mother's new abode was another link in the chain that decided my future destiny in the drama of life.

His new home was comfortable and his stepfather was much concerned for his own and his mother's comfort and he lived happily there for close on three years, but at age of thirteen he began to 'sigh for deliverance from the restraints of home.' He was employed in the pleasure grounds of Blenheim Palace, but as he could think of nothing but the sea his mother gave way and mentioned his desires to Lady Spencer. The result however was not altogether fortunate. Lady Spencer mentioned Samuel Leech to Lord Fitzroy whom Samuel's father had served as valet, and Lord Fitroy who was then expecting the command of a frigate and happened to visit Blenheim sent for young Samuel.

Trembling in every joint I was ushered into his presence. He enquired if I should like to go to sea. 'Yes my lord, I should', was my ready answer. He dismissed me, after some further questionings, but was heard to say, before he left, that he would take me under his care and see to my future advancement. These dazzling prospects not only well nigh turned my brain but decided my parents to send me to sea. To have their son an *officer* in the navy was an unlooked for honour; and they now entered into my plans and feelings with almost as much ardour as myself. Alas! We were all doomed to learn how little confidence can be placed in the promises of nobles!

Not long after Lord Fitzroy's departure, we received a letter stating the fact of his appointment to His Majesty's Frigate *Macedonian*, which, being out of dock, was rapidly preparing for sea. This intelligence was the signal for bustle, excitement, preparation and I know not what. Friends and gossips constantly crowded in to administer their gratuitous advice. . . At last, after much ado, the long expected day arrived when I was to bid farewell to home and friends, to venture abroad upon an unknown future. . . I leaped gaily on to the outside of the coach and in a few minutes, enveloped in a cloud of dust, was on my way to London filled with the absorbing idea 'I am going to sea! I am going to sea!'

With his mother, he visited Wanstead on the way to London; then to Gravesend where he bought

G

a complete set of sailor's apparel; a tarpaulin hat, round blue jacket and wide pantaloons. Never did young knight swell with loftier emotion when donning for the first time his iron dress than I did when in sea dress. I trod the streets of Gravesend. This had always been my highest ambition. The gaudily dressed soldier never had charms for me; but a sailor, how nice he looked! . . . Thus equipped we once more hired a boat and descended the river two miles below Gravesend, where lay the *Macedonian,* in graceful majesty on the sparkling waters.

The first guest we met on board was disappointment. From the promise of Lord Fitzroy we very strangely supposed that he felt my importance nearly as much as did my father or mother. Judge then how we felt when we learned that no-one knew anything in particular about my veritable self; yet as his lordship was absent they said I might remain on board until his return. This was rather a damper on my spirits, but flattering myself that all would be right on his return I soon rallied again.

The morning after my arrival I was put into a 'Mess'. The crew of a man-of-war is divided into little commissions of about eight called messes. These eat and drink together and are as it were so many families. The mess to which I was introduced was composed of your genuine weather-beaten old tars. But for one of its members it would have suited me very well: this one, a real gruff old 'Bull-dog' named Hudson took into his head to hate me at first sight. He treated me with so much abuse and unkindness that my messmates advised me to change my mess.

This unkindness of the brutal Hudson rather chilled my enthusiasm. The crew too, by some means, had an impression that my mother had brought me on board to get rid of me and therefore bestowed the bitterest curses on her in the most profuse manner imaginable. Swearing I had heard before, but never such as I heard there. Nor was this all: in performing the work assigned me, which consisted of helping the seamen take in provisions powder, shot, etc. I felt the insults and tyranny of the midshipmen; their word was law and woe betide the presumptuous boy that dared refuse implicit obedience. But although somewhat grieved with my first experience of sailor's life, I secretly struggled against my feelings and with the most philosophic desperation resolved to make the best of my condition.

We were kept busily at work every day until the ship's stores were all on board, and our frigate was ready for sea. Then two hundred more men, drafted from receiving ships, came on board, to complete the number of our crew, which after their addition, numbered 300 men. The jocularity, pleasantry, humour and good feeling that now prevailed on board our frigate somewhat softened the unpleasantness of my lot, and cultivated a feeling of reconciliation to my circumstances. Various little friendships which sprang up between me and my shipmates threw a gleam of gladness across my path; a habit of attention, respect and obedience in a short term secured me universal goodwill. I began to be tolerably satisfied.

Not very long after, the *Macedonian* sailed round to Spithead and then conveyed between two and three hundred troops to Lisbon. On this, his first long voyage, Samuel was somewhat seasick and wished he had never come to sea, but he soon got over the former but not the latter. From Lisbon they cruised off the Portuguese coast and in various tasks for his master, the surgeon, he not infrequently went on shore and saw something of the country. Indeed, in respect of shore leave, the crew of the *Macedonian* seem to have been more fortuate than many though

the liberty to go on shore, which is always granted while in port, was sure to be used from drunken purposes.

The news of some French frigate cruising off the Spanish coast took them to sea again, but, though they failed to locate the French, they did manage to save the crew of a ship from Greenock. Leech says that this was

a really higher result than if we had found and beaten the French, and had returned in a crippled state, leaving some hundred killed and wounded.

This cruise was particularly unfortunate for Leech as one night while reefing topsails the Sailing Master, Mr. Lewis, threatened to flog some of the men. This the Captain regarded as his own prerogative, and a row followed which resulted in Mr. Lewis being put in irons. At the subsequent court martial both officers were dismissed from the ship and Samuel Leech, who had continued to hope for advancement from Lord Fitzroy was 'condemned to the Forecastle for life'.

It was also a change for the worse for the sailors. The new Captain, Waldegrave, was far more severe than Fitzroy.

Punishment was now an almost every-day scene; even the boys were not permitted to escape. They were consigned to the care of Mr. Hope, the first Lieutenant, who took especial delight in seeing them flogged.

There were frequent desertions and Leech himself had thought of running away,

as opportunities frequently offered themselves. But, being ignorant of the Portuguese language I wisely concluded that my condition among them, if I got clear, would, in respect of my present state, bear about the same analogy as the fire does to the frying pan.

However, Leech himself continued to get shore leave though on one occasion with the other boys, he missed the boat and spent all night on shore and only escaped a flogging largely because one of his companions was the First Lieutenant's servant.

As a result of a fall and a sailor emptying a bucket of water over his still wounded head, Samuel was for a time very ill and expected to die though

by the mercy of a watchful providence, the aid of a sound constitution assisted by the skill of our surgeon, and the kindness of my shipmates, I was at last able to leave my hammock.

As a result of his illness he ceased to be servant to the surgeon and became messenger boy and shortly after servant to the Sailing Master.

The *Macedonian* was then ordered to proceed to Norfolk, Virginia, with despatches and it was while there that the officers visited the frigate *United States*. Leech remarks:

I remember overhearing Commander Decature and the Captain of the *Macedonian* joking about taking each other's ships in case of war: and some of the crew said that a bet of a beaver hat passed between them in the issue of such a conflict. They probably little thought that their joking over a wine cup, would afterwards be cracked in earnest, in a scene of blood and carnage.

After a short stay they returned to Lisbon and from there escorted a convey of merchantmen back to England. While at Lisbon they received mail.

During the two years of our absence I had received several letters from my mother, which afforded me much satisfaction. To these I had faithfully replied. I now experienced the advantage of the primary education I had received when a boy. Many of my shipmates could neither read nor write, and were, in consequence either altogether deprived of the privilege of intercourse with their friends or were dependent on the kindness of others, to read and write for them. For these I acted as scribe. I also solaced many weary hours by reading such works as could be obtained from the officers: and sometimes I perused the Bible and Prayer Book which my mother so wisely placed in my chest on the eve of my departure.

There is no doubt that Leech was a bit of a prig as his account of a run ashore by three other boys indicates. They returned

in a state what a sailor would call 'three sheets in the wind'. They blustered, boasted of the high time they had enjoyed, and roundly laughed at me for being so unlike a man-of-war's man: while they felt as big as any man on board. The next morning however, they looked rather chop fallen when the Captain, who had accidentally seen their drunken follies on shore ordered them to be flogged and forbade their masters to send them ashore while we remained at Plymouth. Now then, it was pretty evident who had the best cruise; the joke was on the other side; for while their drunken behaviour cost them a terrible whipping and a loss of liberty, my temperance gained me the *real* approbation of my officers and more liberty than ever, since after that day I had to go on shore to do errands for their masters as well as my own.

The *Macedonian* had now been in commission for two years and she was placed in dry dock at Plymouth for a couple of weeks, the crew being boarded in an old hulk. There followed a period blockading the French coast, the monotony being broken only by the capture of a French prize and by the recapture of two escaped French prisoners who were trying to escape from England in a small boat.

Then, following the declaration of war against the United

States, which was carefully kept from the crew, (probably, as Leech suggests, because there were a number of Americans on board,) the *Macedonian* sailed for a cruise in the Atlantic during which she met and was defeated by the frigate, the *United States*. Leech himself, with the rest of the crew, was taken as a prisoner to Newport, Connecticut. There the officers left and Leech had sufficiently ingratiated himself with his master to write:

> When my master, Mr. Walker, took his leave of me, he appeared deeply affected. Imprinting a kiss on my cheek, the tears started from his eyes, and he bade me adieu. I have not seen him since.

The need now, however, was to ingratiate himself with the Americans and this he succeeded in doing in the following way. Having moved to New York,

> we were favoured with abundant visitors, curious to see the captive frigate. Finding these visitors extremely inquisitive, and being tolerably good-natured myself, I found a profitable business in conducting them about the ship, describing the action, and pointing out the places where particular individuals fell. For these services I gained some money and more goodwill. The people who had been to see us used to tell onshore how they had been on board of us, and how the English boy had conducted them over the ship, and told them the particulars of the fight. It soon became quite common for those who came to inquire 'if I was the English boy that was taken in her.' This civility on my part was not without motive; it was productive of profit and I wanted money to aid me whenever I got clear, which I was fully determined to do, the first opportunity.

This he succeeded in doing with another boy. In fact, a large proportion of the crew of the *Macedonian* escaped and settled in the United States, doing a wide variety of jobs, a number of them enlisting in the United States Army and even fighting their fellow countrymen. Others went to sea in American ships though only a few ended up in the Navy as this meant almost certain death in the event of capture.

The remainder of Samuel Leech's life is not strictly relevant to a history of the Royal Navy though it has some interest in its own right. After working for a shoemaker for a while, he heard that his cousin George Turner was on board the *United States*. There he visited his cousin and abandoning shoe making, of which George Turner disapproved, went to stay with his cousin's wife at Salem. Still drawn by the sea he enlisted under his own name in the U.S. Brig *Swan*. He enjoyed the life on board considerably more than on the *Macedonian*. Not that conditions were much better; but the treatment he received, especially from the Captain, compared very favourably with the insults and above all the constant threat of flogging that had made his life in the *Macedonian* such a nightmare. The voyage however ended disastrously for they were captured by the British man-of-war *Medway* and Leech was most fortunate not to be detected as this would have resulted in his being hung from the yard-arm.

However, the prisoners were landed at Simonstown and they were imprisoned at Cape Town for the rest of the war. Then they made the passage to England in British warships and Leech was terrified all the time of being detected and going to the gallows, especially when 'Boy Leech' was sent for—though this turned out to be a namesake. He was lucky, and in spite of a period spent in England he got back safely to the United States. Then after a brief period of riotous living ashore which cost him more than a hundred dollars he joined the U.S. Brig *Boxer* for another two years. This ship was almost worse than the *Macedonian* as in the *Boxer* even the Lieutenant or officer of the watch could send a man to the gangway and order the boatswain to 'lay on' with the rope's end. Once when a pilot was illegally given one hundred lashes, Leech writes:

> Had he complained it would doubtless have been to his own injury; for law, and especially naval law, is always on the side of the strong.

And off Ship Island a man was flogged through the fleet.

> His was the only instance of the kind I saw while in the American Navy, and although his back was most brutally mangled yet I do not think he suffered equal to those who are flogged through an English fleet. Still the indignity and brutality are the same in kind, though differing in degree: a MAN should never be made to endure it.

On their return to the station, Leech deserted. After a miserable time he was eventually helped by an old shipmate from the *Macedonian*. He did a series of different jobs and having for some time been interested in religion underwent conversion in the Methodist Church.

> Though I have not gained all that is desirable and that is offered in an abundant gospel, yet I have been trying to stem the torrent of my iniquity, which runs through the earth, and striving to make my way to the path of Glory.

The fact that both Samuel Stokes and Samuel Leech were 'converted' might lead one to suppose that this was common among sailors of the period but Leech himself says that of the three hundred men and boys who sailed in the *Macedonian* many were killed in battle but of the rest only one, John Whisky, one of the quarter masters 'embraced religion.'

Leech wrote to his mother, but dared not return to England. In time he prospered and bought a store and married. After a number of years he visited England having been assured by the Churchills, his mother's employers, of his safety. There he saw his mother for the last time.

There is little more to be said about Samuel Leech himself. His desertion to the United States, the King's enemies, though understandable, would be no more tolerated now than it was then. The large number who did desert only emphasises still further the dissatisfaction felt by so many sailors with His Majesty's Navy. This dissatisfaction, however, does not mean that they did not fight bravely.

Leech may have been a biased witness. He wrote for an American rather than an English audience, but he had many good reasons to loathe the King's service. As is the case with most of the other seamen three elements stand out as the major reasons for his hatred of the Royal Navy—the harsh discipline, the treatment meted out by the officers and the moral degradation encouraged in ships of war.

Flogging forms a significant part of Samuel Leech's case against the Navy but as Jack Nastyface has already been quoted in full on this subject no more needs to be added here.

Of the officers Leech writes:

> The difficulty with naval officers is that they do not treat with a sailor as with a *man*. They know what is fitting between each other as officers; but they treat their crews on another principle; they are apt to look at them as pieces of living mechanism,

born to serve, to obey their orders, and administer to their wishes without complaint. This is alike a bad morality and a bad philosophy. There is often more real manhood in the forecastle than in the ward-room.

Comparing the American service with the British he writes:

The (American) captain and officers were kind while there was a total exemption from that petty tyranny exercised by the upstart Midshipmen in the British service.

Of these Midshipman he had previously written:

These little minions of power ordered and drove me round like a dog nor did I and the other boys dare interpose a word. They were *officers* their word was law and woe betide the presumptuous boy that dared refuse explicit obedience.

This was very different from the American ship where he refused to wash a Midshipman's clothes when ordered to do so, and he heard no more of it.

However, not all Leech's remarks about the officers were harsh: Though I have spoken severely of the officers of the navy, let it not be thought that the whole class of naval officers are lost to the finer feelings of humanity. There are many humane, considerate men among them, who deserve our highest respect. This was the case with the second lieutenant of the *Macedonian*, Mr. Scott. He abhorred flogging. Once, when a poor marine was under sentence, he pleaded hard and successfully with the captain for his respite. This was a great victory; for the captain had a profound hatred of marines. The poor soldier was extremely grateful for his intercession, and would do anything for him to show his sense of obligation.

On the effect of life on board ship on the character of a man, Leech has no reservations:.

There are few worse places than a man of war for the favourable development of the moral character in a boy. Profanity in its most revolting aspect; licentiousness in its most shameful and beastly garbs; vice in the worst Proteus-like shapes, abound there. While scarcely a moral restraint is thrown round the victim, the meshes of temptation are spread about his path in every direction. Bad as things are at sea, they are worse in port. There boat-loads of defiled and defiling women are permitted to come alongside; the men looking over the side, select whoever best pleases his lustful fancy and by paying her fare, he is allowed to take and keep her on board as his paramour, until the ship is once more ordered to sea. Many of these lost unfortuate creatures are in the springtime of life, some of them not without pretensions of beauty. The ports of Plymouth and Portsmouth are crowded with these fallen beings. How can a boy be expected to escape pollution, surrounded by such works of darkness? Yet some parents send their children to sea because they are ungovernable ashore!

His other main target was drunkeness.

To be drunk is considered by almost every sailor as the acme of sensual bliss, while many fancy that swearing and drinking are necessary accomplishments in a genuine man-of-war's man. Hence it almost universally prevails. In our ship the men would get drunk, in defiance of every restriction. Were it not for the moral and physical ruin which follows its use, one might laugh at the various contrivances adopted to elude the vigilance of officers in their efforts to procure ruin. Some of our men who belonged to boats' crews provided themselves with bladders; if left ashore by their officers a few moments they would slip into the first grocery, fill their bladders and return with the spoil. Once by the ship's side the favourable moment was seized to pass the interdicted bladders into the portholes, to some watchful shipmate, by whom it was carefully secreted to be drunk at the first opportunity. The liberty to go on shore, which is always granted in port, was sure to be used for drunken purposes.

The Sabbath was also a day of sensuality. True, we sometimes had the semblance of religious services, when the men were summoned to hear the Captain read the morning service from the Church prayer book; but usually it was observed more as a day of revels than of worship. But at Christmas the ship presented a scene such as I had never imagined. The men were permitted to have their 'full swing'. Drunkeness ruled the ship. Nearly every man, with most of the officers, was in a state of beastly intoxication at night. Here, some were fighting but were so insensibly drunk they hardly knew whether they struck the guns or their opponents; yonder a party were singing libidinous or bacchanalian songs, while all were laughing, cursing, swearing or hallooing; confusion reigned in glorious triumph; it was the very chaos of humanity.

Finally, his explanation of the apparent conviviality that would strike a casual visitor on board a man-of-war: one of the sailors who had deserted, because he managed to return on board voluntarily was excused flogging and the crew were so joyous at his escape from punishment that they insisted on his giving a concert:

Seated on a gun surrounded by scores of men, he sang a variety of favourite songs, amid the plaudits and encores of his rough auditors. By such means as this, sailors contrive to keep up their spirits amidst constant causes of depression and misery. One is a good singer, another can spin tough forecastle yarns, while a third can crack a joke with sufficient point to call out roars of laughter. But for these interludes life in a man-of-war with severe officers, would be absolutely intolerable; mutiny or desertion would mark the voyages of every such ship. Hence officers in general highly value your jolly, merry-making, don't care sort of seaman. They know the effect of their influence in keeping away discontented thought from the midst of a ship's company. A casual visitor in a man-of-war, beholding the songs, the dance, the revelry of the crew, might judge them to be happy. But I know these things are often resorted to because they feel miserable, just to drive away dull care. They do it on the same principle as the slave population in the South (of the United States), to drown in sensual gratification the voice of misery that groans in the inner man—that lives with us, speaking of the indignity offered to its high nature by the chain that eats beyond the flesh—discoursing of the rights of many of liberty on the free hills of a happier clime, while amidst the gayest negro dance, not a heart among the laughing gang but would beat with high emotions and seize the boon with indescribable avidity, should it be offered its freedom on the spot. So in a man-of-war, where severe discipline prevails, though cheerfulness smiles at times, it is only the forced merriment of minds ill at ease; minds that would gladly escape the thralldom of the hated service to which they are bound.

5

CHARLES PEMBERTON

(1806-1812)

ROBERT HAY

(1802-1811)

THOMAS BLACKEY alias THOMAS TAIT

(1806-1808, 1812-1815, and 1837)

BETWEEN THEM NICOL, Jack Nastyface, and Leech cover the period of the 'Great War', and indeed, one or other of them was present at most of the major-named actions, but it may well be objected that they give a misleading picture of the life on the lower deck, and others would view it more favourably. In particular, Jack Nastyface, a deserter, deliberately set out to castigate the naval service largely as a result of the brutal treatment he received at the hands of a particular captain, the Honourable Sir Charles Paget, who was not a typical example of a Naval Captain. Also, as we have already noted, if Jack Nastyface was indeed William Robinson then he had an additional reason to detest the service as he remained in the lowest rating throughout his service whereas all his contemporaries had been promoted to Ordinary if not Able Seamen and some who joined with him had become Petty Officers by the time he deserted in 1811. He was, therefore, not merely a discontented seaman but also an in-efficient one—a natural trouble-maker. As to Samuel Leech it can be argued that he was exceptional in that he entered the Navy under the misapprehension that he had a good chance of be-coming an officer and he never got over the disappointment of Lord Fitzroy's failure to take any interest in his welfare. Under the circumstances, it is hardly surprising that he deserted to the United States, especially after having been captured by them.

There is undoubtedly some truth in all this as other sailors were less discontented than these two, but nevertheless Jack Nastyface and Samuel Leech were not untypical. A great number of British seamen did desert. Jack Nastyface hardly exaggerates when he says that the *Revenge* was 'thrice manned'. In the period there are over two thousand names on the ship's books for a crew of seven hundred and fifty. Of course not all deserted, but the number of those who did was enormous and marines *were* placed on the gangways with orders to shoot if any rating attempted to escape. A great number of British seamen did desert to the United States, particularly as their pay and conditions were better and they had no Press Gang.

Life was not unbearable for the sailors all the time; there were periods of frolic and amusement—'hands to dance and skylark!' Most of them must have enjoyed life some of the time— at least when they were rolling drunk—and some of them, most of the time. They did not all desert; they did win battles though more in the early stages of the war under men such as St. Vincent, Collingwood and Nelson, rather than in the later period under men such as Gambier. Nonetheless, life was unpleasant almost beyond our wildest imaginings. As we have seen, the battles themselves were terrible. Jack Nastyface may joke about an officer being knocked down by a man's flying head, but that is really all one could do beyond cry!

Life ashore may have been unpleasant enough in the industrial towns of the Midlands and North, but the hardships that every seaman had to accept as part of his daily duty were such that only someone like Sir Francis Chichester would today ever begin to endure. Not that this aspect of life on board receives much attention from any of the seamen, but in order to paint a fuller picture of life in the Old Navy five further seamen are worth examining, three briefly and two in detail.

To take a 'pressed' man first; C. R. Pemberton at the age of seventeen ran away from home with another boy and was picked up by the Press Gang in Liverpool. They were interviewed by a naval officer who gave them a shilling each and they were per-suaded to join the navy. Pemberton's career is not worth follow-ing in detail here. He served in the navy for six years and was involved in a number of minor engagements. Later he became an actor, but his full career need not concern us. He wrote a long-winded, evasive and rather tedious autobiography called *Pel Verjuice* and in it he attacks many of the same things as the other seamen. He also came from a better home than the others—after all he joined the navy by mistake—and resented the conditions and his companions more acutely. He even disliked his grog 'the sailor's boasted elixir'. As to his companions,

> I was now one of themselves, to toil as they toiled, washing and holy-stoning decks—to come at a whistle and run at a blow—to scramble as best I could through that congregated mass, some of them the most depraved and abandoned characters, thieves and pickpockets too—to wallow in degradation and misery—to watch continually in avoidance of abuse and beating and to watch in vain—to be scourged with ropes by brutes who were charmed with delight at the sound of the heavy dense blows which they dealt around in sheer wantonness, who rejoiced in their muscular arms, for strength was prized only because it enabled them to strike with greater energy; whose best sport was in watching and smiting at and prolonging the suppressed cries and writhings of their victims. I do not exaggerate. . . .

but he does continue in this vein for several pages without really saying very much more, though it is certainly clear that he had no high regard for the boatswain's mates. He adds that it is those who have been promoted from the ranks who are the most harsh disciplinarians. He does refer here to the guard ship and he is not quite as harsh about the frigate *Alceste* to which he was sent and even admits at one point that he became quite proud of his ship though he also adds,

> Were common sailors to write truly and thinkingly for themselves, their drawing would be a very gloomy one.

Shore leave was given from the *Alceste*, but here again it was used by the sailors for the usual purpose—to drink themselves into a state of helpless infirmity. Pemberton adds that not to do so was considered 'lubberly' and 'cowardly'.

One factor, though, stands out clearly in Pemberton's as in other memoirs. What really made the difference was the Captain. With one particular Captain, Maxwell, the crew put all their strength and skill into what they did because he was merciful and considerate in his discipline. This was not, he adds, true of other Captains.

However, there were officers who were like Captain Maxwell or even better as another seaman, Robert Hay, shows Admiral

Collingwood to have been. Hay himself was far more suited to the navy than many. Like Jack Nastyface, he ran away to sea and was fortunate to be sent to the *Culloden* under Admiral Collingwood though not before, like Pemberton, he had had a very hard time of it on the guard ship, the *Salvador del Mundo*, a ship of which Pemberton also complained so bitterly. In the *Culloden*, though, he was extremely fortunate. This was certainly because the Admiral, Collingwood, took a particular interest in the training of the boys in the ship. He inspected them daily and they were encouraged to climb the rigging in order to train aloft, but they were not allowed to go very high, and an incident in which Hay broke this rule clearly shows the understanding and interest of Collingwood. Part of the daily inspection was a race to the cross trees and one boy, bigger and stronger than Hay, nearly always beat him, and was allowed higher up the mast. Hay, in order to prove himself, went as high and was immediately summoned to see the Admiral who had witnessed the incident. He expected to be flogged, but Collingwood, while criticising Hay for his recklessness, also commended him for his courage, with the result that Hay came to hold the Admiral in highest esteem.

A better seamen, a better friend to seamen—a greater lover of his country's rights and honour, never trod the quarter deck.

In addition, Hay was particularly fortunate in the attention paid him by Mr. Locker. One of the usual jobs given to boys was that of Officer's Servant, and of course it made a considerable difference as to who the officer was. Mr. Locker, whom Hay served for a time, was exceptional. He was the Admiral's secretary and carried a considerable library on board. To this he allowed Hay free access, and, more important still, gave him instruction and encouragement.

Yet, in spite of all the encouragement he received Hay three times deserted from the service. The first occasion was before he went to the *Culloden*. All he had to do was simply to walk off the ship he was temporarily serving in, but, having spent the night ashore, cold, wet, hungry and miserable, he found it preferable to return. He was able to do so without the captain realising that he had intended to desert, which was indeed fortunate for him! At this time he was only fourteen.

The second occasion followed the wreck of the frigate he was serving in. He managed to get ashore from the wreck and he again simply ran away. This time he did not give himself up, but was later taken by the Press Gang. He could not be held and with another pressed man he managed to escape though the ship they were in was heavily guarded and several miles from the shore. This time he strapped four inflated bladders round him and swam ashore, steering by the 'large comet of 1811' which was over the headland at which they were aiming. After this he returned to Scotland from where he had run away nine years before, this time not to be recaptured.

If we look for a reason why he deserted from the frigate *Amethyst*, the answer at least partly lies in the fact that being in the carpenter's crew he did not get on at all with the carpenter, a Mr. Snell, a former shipmate with whom Hay had previously served as an equal. He writes,

We had many disagreeable bickerings so that, on the whole, my time on board was spent rather uncomfortably.

Nonetheless, it is clear that, though Collingwood had inspired Hay with personal loyalty to himself, this was not really transferred to the service as a whole. Another reason for deserting is given in Hay's answer to the officer after he had been pressed, when he was asked why he was not prepared to volunteer.

Because I get much better wages in the merchant service and should I be unable to agree with the Captain I am at liberty to leave him at the end of the voyage.

And indeed liberty was most important and this was not the 'liberty' to 'volunteer' having been pressed.

What injustice and mockery, thought I, first to have that best of blessings, liberty, snatched from me and then insulted by a seeming offer of allowing me to act with freedom! But my doom was fixed and I was thrust down among five or six score of miserable beings who, like myself, had been kidnapped and immured in the confined and unwholesome dungeon of a press room. . . .
. . . A few hours before I had entered London, possessed of Liberty and buoyed up with animating hope. Now I was a slave immured in a dungeon and surrounded by despair. . . . I was left all that day without food.

ABOVE   *Sailors on a Cruise*. A caricature by Cruikshank. Sailors seem to have been fond of dancing on the roof of a coach in motion! (See Samuel Leech p. 84. and Appendix 1.)

BELOW   *The Point of Honour*. A caricature by Cruikshank of a sailor about to receive the "cat-of-nine tails". (See Jack Nastyface p. 46 and Appendix 1.)

Sailors in a Fight by Thomas Stothard. A group of sailors prepares one of the 'Great Guns' for firing.

Having been left all that day and nearly another without food it is hardly surprising he deserted again.

Still, the drunkenness of the sailors is one of the major points that Hay notes.

So great is the predilection of seamen to the use of spirits that when assailed by temptation no consideration can induce them to practise abstinance.

These particular remarks arose from an incident in the *Culloden*, then under Admiral Pellew who succeeded Collingwood. They had captured two coasters containing a considerable quantity of goods, including a large amount of liquor. The sailors knocked off the heads of the bottles and proceeded to indulge themselves without restraint. As a result, within a few hours, over a hundred of ship's company were hopelessly intoxicated and unfit for duty. It is hardly surprising that Hay wrote, 'The Admiral was exasperated.'

With Pemberton, and almost certainly every other sailor, he really hated the guard ship, but even there not all the officers were callous. In particular Captain Dilkes, when written to by Hay's father who had not heard from his son Robert for a long time, wrote back that Robert was away at sea but on return would be instructed to write home. On Robert's return, Dilkes sent for him and ordered him to write home, which he did. Possibly the most significant aspect of this incident is that Robert had by this point forgotten how to write.

As I had in a great measure forgotten my writing, the Captain's clerk wrote a letter in my name.

It is particularly fortunate that Hay became a servant to Mr. Locker or we might not have had his memoirs.

The third sailor Thomas Blackey, alias Thomas Tait, left no memoirs, simply a petition to their Lordships of the Admiralty. In this he gives a brief account of his career. It was similar to thousands of others. He was in the merchant service when he was pressed at Malta in 1806 and after serving in the *Philomel*, and taking part in a number of minor engagements, after about three years his ship returned to England.

We were then ordered home with dispatches, and arrived at Plymouth. When I arrived at Plymouth, I went on shore with

H

the officer, and being so long from England, I went up the town to see if I could get any intelligence of my mother. In a resting I met a man who told me my mother was ill. When returning to the boat, to my misfortune the officer had gone on board with the boat. I was distracted what to do, I did not know, there being a man at the same time who was to have been flogged through the fleet. I dreaded being flogged more than I dreaded to face my enemies, which I faced with courage; as my officers, if any alive, can testify what courage I showed both night and day in the face of my country's enemies' shot. My father Joseph Blackey lost his life when boarding a French Frigate after taking the highest bounty, when I was only two years of age, my mother being left with two children. After my father was killed in the defence of his country, my mother married again to a man named Tait, both me and my sister were called by the name of Tait and Blackey.

He needed to explain his two names as no service counted under an assumed name and therefore he could not claim pay or bounty. It was not uncommon for seamen on being pressed to give an assumed name as it made desertion easier. He continues,

I went to the West Indies and entered our H.M. ship *Sappho*, in the year 1812 to serve my country, having heard there was a proclamation given that all who had deserted the service returned again, should be forgiven and receive his wages and prize money which was due to him. After I was paid off from the *Sappho* by the name of Tait I was sent or otherwise entered again on His Majesty's ship *Harrier*, and was paid off in the year 1815, on the twenty-fifth of August. My commander Sir C. Jones' words was this; 'Thomas Tait are you going to leave, I thought you the last man who would leave my service.' I asked him the liberty to tell me the reason, he said he always found me to be the foremost man to go through fire and smoke, and would report to the Admiralty for my good conduct, you will please to see if my Commander did not do so, I have always done my duty day and night in the hottest of fire in my enemies' country.

In one respect Thomas Blackey was exceptional. After twenty-two years, when he must have been at least forty-seven, he again joined the navy.

I again entered H.M. Ship *Redwing* in the year 1837, and received an accident at my duty, the total loss of my right hand's use, my middle finger being cut off, and the leaders of my palm taken out so that I am not able to use my hand whatever. The accident happened on the twenty-eighth September 1837.

After this he was no more use to the navy and though the Admiralty Board passed him fit, the Doctor in the *Redwing*,

told me there was no employment for me being so disabled in my right hand, I was unfit for service. I never received my victualling money that was due to me from the sixth of September to the twenty-eighth of September being the time I was on board the *Redwing* before my injury which is twenty-two days at one shilling and eightpence per day is one pound sixteen shillings and eightpence which money I never received.

He then presumably found some other occupation, but by the time he wrote this petition in 1851 he was clearly destitute. We may smile at his demand for one pound sixteen shillings and eightpence, but it was no joking matter for him. He was far worse off than another of the sailors, George Watson, who obtained for his injuries (received, it is true, in battle) a pension and a snug berth at Greenwich.

6

GEORGE WATSON
(1806-1814)

The Adventures of a Greenwich Pensioner

GEORGE WATSON'S MEMOIRS suggest that he was probably more contented than any of the others whose records have survived, and he himself had good reason to be satisfied. He had the good fortune to be a Greenwich pensioner as a result of the wounds he received. We might not today regard Greenwich Hospital as a haven of rest, but it did mean that he would never suffer want and would be honourably treated.

The engagement in which Watson received his wounds occurred off the mouth of the River Po at Gora on the 17th of September 1812. It was not a major action as by this stage of the war only very rarely did any French warship put to sea. In order to bring the enemy to action, it was not uncommon for the ship's boats to go into an enemy port and 'cut the enemy out'. Enterprises of this nature, though not infrequently attempted, could be somewhat hazardous, especially where there was a strong shore battery. In this particular incident, three boats from the *Eagle* were sent out to see what they could achieve. They set off sailing close to the shore from the ship and

> when the sails were spread, we spent the first two or three hours in singing sea songs, recounting past adventures, describing our anticipations and the time passed cheerfully away, after which some part of us slept.

In order to find out the lie of the land, they boarded some fishing vessels who informed them that at Gora a number of merchant vessesl were being protected by a gun boat. They waited off Gora until daylight and were then worried by a number of sharp-shooters from shore. Though the batteries did not fire at them, the gun boat did, and there was a discussion between the officers as to what should be done. The officer in command of Watson's boat, Mr. Cannon, proposed to go in and destroy the gun boat, but another, Mr. Moore suggested that they drew the enemy out rather than risk a broadside from the battery.

I and most of our crew approved of Mr. Moore's proposal, and signified the same to our commander, but he was bent at all hazards to punish, what he thought the impudence of the Frenchmen and therefore paid no attention to what we said and ordered us to load our guns, gird on our cutlasses and prepare for boarding; all of which we did accordingly.

All three boats then made for the gun boat, but the other two went aground. However, they jumped overboard to launch them and this relieved the green barge, which Watson was in, of much of the enemy's fire. Still one volley from the gun boat did considerable damage and

they were loading their bow gun to give us another dose, which had they, they might have sunk us, but Cannon seeing them cried 'Up and fire my lads! for if they get that gun discharged at us they will disappoint us'. We fired and drove them from the gun and gave three cheers, then drew out our swords and stood up to board, and as our boat had good way, we laid on our oars and run up alongside. When we came up the Frenchmen were ready to receive us. and had kept out their sweeps to prevent us from reaching their sides; this hindered us from getting on board as readily as we otherwise would have done, but— 'They conquer who believe they can', so we pushed on and when they saw us determined to come along the sweeps, full of desperation, they hauled down their colours and acknowledged our prowess. We had one man killed boarding the vessel, which we thought little to lose considering the danger we were exposed to; by this time Moore and Festing came up, having got the boats off unhurt and congratulated us on our victory, and the gallant manner we had attained it. The battery now began to play on us afresh, so we hauled a little further to the other side of the harbour into the midst of the shipping that was there, several of which had Turkish colours flying to indicate their neutrality. This movement of ours made the enemy cease firing, lest they should injure their allies and friends, and we began to look around for more prizes: not far from us we described a beautiful lateen-rigged galley, with six brass swivels mounted which we boarded and captured without opposition; her men amounting to about twenty were all below. It would appear from the crew of this vessel being off deck that they had been stationed near the gun boat, to assist her against our three boats, had they come up; but seeing us advance with the green barge alone, they had hid themselves, lest we discovering them, might return and disappoint their hopes, which was our defeat, of which they made themselves certain, and now beholding the face of things changed in our favour, they still kept below, thinking by this stratagem to elude our vigilance. There were thirty-six men belonging to the gun boat when she came into action, part of whom jumped overboard as we boarded her, and swam to the shore; she also had three guns whereas we had only one small cannon and twenty-three men. We manned the two prizes with ten men out of our boat and one or two out of each of the others. This diminished the crew of the green barge by nearly a half; then this being done we prepared to proceed on board of our ships, wishing only that we had another prize to make one a piece.

I remarked to one of my companions that we had gained our victory very easy considering the number of the enemy and their advantageous position, 'Aye' replied he, 'but perhaps the next we get may not be won so easily, yet I wish we had another Frenchman to cope with that we might have one at the stern of each barge to tow alongside of the *Eagle*.'—You may learn from these observations the true spirit of British sailors; they think, you see, that they have only to meet an enemy to conquer him, and this confidence bears them above the prospect of defeat and often leads them to victory and enables them to perform almost miracles. It was now about seven o'clock in the morning, and the noise of the cannon had roused the inhabitants of the town who came in numbers to the margin of the river to behold us. We had got our prow turned towards the main, and were steering outward, with cheerful hearts, our prizes in the rear, coming after us, when suddenly from different signal posts, we perceived various flags ascending and descending; the battery also opened fire on us again, to draw our attention towards them awhile; not imagining the snare that was laid for us we loitered too long trifling with them. In a short time a fleet of twenty-three sail appeared in our view, coming round the point opposite that on which stood the fort that fired on us, and extending about a mile further out to sea towards Ancona. The river ran between them and formed the harbour in which we were lying.

We were pleasingly astonished when we first beheld them, and believing them to be merchant men we concluded that we had made a good landfall and imagined them already our own. The wind being right into the port they came rapidly upon us, and we also advanced to meet them and as they arrived within gunshot of us they lowered their sails and formed a line across the entrance of the harbour and blocked us entirely in.

This made us look about us and on Cannon taking his telescope to observe them, he discovered three of the foremost to be national gunboats; here was a-piece with a vengence! He communicated what he saw to Moore and Festing, who thought that if we each attacked one, we might defeat them easily enough, or at any rate fight our way through them, by leaving our prizes behind us—Cannon did not approve of their being left, but thought, that if they were brought into action, they might divert and divide the fire of the enemy, and thus prove of great service. His opinion being agreed to, the commanders of the prizes were secured below, and their men put into their small boats and sent on shore, that they might not rise against us in the conflict. This being done, we drew up our little line, with our best, the green barge, in the front to lead the way as a forlorn hope, manned only with ten men and the commander. We now saw the force of the enemy more clearly, and what was our consternation when they fired! Instead of three cannons from the national war sloops in the van, from right to left in tremendous explosions we perceived more than twenty discharged at us at once. What could we hope now with five badly manned open boats, to oppose twenty-three armed vessels, some of which carried three pieces of artillery. Every heart seemed appalled for the moment, but, recovering ourselves we determined not to be taken for nothing, and animating each other with three cheers, we seized our oars, and made towards them. I felt alarmed in common with my companions, but soon resumed my fortitude. I knew very well that the race is not always to the strong but is disposed by him who overrules all events.

I therefore resigned my soul and person to the will of heaven, and having done this, my courage returned with redoubled ardour, and, having devoted my spirit to its maker, I prepared to devote my body and its services to the cause of my King and country; from that moment, I never sat down in the boat, but pulled my oar standing. I felt the true ferocious characteristics of war fire my bosom on that occasion, though in general I was naturally averse to it.

The grape shot now flew about us like hail, and it seemed to us as if nothing short of a miracle could prevent them destroying us; our main mast where floated Brittania's pendant, was chipped away on every side both below and above our heads; it put me in mind of a cabbage stalk that has been eaten by caterpillars; this is a homely idea I confess but it will portray the appearance of our mast better than any other I can at present think of. As we approached, I often looked at Cavalier Moore, whom I beheld as usual, as composed as if he were counting the stars, with his eyes steadily fixed upon the vessel he intended to board. Festing had sheered to a distance, and had got out of the line of the gun boats and using his cannonade, which we and Moore did not, he sank a vessel a little in the rear of them and put many more into confusion. We now entered the line of the enemy and two of the gun boats being close in our fronts we were exposed to the fire of them both, and did not know which to board:—Cannon asked me, (for I was near him) which of the two we should assail. I replied, they seem much alike and that we had better try the nearest. He immediately ordered the cockswain to lay him alongside of a vessel with a white bottom, which he supposed to be the commodore! We turned towards her, she fired, that instant, Cannon fell, receiving two balls in the breast, below the collar bone on each side; he did not die immediately, but he never stirred from where his wounds laid him; however, he supported himself as well as he could through the whole of the engagement which lasted about two hours after, and enquired of the success etcetera that attended us, while a young Irishman who remained by him, to give him relief etcetera informed him from time to time until the battle was over. As soon as Cannon was fallen, we called to Mr. Moore to take command, who seeing the danger we were in, came to our aid instantly. We turned our boat from the vessel that wounded our Lieutenant, and swung alongside of another, which proved to be the Commodore's; from my situation, I was necessarily called to board first. I had set my foot on the side of the enemy, and raised my cutlass to defend my head from the attack of my opponents who waited on the gangway to receive me. Two of my co-partners ascended with me, one on each side—at that moment, a gun on the quarter deck was pointed at us, loaded with cannister shot, and fired; it was not more than six feet off us— we felt its contents and all three tumbled headlong into our boat—I fell on my back, and my live comrades below me. Two balls struck me; one passed through between my fingers and wounded one of them; the other went through my right thigh, and shattered the bone just below the hip. The shock was instantaneous, and, for a minute or two deprived me of all sense, the pain I felt was not poignant, but a kind of indescribable sensation, which benumbed me all over. I thought afterward and concluded from it, that to be shot dead would be a very easy way to be sent out of this world. As soon as I recovered myself, I looked around me and saw the same vessel that wounded Cannon, and the other gun boat, still firing upon us, and at the same time, I saw some of my shipmates of Moore's crew, upon the deck of the vessel that wounded me, and her colours down, therefore I knew she was conquered. Seeing this I wished to be taken on board, but one of my messmates told me they were too busy at present to attend to us. I endeavoured however, to get on board myself, but in the attempt my thigh bone snapped in two, and I tumbled on my face, and would stir no more until I was lifted up by my colleagues. When I fell a second time, my face rested upon that of another of my boat mates, who was lying on his back; he opened his eyes, and knowing me said, 'I am done W . . .!' to which I replied. 'I am down too, but I hope not done yet!' Here we lay, till Moore's crew captured the vessel and then they took us on deck out of the boat and renewed the action. There were five of us knocked down at the time I was disabled, every one having two balls piercing him— this was a heavy blow, five out of ten! and the remaining five to engage thirty six, the number of the gun boat's company, with every disadvantage, and the enemy certainly would have overwhelmed us, if Moore's timely assistance had not turned the scale in our favour.

From the time we advanced to meet the fleet, which was a good distance from the shore, until the conflict ceased, the beach was crowded with people of every description, expecting I suppose to see in the sequel, their victorious war-sloops coming triumphantly into the harbour with us as prisoners at their stern, but in that they were disappointed. As soon as the Commodore was taken, our men turned his bow gun which was loaded, upon the boat that wounded Cannon; she was lying close under the bow, and having raked her once, she hauled down her colours immediately, and a few hands took possession of her guns; and did the same with another and in this manner succeeded in making twenty-three vessels, each carrying a heavy gun, submit to three comparatively small barges—a thing in itself almost incredible and seldom equalled in the annals of warfare. The Frenchman ran, as soon as our men fired at them, after the Commodore struck—they were not hindered to get away but even made to take their boats and flee, for we knew to keep them would endanger our conquest.

After the battle was over there were not above two or three Britons to each of these vessels, which had brought into action some of them, more than thirty men. In calculation, they amounted to an hundred more than we were, and had more cannon by twenty-six.

Watson was not too seriously wounded and was well looked after by the wife of the French Commander. He was lowered into the hold of the French vessel and when they came alongside he was hoisted on board in his cot. Fortunately for him, the doctor found the wound too high up to cut off his legs, so he splinted it, and put him to bed and later he was sent to hospital in Malta.

The ships that they had captured, however, ran into a gale and most of them were lost, including thirty men from the *Eagle*. Mr. Moore however managed to ride the gale and got through with six or seven others.

To return to his earlier years in the Navy, George Watson's introduction was hardly the happiest. He writes of his first voyage with his father at the age of ten:

It was a little after Christmas and we had a dreadful passage, it blew a gale all the way to Yarmouth roads, and the ship was so leaky that the men were kept at the pump night and day, so that my father could not pay me that attention he willingly would, and which my circumstances required, for I was seasick all the way to London: this made me often think if I were once more safe home, I would never tempt the sea again; but these notions wore off when I got better, so that afterwards, when I might have remained with my mother, I would not. Having got safe to Blackwall Reach a part of the river Thames and not far from the Emporium of our lord, we came to anchor astern of a frigate, that had just arrived from India; about 12 o'clock at night we heard a knocking on the deck, which we soon learned to be the man of war's boat's crew, to impress men from our vessel—we thought it was peace, but a declaration of war between our country and France having been unexpectedly made, and the captain of the Frigate being apprised of it, he had sent his men on board of us immediately: we were all turned out of our hammocks, they would not hear any remonstrance, my father and every soul on board except the master, two small boys, and myself (a mere child) were hurried over the side and taken on board on Mr. King's ship. Thus were we left, in the midst of winter, exposed to every blast, the ship badly moored and nobody on board to secure her better. The wind rose and blew a gale, the cable parted and away we went ashore! We knew not where but providentially we drove clear of all vessels and grounded on a sand bank, not far from the East India dock.

Despite these experiences he became an apprentice though he only once saw his father again and that was at Quebec. He soon settled down in the merchant service and 'I began now to think myself a sailor and to be satisfied with a seafaring life'. It must be remembered that here too, life was very hard and 'ship board is a famous school for iniquity.' It did not make very much difference whether it was the King's or the merchant service which only serves to emphasise the point that it was the discipline, especially the flogging and the lack of liberty, that men objected to in the navy. Equally, in the earlier part of the war when the French were attacking the English convoys, the violence of the enemy was as close even in a merchant ship, as is shown by the following incident, which took place when Watson was in the *Osborne*, a transport.

When we were about two-thirds of our passage, we perceived

two or three suspicious vessels dogging the fleet at a small distance, in different quarters for two days; at day break on the third morning, the largest of the strange ships was discovered steaming direct for the fleet, about a mile and a half in our rear with all sail set, the *Champion* (a frigate) made a signal to the *Osborne* to reconnoitre her; we hove our main-top-sail to the mast and waited for her, but we had not long to, no more than a quarter of an hour, when the commodore made signals for the fleet to disperse, and make the best of their way to England: at that moment this large ship was within musquet shot of us, and proved to be a French line-of-battle ship, by hoisting her colours and firing her bow gun upon us; we wore immediately and stood before the wind, and spread every sail to run athwart the enemy's hawse, when we got to leeward; our stern being open to her broadside, they discharged the whole of it at us but fortunately did us no harm; it flew all over our heads, or falling short of us. He did not pursue us, but steered into the centre of the convoy which were flying in every direction to get clear of him. When he got nearly into the middle of the fleet, he brailed up his courses, took in top gallant sails and our boats, then the game began! The boats boarded the merchantman in all quarters, took what was most useful and valuable from each of them and set the vessels on fire with the remainder of their cargoes. You might see smoke and flame ascending wherever you turned your eyes and out of this good and valuable fleet there were only seven or eight who escaped. Fortunately all the troop ships got away.

This was the first time I saw an enemy, or had heard the report of a line of battleship's broadside, roaring like many thunders; I thought it dreadful but was not the least afraid, though I was on the main-top-sail yard, spreading studding sails, when he fired at us under his lea.

Watson was afterwards told that the French man of war was commanded by one of Napoleon's brothers who claimed to have chased two English Frigates and destroyed above twenty sail of Merchantmen, though, in fact, there was only one Frigate—*the Champion*—there.

He sailed in *Osborne* for several years and spent a good deal of the time in South America where at this stage the British were helping in the rather confused war between the colonists, the

Spanish and Portuguese governments and the French. He was present at the storming and sacking of Monte Video, which rather horrified him and also at the failure before Buenos Aires from whence the *Osborne* brought the troops home. But home meant England, not his family, and though he wrote to his mother and sent her some money, he joined the *Scipio*, another transport, with a townsman William M'K . . . of whom he was particularly fond.

After a voyage to Gibraltar they returned to Falmouth and here M'K got drunk and stayed ashore all night and 'entered on board the *Fame 74*, then lying in port.' George Watson followed suit.

I never joined the *Scipio* again; in the afternoon I parted from the cook, and went on board of the *Fame 74*, which was still lying in the harbour to see my townsman William M'K . . . who still was dear in my estimation. I spent the evening with him very pleasantly and the sailors of his mess, as their manner is in men-of-war, procured us plenty of wine, and everything that could be got to make a stranger comfortable; when morning came I started to go ashore, I felt reluctant to part with my friend and instead of doing so, I volunteered to serve his Majesty. This was the first step in my martial career, the portal to many hair breadth escapes by 'flood and field'.

Watson was certainly fortunate in the Captain of the *Fame*, R. H. A. Bennett who was a considerate and able officer.

Our Captain loved order and used every means to make his men expert in every naval and military exploit, without being a burden to them so that every man obeyed him with cheerful manner and alacrity instead of being weary and disgusted with his commands. He gave great encouragement to all who distinguished themselves by activity, sobriety and cleanliness.

He constantly changed the jobs that the crew did so that everyone came to learn the different duties in the ship—an unusual circumstance as normally the untrained landsman would get almost no opportunity of going aloft. He also divided the crew into quarter watches—again an unusual act at this time—so that some hands got all night in.

They were stationed in the Mediterranean, but their duty was generally monotonous with an only very occasional decent on the enemy shore or a harbour.

The worst of the season being past, we put to sea again and cruised off Toulon, as usual, doing nothing but tacking back and forward, from and to the land, watching the manoeuvres of the French fleet, which sometimes came out of port to plague us, to make sail, and clear for battle and then run away from us like wild geese, giving us a wild goose chase after them beneath their batteries, carrying with them the curse of many a hard-mouthed Tar, for their wanton cowardice.

Excitement of another sort came to Watson and in the process he very nearly lost his life.

It was afternoon, and shortly before the time the Fleet generally reefed topsails for the night, and as I was stationed in that duty next to the man at the earing in the starboard fore-top-sail yardarm I thought it would be to our advantage to get the earing doubled before hand, so for that purpose I went aloft and descended on the leech of the sail, (the leech is that part that extends itself from the higher yardarm to the lower when the sheet is hauled out); just as I got upon the sail, about four feet below the yard (a dangerous position at any time) the signal was made by the Admiral to form the line of battle; our ship was in her station and the *Superb 74*, was on our weatherbow and in answer to the signal was bearing down athwart our hawse, to get in her's; as our Lieutenant thought we might come in contact with each other, in the direction we were steering, he ordered the fire topsail to be shivered (that is shook) to cause our ship to drop astern, the topsail shook, and I was hanging by it, with nothing to support me; it blew pretty fresh and every moment threatened to shake me off; I was first thrown one way and then another, till I gave up every hope of life; I caught hold of some of the points by which the sail is reefed, that were nearest to me and twisted them round my wrist, and kept my hold till the skin was torn. My shins were also chaffed much at the same time, the sailors, both in the top and on the deck, when they saw my situation told the Lietuenant, that he might fill the sail; he said he could not, owing to the position of the two ships, and concluded by saying 'what is the fool doing there?' So much for the pity of that worthy personage; by this time I was nearly exhausted, my shipmates advised me to throw myself clear of the ship, into the sea as my only resource for safety, for if I fell by the fluttering of the sail, I might fall on deck and be instantly killed; I came to the resolution recommended and cast my eyes down below me to see how I might drop clear of the fore yard; at the same instant I diverted my thought in prayer to Him that is alone able to save; at that awful moment, a rope called the sliding sail halliards flapped close to me and knowing an opportunity like it might not occur again, I let go my doubtful hold, and risked the seizure of it, which I providentially accomplished, and rapidly descended until safely upon the fore yard arm. When I found a rest for my foot, I was so weak, that my shipmates were obliged to come and assist me into the rigging and by their aid I got securely landed on deck to the great joy of myself and the satisfaction of all who beheld me.

He served in the *Fame* for a year or so and then, when the *Fame* was ordered home, was transferred to the *Eagle*, where conditions were not quite so good, though even so, Watson was generally content. However one incident occurred which would certainly have turned a less well-disposed man. One afternoon, when he was off watch, the Captain of the Top, a Petty Officer, had ordered him aloft. Watson was reluctant to obey and a fight started and the Captain of the Top reported him to the commanding officer, Captain Rowley. Watson was sent for, but he met the Captain on the way and Rowley discovering who he was

without saying another word he gave me a dreadful blow on the head with a stick, which he held in his hand; it cut through my hat and tore my forehead; but that was not all. He repeated the attack and belaboured me till my sides and arms etcetera were black and blue and the weapon being broke, he threw the remnant of it overboard and to finish off the work properly, he kicked my breech, and ordered me aloft again when I was fitter to be put to bed.

Even this was not the end, as Watson hoped. A few days after when the hands were turned up to witness punishment; after two or three offenders had been dealt with Watson was called out and given a dozen lashes with the cat o'nine tails. This seems to have done him some 'good' for the claws which he says were worse than those of a real cat and

I felt them so keenly, being the first and the last time they scratched my back, that I thought I would rather let the rogue that caused what I endured kick me overboard another time, than have those unnatural devil cats at my shoulders.

This, of course, was supposedly the point of flogging, but it should be noted that Watson was the only one among all these sailors who was able to view it in this light. For the others, though they would not have described it so, flogging was the product simply of the sadism of the officers and the boatswains' mates. In spite of the Captain's action, Watson continued to regard him with some affection.

It is but justice to say there could not be a better commander to his crew when the ship was safe in port, and your duty done; in such cases you might indulge in every meriment and festivity with impecunity.

He also praises the Captain for allowing regular shore leave to the whole ship's company in turn whenever time permitted, and even Rowley's fondness for bestowing corporal punishment, especially for drunkenness at sea.

This is not to be wondered at, as so much depends upon sobriety in vessels exposed to a continual warfare as we were; besides, there is such diversity of characters in a ship of war that it is necessary to deal harshly with some for the comfort and security of others.

Watson has no illusions about his ship mates.

A man-of-war may justly be styled an epitome of the world, in which there is a sample of every character, some good men as well as bad, but in general the latter are predominant—here are (in disguise) highwaymen, burglars, pickpockets, debauchees, adulterers, gamesters, lampooners, bastard-getters, imposters, panders, parasites, ruffians, hypocrites, threadworn beaux jack-a-dandies, these with their roses faded and their lilies soiled, walk the deck in utter contempt, dejected and forlorn, with the old tarpaulin jacket, dirty shirt and pad straw hat.

A somewhat different aspect of the ship's company were the animals they had on board.

We had livestock on board of every kind in abundance; bullocks, pigs, sheep, goats, geese, ducks, turkeys, chicken etcetera, many of the creatures being domesticated, were spared the general slaughter and had names given to them by the Tars. There was Billy the goat; Jenny the cow; Tom the sheep, Jack the goose and many others; Jenny the cow, after being two years on board, ran dry, and therefore was killed; . . . poor Tom the sheep was killed by lightening and I know not what became of Billy: as for Jack the goose, he saw them all out, and I believe, was in the ship when I left her; it was a very tame creature, so remarkably so, that he would come out of his coop, and join the assemblage of forecastlemen, when they have been in a group, talking about anything and seemed quite at home amongst them: as for the old boatswain, when he was on deck he was seen to have Jack for his companion who walked back and forward with him, and made his turns as regular as Pipes himself.

For the First Lieutenant, Cannon, who was killed in the battle at the mouth of the Po, Watson had a very high regard. There was, on the other hand, a midshipman who was the exact opposite. Watson heartily detested him. He

was haughty, ambitious, ignorant, vain as a peacock, implacable, revengeful, cowardly, contemptuous and contemptible, hated by all over whom he had any contact. He was one of those creatures that are most useless and offensive in His Majesty's Service, and only calculated to create and nourish sedition and mutiny, but their unreasonable enjoyments, without regard to impediment or the excuse or advice of the experienced. Such fan the flame of discord, and light the torch of rebellion, in the breast of everyone who is subject to their caprice and tyranny, and though the Government under which, such have authority be of the best description, yet it become loathsome, when represented by animals like these, for even seamen, so rude and boisterous in their manners, expect better things in those that rule them and never fail to notice and condemn, the commander that wants them.

Their duties in the *Eagle* were very much what they had been in the *Fame*, though there were a few more excitements. In particular, they made a very successful attack on a harbour between Trieste and Lissa. There they cut out and towed away four vessels and destroyed several others. Watson himself was wounded and was off duty for six weeks. On their return to Malta they were

J

warmly welcomed; the list of prizes they had captured had reached
Malta before them and all and sundry were anxious to do well out
of them.

Watson was wounded again at an attack on a fort near Zante
where some of the men got drunk much to Lieutenant Cannon's
anger and Cannon 'thrashed their backs with the flat part of his
sword, which they well deserved'.

Not long after this Watson received the wound that forced him
to be invalided home.

While he was in hospital in Malta he was well looked after and a
number of his shipmates visited him, including Mr. Moore and
some of the officers, but one particularly unfortunate incident
took place when a fight developed in the ward and one of the men
fell on Watson's only half-healed thigh and broke it again. He was
not fit to travel back in the *Eagle* but after some months was
finally allowed to return in the *Repulse*. He was still not well and
he had a pretty uncomfortable voyage, though the members of
the crew did what they could. On arriving at Plymouth he was
transferred to the hospital there, but then the nurses paid him a
different sort of attention.

Some of them had several husbands, or men they called by that
name all living on board different ships and as there was seldom
more than one of these in port at a time, they equally enjoyed the
caresses of their pliable spouses in happy ignorance of their dis-
honour, being accustomed to the manner and association of
sailors, these ladies are exceedingly bold. . . . . . I had a great deal
to do to repulse the temptations I met with from these syrens,
the more so as I was naturally fond of the society of women.

He left Plymouth hospital before he was fully cured, as he had
received a letter from his mother who was anxious to see him as
soon as possible. He went to the dockyard to receive his pay—
some £120—and then went to London to arrange his pension. He
received half a year in advance. Finally he made his way back to
his home in Newcastle and his mother scarcely recognised him.

I did not appear to be the once rosy-cheeked boy that had left
her ten years before; but having examined my chin, where was
a particular mark, she was satisfied . . . . . and we rejoiced in the
goodness of the Almighty who had, through a series of troubles
and uncouth adventures, brought once more to his paternal
shed the GREENWICH PENSIONER.

7

SAMUEL STOKES

(1806-1807 and 1809-1815)

His life in the Merchant
and Royal Navies

THE LAST SAILOR of the French Wars quoted here is particularly interesting for two reasons. First, the journal that he wrote is still the possession of a direct descendant and has never been seen outside the family circle. Second, since he writes about his service in both the Merchant and the Royal Navy, a direct comparison can be made of conditions in the two.

There is no doubt which of the two Samuel Stokes preferred. He did not volunteer but was pressed, much to his horror:

This was my lot and what I often call my hard fate, for every day I find something to tease and perplex one in this new scene of life.

This took place in 1806 when he was fourteen years old, and he had already had some experience of the navy. His father was a soldier in the 3rd Regiment of Dragoon Guards and, when Samuel was two, was taken prisoner in Belgium. For three years his family assumed he was dead. They lived in Ipswich where Samuel received some schooling and when he was twelve he was sent to learn the trade of baker, but he did not enjoy this.

This was very much against my will; my inclination was so strong for going to sea, I could not bend my mind to anything else, though often persuaded by my parents not to go to sea, especially as my grandmother who was very fond of me and often told me that if I ever went to sea she should never see me any more and it proved a prediction. In the latter part of May 1805 I shipt myself without asking my father's leave on board the *Hazard* bound to Maidstone in Kent, and on the 30th May my grandmother died and was buried before my return. She was 72

years old but was as well in health as she had been for several
years when I left home and I was only thirteen days away. At
the end of this short voyage I should have been willing to give
up going to sea for I was very sick at sea and often wished I was
in the Baker's shop again, but I was afraid to own that I dislik'd
it as I had been without my father's consent though everything
concur to make me dislike it. The loss of my uncle was very
much impressed on my mind though I never knew him. He was
drowned at London the first voyage after coming out of the
Blue School, on the 1st of March 1788, and was found the 4th. I
think this was one great reason my grandmother was averse to
my going to sea and she told me I was very much like my uncle
both in temper and look. I have been many times told the same
from others that knew him. I had several reasons for having a
dislike to the sea but I did not express one as I run myself it, but
said I liked it very well.

He made several small voyages in the *Hazard* and then sailed in
the *Nottingham* for Liverpool. After rounding Land's End they
ran into a very heavy gale and the cargo shifted, but eventually
they managed to crawl into Waterford where they rode out the
gale.
The next part of their voyage was even more unfortunate.

On 26th of March we was favoured with a fair wind and got
under way with our consort the *Port Packet* and twelve sail of
ships beside all bound for Liverpool. We had very little wind all
this day and all night. At daylight the next morning a fresh
breeze sprung up off the land. A Brig called the *Favourite*
belonging to Dublin being the only one in the fleet that was able
to hold way with us, for before twelve o'clock a.m. the other
twelve sail was out of sight. The *Port Packet* lost sight of us
this time to join us no more, but in a few hours we was joined
by a French privateer. We first see her when the watch was
called at twelve o'clock. One of our men took the spy glass to
look at her as she pass'd us to Leeward and told the master he
was certain she was a privateer, but the mate persuaded the
marster to the contrary telling him he was sure it could not be a
privateer so far round Land's End. But when the watch was
call'd at 4 o'clock P. M. the case was decided. Our marster took
the telescope to reconnoitre the privateer and see him send his
boat and board the *Favourite* and then bore away for us, but just

at that instant it fell calm and all hands went below to pack their things up intending to make their escape. But I was sent to the helm and though I was not of any use there I was threatened if I left there they would punish me, therefore I had no time to get any of my things. The three foremost hands come on deck with their clothes determined to make their escape. They cast the long boat's gripes off and launched her overboard, and when they got into her called me and told me that if I did not make haste they would leave me. The master and mate had agreed to stop and told me I had better stop that I should not take any harm. Now I did not know what to do for the best. I could not bear the idea of leaving my cloths and not a minute to spare, but me great coat being on deck at the time, I hastily took it up and jumped into the boat for it occur'd to my mind in a moment what my father had suffered in French prison for I have ofter heard him relate the difficulties he met there. We left our ship off the Saltees about three leagues from the land, on the 27th March 1806. The privateer's shot come very close to us after we left the ship but all fell short. The following morning we fell in with a Waterford packet bound to Waterford. They tow'd us into Waterford harbour, and give us some refreshment, for we was very much fatigued as we had been rowing hard all night, and then we pulled the boat up to the town and the man sold her for five guineas and gave me the odd five shillings as my share and then left me to manage for myself. I did not see any of them after until I see them in Ipswich which was very near two years after. I was left to make the best use I could of my five shillings in a place where everybody was strangers to me and I was very little more than fourteen years old. Now I wanted that parental advice I had very often refused. Now I begin to know trouble. The Lord is correcting me for disobeying my parents.

It was indeed a very unpleasant position for a fourteen year old boy to be in. His sole hope was the Navy, and they were only interested in getting him into the service.

The Captain of the tender that was laying there for the purpose of impressing men for His Majesty's Service sent his boat ashore to take me on board. They told me they only wanted me to go with them in chase of the privateer that had taken our ship. They told me that I should know our ship if I should see her. But it was not for that or any other service that I could do to them. They hoped they should persuade me to volunteer for His Majesty's Service before we come back. We sailed from Waterford and cruised the Irish Channel about a week before we got any intelligence of the privateer. Then we spoke a Guinea Man homeward bound who told us they saw the privateer about twelve leagues northwest off Cape Clear. They chased her for several hours and found she went from them so they gave up the chase and we returned to Waterford. I did expect to get my liberty as soon as we arrived at Waterford according to promise. But I was very much mistaken for they used every means to persuade me, for I told them I was an apprentice to the owner. They kept me on board two or three days after we returned off the cruise. Every day they had me on the quarter deck and told me I should not get clear and it would be better for me to enter but I was determined never to volunteer. On the 10th April the captain sent orders on board to let me go ashore.

In the end, after having spent all the five shillings and even sold his great coat for three shillings, the only way he could get a vessel was by binding himself apprentice. This he did, though intending to break it as soon as he could. When they got to Liverpool he found the *Port Packet* there and Captain Christie willingly gave him a passage home, but the result was unfortunate.

On this passage we had very fine weather indeed, light winds but fair. We spoke several ships in the Channel, and they told us there had been two or three privateers seen on the coast and several English vessels had been taken. On hearing this we bore away for Spithead to wait for a convoy going to the Eastward. There being a convoy coming at the time he was going in, the *Commadore* hove us too and sent his boat to board us. I was very much inclined to stow myself away in the hold, as we expected they was coming to press. If I had done so I should have escaped, but Providence had ordered otherwise. My master told me he was sure they would never take me as I was so young, but the fact is they took me and only me. Nevertheless Captain Christie used every possible means to prevent it, but all to no purpose.

His first stretch in the Navy was not very long. This is how he describes it.

I was pressed and taken on board His Majesty's Brig the

Richmond May 13th 1806. My face is again turn'd from home, and my parents are disappointed of seeing me so soon as they expected, for I am going now to Gibraltar without any prospect of knowing whither, when, or ever I may reach home. Our passage was very short to Gibraltar. We laid here but a very short time before we was sent to cruise off the coast of Spain under the command of Admiral Harvey who was cruising off Cape Finistere with six sail of the line, and he sent us to cruise off Vigo to blockade a Spanish privateer that was riding in that harbour. We had not been cruising many days, before our Captain received a letter from some person who was living at Vigo. The letter contained a full description of the privateer and his intention of coming out to take us. The hands was turned up and the letter read to the ship's company. I think it was about seven or eight days after, on the 7th of June in the morning as we lay to off the harbour's mouth, we see the privateer get under weigh and proceed to sea. Accordingly we made preparations for what we expected might be the event. The privateer having a superior number of men, he intended to run alongside and board us. We expected this to be his plan, as we had watched his motions very close and while he was in the act of shearing alongside, we gave him a broadside, and knocked away his foremast, and while he lay confused in this disabled state we sent our shot into him so fast, the proud Spaniard haul'd his colours down in sight of his own harbour and very probable in sight of some of their homes. Their loss was very great, ours was very little compar'd with theirs. As soon as we had cleared the deck and secured the guns, we took our prize in tow, and the next day in the afternoon we joined the Admiral, and the prisoners were sent ashore with a flag of truce two or three days after, and we went to Gibraltar to refit. We was near a month at Gibraltar this time, and then was sent to cruise on the coast of Spain. We took several fishing boats and small vessels one of which we made a small cruiser of but very soon lost her for we were obliged to cut her adrift in a heavy gale of wind, as she was too large to tow in a heavy sea. The latter part of the gale we chased a large American ship into Lisbon. She was load with a Spanish cargo. Lisbon being a neutral port at this time, he was safe as soon as he got over the bar. Nevertheless we went into Lisbon too, and lay there until the ship came out again, and a very few hours after she sailed we followed her out, and the same afternoon we made a prize of her, and sent her into England. She had a very valuable cargo, but what it was I never knew, for it was kept quite secret, and I run away before the prize money was paid, for we returned to Lisbon and was appointed to take a convoy to England. Before we sailed, our Captain purchased a small four oar boat for a gig and I was choose for one of the crew. This suited me exactly for I was very desirous of belonging to a boat. This gave me great hopes of gaining an opportunity to run away as soon as we got in England. We sailed from Lisbon in the month of September 1806 with about twenty sail of merchantmen and about three weeks after we arrived at Spithead, and two or three days after we sail'd for Cork to cruise on the Irish coast. We pass the winter on this station and nothing happened worth mentioning as we lay the greater part in harbour. On 27th May we sail'd from Cork for Portsmouth to refit, and arrived at Portsmouth the 3rd of June 1807, and on 5th June, after putting the Captain ashore at sallyport he gave me leave to stop ashore until the next day. I slept in Portsmouth that night, but my mind was very much agitated all night what I had best do. I was very much inclined to run away, but the dread of being punished if I did not get clear without being stopt almost deter'd me from making the attempt, and the thought of returning was a torment to me. Therefore I determined on making my escape whatever might be the event. Accordingly I rose very early in the morning and got safe out of Portsmouth before the sun rose. I was obliged to be very cautious not to travel through any town I could possibly avoid, as the soldiers at that time would stop all travellers that had the appearance of sailors. on the third day after I left Portsmouth, I got to London and went to Mill Stairs where the Ipswich corn vessels generally lay at that time. I found several there. I went on board the *Griffin* and told the master my case. He offer'd me some refreshment which I readily expected as I had not eat any thing since the night before I left Portsmouth, The following day I left London in the *Daisy* a small vessel bound to Ipswich. Now I thought I was quite out of danger. but when we got down to the Nore, we found the man-of-war's boats was pressing very sharp. This a little surprised me and I was obliged to stow myself away in the hold with two others that had run away as well as myself and we pass'd through the fleet unnoticed or at least without being stopt. We had now only to fear being boarded going in Harwich, but Providence smiled on me to the end and the same night we got into Ipswich river. And the next tide we got up to Ipswich quay and I went home quite unexpected on the 12th of June to the joy of my parents. For they had not heard from me but once since I was pres'd.

There is no doubt that one factor that helped deserters considerably was the assistance given them by merchant service captains and crews. This was, of course, not surprising as there were few who had not been molested by the Press Gang and there was, inevitably, considerable hostility between the two services, in spite of the protection given to merchant ships by the Royal Navy.

It was not difficult at this time to get a berth on a merchant ship owing to the great shortage of seamen. Stokes soon found a ship but he changed after two voyages much for the worse as the Captain was 'the cruelest tyrant I ever sailed with in the merchant service' and the one after that was not much better.

. . . while he was getting drunk ashore he made me wait for him in the Boat, and very seldom came on board before three o' clock in the morning and sometimes not so soon. Thus night after night I was deprived of my rest and exposed to cold frosty nights and in the day was not allowed sufficient food to satisfy hunger and that very bad in quality and many other things I had to endure too numerous to mention.

As in the Royal Navy, the Captain made all the difference to life on board, but there was a great difference between the two services. In the merchant navy if you did not like the Captain, you could change your ship at the end of the voyage.

. . . as soon as we got home my father was on the quay and ordered me to come ashore as soon as the vessel was moor'd and told my master he had heard of his ill treatment to me therefore he would not let me go with him any more.

He sailed in several further ships, but became increasingly afraid of being impressed. There was one solution to this and that was to be bound apprentice as this gave protection. Samuel's father was very much against this and although Samuel does not say so, it was almost certainly because the father would have to give some assurance for his son. Knowing that Samuel was quite likely to move on when he pleased, he was not prepared to give this assurance.

The matter came to a head when five months later a brig in which he had just been serving 'was taken about ten days after she sail'd' and it was ten years before any of the ship's company got home. This persuaded Samuel's father to agree to his being bound and in October 1807 'I bound myself apprentice for three years to Enos Page, to learn the art of a mariner and fisherman.'

To begin with all went well. Samuel worked hard but did not get on with the other apprentices. He says that the others told tales against him and these were accepted by his master. He also adds that his master went to the Baptist Chapel whereas he went to church and this made him unpopular. Whatever the reason, he soon fell from favour as anticipated:

> Now I find my father's words is coming true, for I begin to think of running away, for I find it quite out of my power to give my master the least satisfaction in anything that I did. Everything went wrong, and by that I was encouraged to leave him, for I thought he would not trouble himself about me, but he sent for my father and promised to behave better to me in future, so that my father prevailed on me to go back.

Shortly after this his father died and the situation rapidly worsened again. He tried to run away but was caught and threatened with the Press Gang and service on board a man-of-war. Finally, however the Captain struck him. This was the end. Stokes decided to leave Ipswich and join the Revenue Service. Here he would be safe from the Press Gang.

> I went to Harwich with several more and ship'd at Harwich Custom House to go on board the *Rattlesnake* on the Revenue Service. She was lying at Deptford fitting out, and the latter part of the week I was sent with several more to join the *Rattlesnake* at Deptford. I got a good protection when I join'd this vessel. I could go ashore or anywhere I please without being afraid of being pres'd.

The Revenue Service was a fairly monotonous job, but it did mean freedom to go on shore and safety from the Press Gang and there were moments of excitement. One such incident turned out very much better for Stokes than he deserved.

We sailed from Deptford the beginning of March 1809 to take

our station in the Downs where we lay moor'd all the time I belong to her. Our principle employment was to join the boats along shore to look out for smugglers. We took one after we had been very near three months, landing her cargo on the beach under the South Foreland, with seventy-two tubs of gineva and a great quantity of dry goods. This was the first prize I had been at the taking of since I had been in the Revenue Service. I did not expect we should be allowed to make so free with the liquor, for we drank it out of the casks as if it had been small beer, until there was not a sober man in the three boat's crews except the chief mate. The Boatswain was officer of the boat I was in. He was not only drunk but very quarrelsome, and as we had got some liquor in the boat he threatened to report us to the captain and have us all sent on board of a man-of-war. Thus he urged all the boats crew to quarrel with him, and he more particular alluded to me for he said it would not be much trouble to get me there as I had run away once. In a moment determined to have my revenge on him I took my pistol up and without a moment's hesitation I should have shot him, if the man behind me had not given my hand a sudden check and shaked the pistol out of my hand. I cannot describe my feelings at the time, for that kind Providence that prevented me from doing murder, also brought me to my senses, and made me ashamed of it, and fearfull of what might be the issue. I did not get any sleep after I got on board although I went to bed. In the morning the Boatswain reported me to the Captain. I was ordered on the quarter deck and all the Boat's crew. I expected nothing less than a man-of-war to be my sentence, but after Captain Dobbin examined the whole and found the Boatswain was drunk, he told the Boatswain he thought he was the most at fault, for by getting drunk set a very bad example for the boat's crew. I was now in hopes I should get clear, for the Captain said it was the liquor that had tempted me to shoot the Boatswain, but as it was the first complaint in the whole proceedings, he considered that the Boatswain had very much aggravated me, and therefore he dismissed us from the quarter deck. But sent for me again and told me if I only consider'd the consequence of being intoxicated I should not get drunk any more, and if ever I did when I was on my duty he should send me on board of a man-of-war. He gave me very good advice. I promised to act according to it, but it made no lasting impression on me, for I was seldom sober when I had it in my power to get drunk.

Drunkenness—so prevalent in the British Navy—once again got Stokes into trouble. He left the Revenue Service and travelled to London where he had difficulty in getting a ship. Eventually he joined the *Greyhound*, an American ship due to set sail from Gravesend on the next day, and bound for Cadiz and Vera Cruz.

The same evening I went on board the *Rattlesnake* to get some things I had left and I found that eleven of the fourteen that had left her had joined her again, and unknown to me, someone sent to let the Chief Mate know that I was on board. He soon made his appearance and told me he hop'd I would join her again for Captain Dobbin would forgive all that was past, and my wages was still going on as my name had not been cross'd off the books. I promised to join her the next day, and had appointed the time he was to come for me, when the Captain would have been ashore. But the next morning I was very much surprised to see the signal for the convoy to get under weigh and by ten o'clock the fleet was all out of the Downs. This was a great disappointment to me for I was determined to leave that day if we had not sailed so early, for I repented that I had undertook this voyage, but it was too late, but the wind was fair and two days after we took our departure from the English Land as I thought for at least two or three years.

This was most unfortunate for Stokes, and not merely because they ran into a severe gale which separated the fleet and caused considerable damage.

The morning after the gale ceased and we was all hands employ'd repairing the damage, we saw a ship on our weather quarter coming up very fast, which we at first thought was a French privateer. We made all the sail we was able, to get from him, but not being able to, set our sails fair. He come up with us after four hours chase, so that we could see that he was an English man-of-war, and we hove our ship too, and as soon as they come up with us, sent their boat on board to overhaul us, and press'd me and another man because we had not got American protection, and sent two Irishmen on board in our room.

The Americans certainly had every reason to complain, especially as the Captain claimed that Stokes was an American, but worse was to follow.

Now I am again forced to serve His Majesty again on board the *Helena* sloop-of-war press'd at sea in the Lattitude of Cape Finistere on the 20th of June 1809. I was call'd on the quarter-deck and to my surprise see an officer that was a shipmate with me when I run away from the Richmond gun brig. The sight of this man made me think of changing my name for I was not afraid that he would know me by anything else. Captain Worth asked me how long I had been to sea, my name and where I belonged, and many more questions, but he was not satisfy'd with my answers and especially when I told him I was born in America, for he said he was sure I was an Englishman. And there stands a gentleman that have sailed with you in the Richmond gun brig. I told him I never had my foot on board of a British man-of-war before, and I hoped the American Consul would soon get a discharge for me. He asked me a great many questions about the part of America I belonged to. I answered them so correct that the Captain told Mr. Robinson my old shipmate he must be mistaken, but he said, if it was so he never saw so much alike before. I was stationed in the fore-top where I discharged my duty to the satisfaction of the officers and was very soon mark'd for a smart sailor and Captain Worth told me if I would volunteer he would give me a better rate, but I did not like the service well enough to enter for the sake of a Bounty, for I expected to be discharg'd for an American the first time we went to England, and so it was the first time we went to Plymouth our ship had not been moor'd above three hours when my discharge was sent on board, but I did not know it for several months after, and then the King's Proclamation was out to pardon deserters and I gave myself up, and the Captain told me if it had not been for Mr. Robinson he should have given me my discharge.

He only remained in the *Helena* for a few months, but during this time they succeeded in chasing and capturing a French privateer and also recapturing a British merchant ship. The *Helena* then needed repairing, so Stokes was sent on board the *Dreadnought* of 98 guns under Rear Admiral Southerby. He was initially rated 'landsman', but this was later reviewed and he obtained a rating of Able Seaman. The picture he paints of this ship is not entirely credible and he may have been exaggerating a little, especially when it is remembered that later on he became very

religious and ended up as a clerk of a church in Ipswich. The
memoirs were compiled between 1830 and 1835, so there may be
some hindsight in some of his remarks. Still, it is a very intriguing
description:

> I am now in a ship where I can give full scope to every sinfull
> practise, for if ever there was anything on earth that deserve to
> be called a hell, this ship was one, but she was just what suited
> me, for I was only fit companion for the worst in the ship, and
> drunkeness and swearing was to me a delight, and I often
> heard oaths I never heard any before make use of. Neither
> tongue nor pen can describe the sins I practised for several
> years. The Recollection of this part of my life past in so much
> wickedness, is very often a trouble to me, but while I belong
> to this ship, I was counted a merry fellow, as I was always one of
> the first to dance and sing when the hands was turn'd up for
> that purpose, and that was every evening when duty and the
> weather would permit, and the Admiral as well as other officers
> would take a seat near us to see and hear us, and the more sin
> was mixt with our amusements, the more they was delighted.
> The sins of this ship was equal to the sin of Sodom, especially
> on the day we was paid, for we had on board thirteen women
> more than the number of our ships company, and not fifty of
> them married women. Our ship's company I think was very near
> eight hundred men. We sailed from Cowsand bay two or three
> days after the ship was paid, and left the bomb boat men to re-
> pent that ever they trusted the *Dreadnought* a penny. It was
> calculated the ship's company owed two thousand pounds and I
> believe they never got so many farthings. This ship was noted
> for her wicked principles. I had not been but a short time in
> this ship when she was paid, or I might have been a partaker in
> this as well as every other evil, for at this time I was capable of
> doing anything but good.

They did not spend all their time in 'amusement'. During this
time they were stationed off the French coast, and the boat's crew
to which Stokes belonged was often kept all day away from the
ship without anything to eat. Whenever a French ship appeared
they proceeded to chase it. Indeed, they captured a fair number.

However, the evenings were generally free and 'spent in dancing, singing and all kinds of unprofitable amusement, one fool
making sport for another thus the day mostly ended and very

often some one put in irons for punishment the next day for being drunk.' The one occasion on which Stokes was reported for drunkenness several officers pleaded for him, and as it was his first offence he was not flogged, but, he adds: 'I was the first and last that ever Captain Collard forgave for drunkenness while he was in the *Dreadnought* for he was always punish'd very severe and especially for drunkenness.'

Not that it was a happy ship, for on one occasion:

On our passage home, we fell in with the *Snapper,* an English man-of-war schooner, in sight of the Island of Ushant, who gave us information of a Spanish ship being taken by a French privateer and carried into Ushant. Our Admiral was very anxious to cut this ship out, but he was very doubtful the ships company would not fight, as the ship was very near a state of mutiny. We had seven men in irons at the time, which our Admiral said he would try by a court martial for mutiny when we arrived in England, for the ship had been in a general up-roar the night before we fell in with the *Snapper,* on account of the bad usage we had in the ship, and these seven men was in-tended by the Admiral to be punished as an example for the rest of the ship's company. But Providence ordered it otherwise, and the greater part of the officers having a better opinion of the ship's company, persuaded the Admiral to turn the hands up to see who would volunteer. It was accordingly done, and every man in the ship volunteered his service, for the greater part of our ship's company had the honour of fighting in their country's defence at Trafalgar under the command of Nelson, and still maintained that daring spirit which have ever distinguished the British sailor for skill and courage to add honour to the British Crown.

The Nelson tradition was certainly a very real thing and there followed a very brave attack on the Spanish ship. This is Stokes' description:

At three o'clock in the morning, September 9th 1810, we man-ned nine boat loads to cut the ship out, commanded by the first Lieutenant, and pulled directly into Ushant Harbour. I was one of the large cutters' crew this morning, and we was the third boat alongside the ship. The officer of our boat was kill'd about five minutes before we boarded the ship, and the Coxton was wounded with two musket balls in his breast. The ship was moor'd head and stern with four anchors, and some soldiers on board. There had been three hundred all night, but seeing our boats coming in after daylight the greatest part of them made their escape to the shore in the ships boat, and join'd the soldiers that was rank'd along the beach. The French had 500 soldiers and two or three field pieces placed so near the ship that we might throw a biscuit amongst them, and therefore we had a great many killed and wounded before our launch got in to cover us, for she was the only boat that had a canonade, but after she come between us and the beach, she made a very great slaughter amongst the French by discharging grape and canister shot. I think all the inhabitants on the Island was assembled on the beach for there appeared to be so many women and children as if there had been a fair. It was about two hours from the commencement of this action before we got out of the reach of the enemy's guns, for the enemy kept up a smart fire from a hill that was at the entrance of the Harbour long as their shot would reach. This hill was quite perpendicular and form'd one side of the harbour's mouth like a pier, and the entrance so narrow that the ships had but just room enough to come out. As soon as the ship was out of the harbour, I went into the Cabin with two or three more in search of something to drink, and found some wine, and while he was drinking each a glass, a Spaniard who was the mate of the ship crawled out of the stern sheets, and said he supposed the ship was out of the harbour. He could talk very good English and told us we had got a good prize but said he thought we must loose a great many men. He went on deck with us, but he was no sooner on deck, than he was like a man that is struck dumb for several minutes. The first lieutenant spoke to him but he could give him no answer. The sight that was before his eyes struck him with wonder and surprise. Forty five men on the deck killed and wounded and the gangways cover'd with human blood, and that getting cold and congeal'd, was slippery as grease, so that a great many was tript up and was stained with blood. Very few escaped a stain before we could clear the decks, and it being warm weather we was dress'd with white trowsers, which made the blood like more conspicuous. Two of our boats was taken with nine men in them wounded. We lost these boats by the painters being shot through. It was the barge and the pinnace we lost, and the rest of the boats was so full of shot holes we could hardly keep them afloat to get the wounded men on board. We was hove too alongside of our ship just as the bell was striking eight o'clock and while we was employed getting the wounded men on board, the *Poitiers* of 74 guns hove in sight, and while we was burying our dead, she lay too under our lea, and her band played that mournful tune call'd the 'Battle of Poitiers.' After the funeral service was over the Admiral told us he had not a doubt but we should have a very handsome medal and that he would do all in his power for us and would lay it before the board. The loss of the enemy was much greater than ours as was some time after reported in a letter that was sent to the Master-at-Arms by one of the men that was taken. We arrived in Cowsand bay on the 14th September, and our prize with us, and as soon as the ship was moor'd, the Admiral and Captain went ashore together, and we never see either of them since, but a few days after two printed papers was sent on board to be read to the ship's company. One was the thanks of the House of Lords, and the other the thanks of the House of Commons for our gallant conduct in cutting out the *Henrietta*, and about a month after we was paid the sum of 14s. od. a man prize money, but the medal we expected and that was so dearly earned never come to hand, so that fourteen shillings and a thank was the only reward this country would bestow on men forced from their wives and families and friends to fight in its defence, but hard hearted England have discharged hundreds of her Tars worn out in her service without a pension to end their days in a workhouse.

A sad end to a gallant affair, though not altogether surprising. It had not been a particularly successful venture and the historian of the Navy, Laird Clowes, refers to it as an 'unfortunate affair'. It is interesting to compare these two accounts and shows without a doubt that Stokes' account is substantially accurate.

It had been reported to Rear Admiral Thomas Sotheby, who was cruising off the Coast in the *Dreadnought 98*, Captain Valentine Collard, that a vessel was among the rocks on the west side of the promontory. Early in the morning, seven boats, under Lieutenant Pettman, were sent in to bring her out. They were received with a heavy fire from troops and a couple of field pieces on the beach; but they boarded and carried the craft, which proved to be the Spanish merchantman, *Maria*

K

Antonia, prize to a French privateer. Just then, about 600 troops, in a precipice almost immediately above the water, began to pour in volleys of musketry, to which no adequate return could be made. In consequence the attacking party had to retire with a loss of two boats, and 6 killed, 31 wounded and 6 missing.

This was undoubtedly the most outstanding engagement, though Stokes was involved in two other incidents. In one the ship's barge sailed ninety miles up the Tagus where the French army was encamped.

We was employ'd night and day watching the enemy to prevent them crossing the Tagus. We had a great many boats up the river but none wanted employment. We very often alarmed them in the night with a shower of shot from the boats. As there was but a small space between them and the Bank of the River; such was our employment while we was up the Tagus that we only once had an opportunity of cooking any provision for we was forced to eat our meat raw. After we had been fourteen days up the Tagus our pinnace was sent to relieve us.

In the other, when Lisbon was threatened by the French some two thousand sailors replaced the Portuguese in Fort St. Julian to release the soldiers for action. Stokes enjoyed this brief adventure.

Our duty was very easy for we had very little to do besides eating and drinking and walking about a certain distance, with leave for a certain time. It was a pleasure to us to be here. For my own part, I lik'd it much better than being on board, although I had as much liberty as any man in the ship, for I was ashore every day in the gig.

Their next station was the Baltic where they passed a very pleasant summer, but the return was extremely tragic.

We was detained in Wingo Sound about a month longer than was usual for a fleet to stop, by the *St George* 98 getting ashore, and thereby lost her rudder, and was very leaky. So the Admirals and Captains met to decide on bringing her to England, or leaving her in Wingo Sound till the next spring. The greater part could see no danger in taking her to England, and the *Cressy*, a new 74, was appointed to take her in tow, and the *Defence* 74 to attend upon her. The *Hero* 74, with a 20 gunbrig

I think call'd the *Grasshopper*, was appointed to take the convoy; and as there was a large fleet of merchant ships, the Admiral ordered that they should not get under weigh until the men of war was out of the sound; and in the morning of the 21st December the signal was made from the *Victory* for the large ships to get under weigh for England; and as soon as the fleet was out of the sound, the *Defence* and *Cressy* with the *St. George* in tow followed us, and the *Hero* with her convoy brought up the rear. The morning was very fine, but by two o'clock P.M. it blew a hard gale of wind, and by carrying a heavy press of sail hoping to clear the land before dark, we sprung the fore topmast about two foot above the cap. We made it known to the Admiral by signal, and he made a signal for the *Ajax 74*, to keep by us until we repair'd the damage, which we completed just before dark, and our Captain order'd a signal to be made for the *Ajax* to proceed to the Admiral, he being with the fleet so far ahead of us that we could just see them from the deck; and in the course of the night the *St. George*, *Hero* and *Defence* was totally lost. I never heard of more than twelve men being saved out of the *St. George* and not one out of the other two ships. This dismal night England lost more men than ever she lost before at one time. I cannot say I know the exact number of men that belong to these three ships, but I think it was about two thousand, and a twenty gun brig was obliged to run into an enemy's port to escape going ashore, and about five o'clock in the morning we very narrowly escaped going ashore with our ship. The pilots (for we had two on board) expected we was very near the land and was doubtful we should not clear it without going about; and so it was. We could hear the sea break on the Rocks before we could discern the land. Then, as soon as the land was reported, the helm was put a lee, and our ship come about to the astonishment of all on board, for I believe every one thought it impossible for any ship to come about in such a heavy sea and especially as it blew so very hard that we could only carry our three close reef'd topsails and three stormsails; and after the ship was round we appeared so close to the rocks that we might hove a stone among the breakers, and therefore we was in great doubt wither we should fetch off the land under so small canvas. Nothing but death to be expected, the coast of Norway close under our lee and a bad sailing ship. But our fears was soon removed, for in twenty minutes after the ship was about, we lost sight of the land, and as it was foggy, we could not see it at daylight. This was another providential escape from death. The same night so many of our country men perished in the three ships I just mentioned, and I many times since wonder's that God should preserve such a number of wretches as sail'd in the *Dreadnought*, for she was often called the floating Hell, for the wickedness that was practised on board of her; and to my shame and disgrace I must say that I was one amongst the worst in the ship, for I was often told by my wicked companions that I was the wickedest wretch in the ship. This was mostly told me in jest, but I always took it in earnest. For, whenever I was told of my wickedness my conscience would condemn me and bring my past sins to recollection and cause my mind to be troubled concerning a future punishment. But when I was struck with a sense of sin I always got drunk to drive away what I then called Dull Thoughts; and this was the case on the 23rd December. I got drunk for joy, instead of giving God thanks for such a deliverance as we had just been favour'd with. In the afternoon of the 24th we joined the fleet and come to anchor at the back of the Goodwin Sands for the want of a wind. At the turn of the tides we got under weigh and proceeded down channel, and arrived in Cowsand Bay on Christmas Day.

After this the *Dreadnought* was paid off for refitting, and Stokes with some others was sent to the *Ocean*. Here he was made a Petty Officer—Captain of the Fore Top—and he certainly 'enjoyed' this ship much more. Shortly after joining he was paid some prize money.

I think I was not sober one hour when I was awake, while the money lasted. I was several times reported for being drunk and neglecting my duty, but as the ship was in Harbour, the First Lieutenant said it was the only opportunity we had of enjoying ourselves, and by that means I escaped punishment although I deserved it, for I had very much offended the Boatswain by using a good deal of improper language to him, and it was a long time before he could forget it.

But Stokes also had other more concrete reasons for liking the *Ocean*. He had a good Captain and First Lieutenant and was obviously very content.

I was a great favourite of the First Lieutenant and generally respected by all the officers as well as the ship's company, so that I was very comfortable. Indeed, if I had been allowed my choice, I should not have found a better ship in the Navy. For we had not been long in the Mediterranean before she was called the 'Happy Ocean' and such indeed she really was, for every man in the ship was rewarded according to his merit and as much liberty as the service would allow and every other encouragement the officers had in their power to give, and the ships crew sensible of the kind treatment they met with, always ready and willing to obey, so that the *Ocean* had the name for having the best and smartest ships company in the Fleet. This was quite different from what I have said of the *Dreadnought*, and there was as much difference between the two ships as there is between chalk and charcoal.

They were stationed in the Mediterranean and they spent most of the time cruising off the coast occasionally using the boats to sail into a harbour and attempt to cut a French Privateer or a Frigate out. Sometimes it ended successfully.

Sir John Gore sent his boats into Blans to cut out a French Privateer expecting to bring her out without loss, as he was not aware they had erected a battery directly over the place where she lay, and he would not allow our boats to assist. But he was glad of our help the next day to bring his barge out, as he lost her cutting the privateer out. We undertook the task and landed our marines who took the battery from the French, dismounted the guns, and we brought the barge out without the loss of a man, and the next day the Prize was sold to a Spaniard and we shared 3s. 6d. a man.

On another occasion they were not so successful:

We arrived in the fleet just in time to send our boats with the boats of the fleet, to cut out two French Frigates that was moor'd in a small bay about ten miles below Toulon. We no sooner enter'd the Bay than a battery open'd a very heavy fire on us, and the Frigates being moor'd with chains we was obliged to make our escape as fast as we could out of the bay, for we was quite surprised when we found the French had got guns mounted ashore, for we expected to have only the ships to contend with; and after this unexpected repulse the boats come all out without any loss.

In this action Stokes received a slight wound in the hand but rather foolishly he did not report it and as a consequence 'I deprived myself of a smart ticket'.

At another time they gave assistance to the army in destroying a fort on the Catalonian coast and then embarked the troops. This was quite a dramatic occasion:

> It come on to blow very hard, so that the boats could not land to bring anything more off, for the night was very dark and dismal with very heavy rain and dreadful cracks of thunder attended with continual flashes of lightening, so that the elements appeared one continual blaze; and about the middle of the storm, the castle blew up, and the explosion, with the dreadful appearance of the heavens, and the foaming agitation of the sea made a very dismal sight; but thunder and lightening is very common in this part of the world—but this was the heaviest that ever I see.

But in the next storm they suffered more:

> On a Sunday evening in the month of October 1813 we had not furl'd the sails more than an hour, when the heavens was black with cloudes and another dreadfull thunder storm burst over our heads, and not a ship in the fleet but what received some damage from lightening. Our ship suffer'd most, but not a man kill'd. Our main mast and main topmast was so much shatter'd we could not set and sail on them, for several of the iron hoops was bursted off, being melted like lead by the lightening, and our main mast which was much larger in the round than a butt was so shattered that it was nothing more than a bundle of splinters.

While he was in this ship, Stokes spent a considerable time studying navigation though his claim to have acquired 'a perfect knowledge of it' was not substantiated by the later posts he held in the merchant service. He does not seem to have been encouraged much by the officers—though this may have been his own fault. He was obviously not an easy person to get on with, and his knowledge did not seem to have been any use to him in the Royal Navy. There is little doubt that his great handicap was drunkenness.

On our passage for England, I was broke from being the Captain of the Fore Top and disrated, for the Third Lieutenant had reported me to the Captain for drunkenness and neglect of duty at sea, and used all his influence to get me punished, but Captain Plampin told me he thought it would be sufficient punishment to take my rate from me as I was going to leave the ship with only the rate of Able Seaman.

Stokes had only himself to blame, the more so as when, shortly after the *Ocean* was laid up and Stokes was drafted to a Gun Brig—the *Brazen*—with two or three others, they arrived on board so drunk that the First Lieutenant could not even discover who was who. Even the next morning Stokes was not much better. In spite of this, he did his duty well and was in turn promoted to Gunner's Mate and then Boatswain's Mate. He served in the *Brazen* in these capacities for the last fourteen months of the war, and finally in September 1815 was paid off. Even then his adventures were by no means over.

As I was going ashore with six more men in a waterman's boat, the boat fill'd with water and we was obliged to swim for our lives. We was not long in the water before we was all pick'd up, but I lost the greatest part of my clothes with my pocket book containing a one pound note, and some papers no use to anyone by myself. Having about thirty seven pound Bank of England notes in my pocket, I went on board the *Brazen* to dry them, and then went ashore at Woolwich and walk'd to Greenwich in my wet clothes, and there I took coach for London, and the next morning I took coach for Ipswich and that evening I got home and found my mother alive and well, expecting me home, for she had heard from me a short time before.

The war being over, Stokes with many others had considerable difficulty in obtaining a ship, though in the end he succeeded. There is not room here to give full account of his service in the Merchant Navy, but he did change a great deal in the years immediately after leaving the Royal Navy. This came about primarily because he underwent a religious conversion and spent a great deal of time reading the Bible. To show how little difference in many respects there was between the two services, and also Stokes' changed attitude, it is worth while recounting one voyage that he made to Quebec and back, in which almost every hazard seems to have been encountered.

We sail'd from London 21st March 1817, for Calais, and there we took on board four hundred soldiers for Cork, and coming to sea, our ship was struck on Calais Bar, and knock'd a piece of the false keel off, and made her leaky, but as the weather was fine we made our passage to Cork in about seven or eight days, disembarked the soldiers and proceeded on the passage to Quebec; and about a week after we left Cork our ship catch fire by the Pitch Pot boiling over into the cookhouse fire. There being very little wind at the time we put the fire out much easier than we at first expected, for she appeared to be all in flames on deck. This made our situation appear very dangerous, especially as we had thirty seven passengers on board, our ship's company seventeen in number and only the jolly boat clear, the ship more than two hundred miles from land, and not a ship in sight, so that if the fire had prevail'd we must have perished either in the fire or water, but that mercifull hand that had so lately preserved me from sudden death is again stretch'd out to preserve me. I can never be thankfull enough to my God for the mercys bestowed on me so unworthy a wretch.

I read the scriptures a great deal this voyage but I cannot profit as I ought for I have powerful enemys to contend with both within and without, for my shipmates would sometimes call me hypocrite and try to vex me as much as they could. This was a great trouble to me yet I endeavoured as much as possible to avoid giving any offence, so that I found that they soon got more agreeable and I was less disturb'd when I had an opportunity of reading, which was very often in my watch below for we had fine weather all the passage out, until we came in sight of Cape Britton at the mouth of the Gulf of St. Lawrence. There we got beset in the ice two days, and by carrying a heavy press of sail to force the ship through the ice we lost a great deal of copper off the ships bottom. But we got clear of the ice without any other damage and in a few days arrived at Quebec. By this time my shipmates was got very sociable with me, but it did not last long, for our second Mate had several times neglected his duty by getting drunk therefore the Captain appointed me to do the duty of second mate the remaining part of the voyage. This created a great deal of enmity in two or three of my shipmates, who thought they had more right to perform this duty than I had, and took every opportunity to obstruct me in my duty, and to poison the minds of others against me. This was a great

H.M.S. '*Hastings*' by O. Borland. Queen Adelaide the widow of the 'Sailor King,' William IV, is seen on the poop. (See Appendix I.)

The Duel between the 'Macedonian' and the 'United States' by Montardier, described by Samuel Leech (pp. 73–82).

OPPOSITE The Battle of Navarino by Gilbert. Charles M°Pherson's ship, the Genoa, is the right hand one of a group of three in the centre background (See pp. 145–165).

LEFT *Reefing* (Shortening Sail). The crew aloft roll up part of the sail to 'shorten' it and keep it so by tying up the reef points.

RIGHT *Weighing Anchor* from a print by Kohler. The sailors are pushing round the Capstan with the Capstan Bars to haul up the anchor.

The Gun Deck of H.M.S. '*Excellent*'. This photograph shows the deck of the ship after she had been converted to a gunnery school. (See chapter 9.)

trouble to me, as I did not like to make any complaint to the Captain. But it was not long before the Chief Mate took notice of their conduct to me and reported one of them to the Captain who discharged him from the ship as he had by his conduct forfeited both his wages and his cloaths. This was a caution to the rest. For our ship was very comfortable the remaining part of the voyage and I could attend to my duty without any obstruction, and enjoy my leisure hours without being disturbed, so that I was very comfortable the remaining part of the voyage with all the ship's company as I had nothing more to disturb my mind but what arose from the dangers we was exposed to by having a leaky ship. For our ship made two foot of water every twelve hours before we left Quebec, and as soon as we sailed, the leaks begun to increase, and continued so to do untill we was obliged to keep both pumps continually going so that we could not go below to get even our meals, which was very scanty, for man had to labour so hard without any rest, only by setting down by the pumps when we got a spell. Our bread was all expended fourteen days before we arrived in Ireland, and our beef ten days before we arrived. One cask of flour was all our provisions for ten days for seventeen men, and a gale of wind with a heavy sea stove our water casks on deck so that we was deprived of fresh water until the gale was over. We had stowed a butt of water in the after hatchway before we left Quebec, that we might not be short of water, but when we took the hatches off, to our grief we found that cask also was stove by the working of the cargo, and leak'd more than half out. Now our conditions was alarming. The fear of being starved, together with the near prospect of being drown'd if our strength failed so that we could not attend the pumps. But the hope of falling in with some ship or other encouraged us to use every effort in hopes that we might escape death. In this distress I offer'd to God many silent prayers, but I doubted God's willingness to hear me. As I did not know whether I could pray I vow'd that if God would bring me safe out of this trouble, I would henceforth serve him. But I fear I have many times broken my vow since. On the 7th of September about eight o'clock in the morning we see Cape Clear. This created a joy I cannot express. At two o'clock we got a pilot on board and went into Crucks Haven, a small harbour about four leagues to the westward of Cape Clear, with our last puddings boiling in the coppers. We run our ship ashore on the most convenient place in this harbour for finding the leaks, with four feet of water in the hold. After the first tide our ship made very little water, and my shipmates soon forgot their past danger and toil, but it was not so with me. For the Lord had impress'd this mercy on my mind too deep to be easily forgotten. Not that I was any better than my shipmates. No! It is the Lord that make us to differ. I could call to mind how daring and hardened I had many times been amidst great dangers, and the loving kindness of the Lord to a rebel like me, for I was sincerely touch'd with a sense of the undeserved mercy I had received in being brought safe through so many dangers.

Shortly after this voyage he was married, but continued to go to sea for another ten years, though now generally as Mate. He never attained a permanent post as Captain and finally retired from the sea when he became Clerk of St. Peter's Church, Ipswich, where he spent the remainder of his life.

Possibly, looking back, Stokes was a little hard on the naval service though there is no doubt the *Dreadnought* was not a particularly 'good' ship to sail in, in any sense. The hardships in the merchant service were about as great as in the Royal Navy and there was no certainty of the food being any better. There was, however this one great difference which has already been noted. A man could change his ship if he did not like the Captain in the merchant service. This, of course, was impossible in the Royal Navy.

If, then, there is any final conclusion to reach on conditions on the lower deck during the French Wars, it is this—they depended on the Captain. If he was a 'flogging' captain, like The Hon. Sir Charles Paget or Waldegrave, then life became almost unbearable and desertion commonplace (witness the number who deserted when Paget was appointed to the *Revenge*). On the other hand a good Captain like Collingwood could and did make life on board if not pleasant, at least bearable. The Captains were at least in part appointed by the Admiral and here lies to a large extent the significance of 'Nelson's band of brothers'. Jack Nastyface recalls how two of the ships in company with the *Revenge* always beat them at furling and reefing. The reason he gives is most revealing. 'They were not in fear and dread, well knowing they would not be punished without a real and just cause. These men would have stormed a battery or engaged an enemy at sea with more vigour and effort than the other seven.' Whether Jack Nastyface's ratio of two happy ships to seven unhappy ones is a typical one, is doubtful, but it must be remembered that this refers to the latter part of the war after the death of Nelson and the retirement of Cornwallis, Barham and St. Vincent. The navy was for all its superiority in men, material and experience, surprisingly unsuccessful. Only the 'unorthodox', the Cochranes and the Brokes, who were certainly not 'flogging' captains, achieved any real success. For the rest, it was Wellington who won the war.

The position and power of the Captains did not change suddenly. As late as the 1860's flogging was still not uncommon, though by then it would not be given summarily by the Captain, but only by sentence of a court martial. Still, it continued to matter very considerably who the Captain was and one of the most heartfelt tributes was paid by the next author, Charles M'Pherson to his Captain—Walter Bathurst—and this can well serve to bridge the two periods.

He was greatly beloved by the whole crew, who looked upon him as a father, and who always found in him a ready refuge from injustice and oppression. His character of *a good captain* (a title alas! too rare in our fleet) was not confined to this period, or his own ship's company; for during the mutiny of the Nore, the mutineers absolutely forbade, on pain of death, any officer from entering aboard except Captain Bathurst. Such was his character in 1797 and such it continued till his sunset and the brave and excellent old man fell fighting the cause of an oppressed people under the Fort of Navarino.

8

CHARLES M'PHERSON
(1825-1828)

*Extracts from "Life on board a Man-of-War" with a
description of the Battle of Navarino*

IN THE PERIOD immediately following the end of the 'Great War'
against Napoleon the Navy was drastically reduced in size. In 1813
some 140,000 seamen and Royal Marines were serving, but by
1817 there were only 19,000. Thus, in four years, 121,000 seamen
and Royal Marines were thrown out of government employment.
This reduction, which also occurred in the army, resulted in widespread hardship and poverty, especially in the sea ports. It is,
therefore, all the more noteworthy that shortly after the end of the
war, when Lord Exmouth led a naval expedition against the
Moorish pirates in the Mediterranean, he did not find the manning
of his fleet particularly easy. The seamen were required to be
volunteers, and the expedition was fully manned in the end, but
the seamen's hostility to the navy was such that many preferred
destitution to voluntary service in the Royal Navy. As Samuel
Leech put it, 'The hardest crust, the most ragged garments,
with the freedom of your own native hills . . . is preferable to John
Bull's "beef and duff", joined as it is with the rope's end.'

Lord Exmouth's expedition itself was successful. The fleet
bombarded Algiers and did such considerable damage that the Bey
of Algiers agreed to the release of all slaves and promised to stop
marketing them. Not that this promise was worth very much, as
further intervention was needed to enforce it. However this
action emphasised the primary role which the navy was to adopt
over the next fifty years—that of 'policeman'.

Nevertheless the 'Old Navy' was by no means dead yet. This is not the place to describe in detail the 'policing' role that came to occupy a considerable proportion of the navy's time, the tedious and unhealthy war against slavery. Almost as a postscript to the Napoleonic wars the great wooden wall sailing ships fought one last major action—not against the French and Russians but with them—against the Turkish fleet in Navarino Bay.

The Greeks had for several years been rebelling against their Turkish overlords. A number of individual Englishmen—among them Lord Byron—had given aid to the Greeks but the policy of the British Government was officially one of neutrality in the struggle.

All the major European governments wished to retain the status quo leaving power in the hands of those who had traditionally exercised it. The Congress of Vienna, the settlement that followed the Napoleonic War, had been based on this principle. The Greek revolt had upset this status quo and numbers of individuals ardently supported the Greeks, among them Cochrane, who it will be remembered had played an important part in the attack on the Basque Roads, as described by Jack Nastyface. The governments had generally resisted these and other pressures to intervene, but by 1826 the Greeks were everywhere in retreat, largely due to the effective attacks of the Egyptians under Ibrahim Pasha. The fact that the latter acted more for his father Mehemet Ali than for the Turkish Sultan only served to complicate the issue.

At this stage the Russian Government clearly decided that it did not want to see Greece again entirely overrun by the Turks, and the English and French were both anxious to end hostilities there. The outcome was the 1827 Treaty of London between these three great powers, which insisted on an armistice between the Turks and the Greeks. The British Prime Minister, George Canning, believed that there need be no battle and that the publication of the treaty would contribute to a peaceful settlement, but this was not to be. In order to enforce this armistice, the allied powers had only one means at their disposal—their three navies, and it fell to the admirals to carry out what was virtually an impossible task, especially for the English Admiral, Sir Edward Codrington. He was not helped by the fact that his two subordinates were both anxious for a battle, though even he came to the conclusion that the use of force, in the last resort, would not be disapproved of.

The Turks soon rejected the proposals of the Treaty of London and Codrington was left in a situation in which he was expected to prevent 'hostile collisions' without actually becoming involved. The combined Turkish and Egyptian fleet collected in the Bay of Navarino on the southwest corner of the Greek peninsula. Their intention was to destroy the last centres of Greek 'rebel' resistance. To achieve this they had to cut off all supplies to the Greek forces —supplies that included the help given by 'irregulars' such as Cochrane. Codrington did persuade the Egyptian commander Ibrahim to accept a loosely worded truce not to use his fleet until he had heard from Constantinople, but even this truce caused misunderstanding. At one point some of the Egyptian ships sailed to the Gulf of Corinth in order to take supplies to the Turkish garrison at Patras which was threatened by the Greeks and their irregular allies. Ibrahim's argument justifying this breach of the truce was that if the Greeks were allowed to attack the Turks he saw no reason why he should not retaliate if attacked. However, Codrington did persuade the Egyptian ships to return to Navarino without actual hostilities, but the truce ended on October 15th, 1827.

Codrington was left in a position in which he had either to attempt to blockade the Turkish fleet through the winter, which was virtually impossible, or to enter the Bay of Navarino with the allied fleet which could well lead to a pitched battle. He was finally persuaded on the latter course by the fact that Ibrahim was carrying out a considerable land offensive against the Greeks.

From this point many details of the battle can be taken from an anonymous narrative by a sailor in one of the British ships of the line, the *Genoa,* whose name was almost certainly Charles M'Pherson. Unlike Codrington, the sailors on the *Genoa* seem to have been convinced that a battle would occur. The *Genoa* had only just rejoined the main fleet and this may have added to their conviction. M'Pherson talks about the 'impending conflict', but also of the day before the battle writes:

Some doubted that the Turks were cowards, and would not fight after they received our fire, while others again quoted cases to prove the contrary. Many lamented that there would be no prize-money, as the order was currently reported to be, 'to burn, sink and destroy', which would exclude the power of capture. 'There goes the sun under water!' said a Scotsman of the name of Currie, 'Who of us will see another gloaming? What do you say, De Squaw?' The German was sitting on one of the forecastle guns, attentively watching the motions of my messmate Tom Morfiet and another who were playing a game of chequers, totally regardless of the consequences of the impending conflict. De Squaw, as was his custom, when spoken to, did not pay any attention to the inquiry till the question was repeated, and when he turned his unearthly looking visage, it was not to the person who addressed him, but to my messmate. Starting up, he seized Tom by the arm, lifted him on his feet, and gazing earnestly in his face, said 'Morfiet! before tomorrow night, you and I will be playing another game!' He then walked away with his arms across, and took his seat on the boom apart from the rest.

This account may have been at least partly the product of hindsight.

De Squaw much impressed his fellow shipmates with his almost uncanny perception, and M'Pherson may well be exaggerating the incident. Another incident though, leaves little room for doubt that the sailors expected a battle the next day.

I was aroused by my messmate, Lee, who had been looking about the decks for me, to give me the share of a bottle of wine, and to write a letter for him to his mother. He filled the tot and taking my hand, said, 'May we meet again tomorrow!' And having drunk, he filled up to me and I drank likewise, after repeating his wish. He then said that as we were to go into action tomorrow he would like to write home through me; and having borrowed the sentry's lantern, I took the crown of my hat for a table, and the pile of shot on the combings for an easy chair, and after some remarks and advice regarding what he should say, I began, and wrote, according to his dictation, the following letter,

Dear Mother and Sister,

This leaves me in good health, and I hope it will find you in the same. Can't say if ever you'll get another letter from me; for we mean to go in tomorrow to Navarino Bay to beat the Turks so, whether I'll be sent to Davy or not I cannot tell: but you must not fret, dear mother, if I should be called away tomorrow, for you know that death is a debt we must all of us pay. If any of your old neighbours are calling on you tell Susan Clare that—(here Ned made a dead halt, but at last resumed, with the manner of one who was accomplishing some finished piece of diplomacy)—that I have not forgot the little bit of business she knows of, nor the *crooked sixpence*. She will understand what you mean, though you don't. And be kind to her, because as how her father is frail and was an old acquaintance; and tell her I have got some rare shells to bring home.

Now God bless you all, and keep you! I bid you fare well; but I hope to live to see the Turks get a great drubbing, and to weigh anchor again for Old England!

I remain, Dear mother and sister,
Your affectionate Son and Brother,
Edward Lee.

Having sealed the letter with a piece of metal, and finished the bottle of wine, we both went down and turned in.

On 20th October, 1827, then, Codrington decided that the Combined Fleet should enter the Bay of Navarino and anchor. What he hoped this would achieve is not altogether clear, but certainly he hoped that it would not lead to a battle, though inevitably he ordered the ships to be ready and using the famous words of Nelson he added that if a battle did arise 'No Captain can do very wrong who places his ship alongside that of an enemy', and he addressed this to a French Admiral! All this was not directly the concern of M'Pherson who proceeds:

I had a comfortable sleep for four hours, when I was aroused by the boatswain's mate swinging out 'Both watches pass up shot.' There was a line of men made from the shot locker up the main ladder, and we commenced to pass the shot up from one to another, and to fill with it the tubs that were ranged along the decks at regular distances.

We soon had the tubs all filled with shot, and everything else prepared. The sun was just rising as we were called on deck to make sail. The English squadron had kept nearly abreast of the harbour during the night, but the Russian and French ships had dropt four or five miles to leeward. We made a stretch out from the land slowly, to give the latter time to come up, before we stood in for the bay. . . .

At six bells (11 o'clock), the drum beat to quarters, with the well-known tune of 'Hearts of Oak'. The officers mustered the men, and saw all were present. The Lieutenant of the quarters where I was stationed was a young man of the name of Broke, a worthy son of that Captain Broke who commanded the *Shannon* frigate, in the ever-memorable action with the *Chesapeake*, a Yankee frigate of superior size. He gave us a few words to the following effect: 'Now, my men, you see we are going into the harbour today. I know you'll all be right glad of it; at least, I suppose you would be as much against cruising off here all winter as I am. So, I say, let's in today, and fight it out like British seamen, and if we fall, why there's an end to our cruise. I hope, when the guns are to man, you'll be at your stations.' The drum beat retreat, and several went and fell fast asleep between the guns.

We were now within two miles or less of the entrance to Navarino Bay, all sail set, stud-sails low and aloft, when the boatswain piped to dinner, and many a one assembled at the table for the last time.

The probability of never meeting again cast a soberness over the mess, which is generally a scene of banter and mirth. One or two tried to raise the spirits of their messmates by the usual sallies of nautical wit, but the effect was only momentary.

The piper now played 'Nancy Dawson', the well known call for the cook of each mess to go up with his monkey for his allowance (of grog) . . . All drank their allowance after the customary wish upon such occasions of 'May we all meet again tomorrow!' I went on deck with a kettle of pea-soup, and saw that by this time we were within a quarter of a mile of the fort that guarded the entrance of the harbour of Navarino. A gentle breeze was blowing which scarcely filled our sails, and we were not going above a knot an hour. All at once a man jumped from one of the forecastle guns, and roared out, 'There it goes now!' 'What!' said I, 'What's the matter?' 'Don't you see them there two pieces of bunting at the *Asia's* mast head! That's the signal to engage, my lad! Take a good look of it, so as you'll know it again.'

At this instant, the drum beat to quarters. I ran to the head, tumbled kettle and all overboard, and then made the best of my way to my gun. Every gun was soon manned, and already double shotted. The German De Squaw was quartered at the gun before me. We all stood in silent expectation of the order to 'fire'; and as directly to have a dose of the pills the Turks had been preparing for us these ten or twelve days past. We could observe them leaning over their guns, and pointing with the utmost *sang froid* to the different ships as they made their

L

appearance. The flagstaff they had on their batteries had no colours mounted, and everything seemed rather to betoken an amicable feeling. A boat pushed from the shore with a Turkish officer aboard and four men, and made for the *Asia*, that by this time, was clear of the guns of the forts, and about a hundred yards ahead of us. The officer I could see went aboard of the *Asia*, but did not stop two minutes. On regaining the shore he threw his turban from him, and ran up to a gateway in the fortress, where there was a crowd of people waiting his arrival. As soon as he made his appearance the red flag waved on the battlements, and at the same moment a signal gun was fired. The word now flew along the decks. 'Stand to your guns there, fore and aft!' 'All ready, sir' was the immediate reply, as the Captain of each gun stood with the lanyard of the lock in his hand, waiting to hear the word 'fire'. This was a period of intense excitement. A dead silence prevailed and 'the boldest held his breath for a time'. All the while we were 'drifting on our path', and now we were clear of the guns of the batteries, and steering alongside of the Turkish line. The Turks likewise were at their guns.

The pipe went to bring ship to anchor, and to furl sails. I was sent to the fore topsail yard-arm, the outermost man but one, who was Morfiet my messmate. I here had a grand bird's eye view of the whole harbour. . . . In the Bay, and round about us, were ranged in a triple line the Turco-Egyptain fleet. . . . We could see in a moment the situation our ship was placed in—a situation more perilous than any other ship in the whole three squadrons. Right abreast of us, and bringing nearly every gun to bear upon us, lay two of the enemy's line-of-battle ships: a little further ahead on our starboard now lay another two deck ship, and three double-bank frigates were so placed on our larboard bow and ahead, that they could gall us severely with their shot, while a large frigate lay athwart our stern that raked us with success for some time, till a French ship hove down and relieved us from her fire. Nothing can better show the honourable share the *Genoa* had in the action than that out of 460 men, we had 26 killed and 33 wounded, while the *Asia*, out of a crew of 700 men had only 19 killed and 57 wounded.

While on the fore-topsail yard, the report of a gun and small arms reached our ears, and turning round, we saw one of the brûlots, close to the *Dartmouth* frigate, on fire. The Captain of the *Dartmouth*, immediately ordered a cutter to board the brûlot. Lieutenant Fitzroy, with 8 stout men, soon pushed alongside of her, and as the bowman caught hold of her with the boat-hook, another jumped into the main-chain, and brandishing a cutlass, was proceeding to mount the bulwarks, when he received a pistol-ball through the head. At the same time, a volley of musketry was discharged on the crew of the boat, which killed Lieutenant Fitzroy and wounded another four. The remainder of the boat crew discharged their musquets at the vessel, but the Turks were under cover of the high bulwarks and received no damage. By the time the boat reached its own ship the brûlot began to blaze, in consequence of her crew having set fire to her before leaving her. This was the object of attention to my messmates and me on the fore-top sail yard, and the commencement of the carnage and destruction that followed.

About the same time, Sir E. Codrington, wishing if possible to bring things to an amicable arrangement, sent his boat to the Egyptian Admiral's ship, with instructions that if he did not fire upon any of the allied flags, not a shot should be fired at him. Mr. Mitchell, the pilot of the *Asia*, having reached the ship delivered his message, and having a flag of truce considered himself and the boat's crew safe. But as the boat was leaving the ship, Mr. Mitchell was shot while sitting in the stern-sheets of the boat, and dropt into the arms of the man who pulled the stroke oar. One of the men held up the flag as high as he could, with one hand, pointed to it with the other, and demanded the reason of their firing on it. He received no other answer than another volley of small shot, which however had no effect. They pulled for the *Asia*, and immediately on reaching it, a most treacherous broadside was poured into the Egyptian Admiral's ship, that made her reel again.

Tom and I were just making our way down from the fore-topsail yard, when the enemy's guns opened upon us. Morfiet, grasping my hand, exclaimed 'Don't forget Tom Morfiet, M.— farewell!—to your gun! to your gun!' and so saying, he jumped down on the maindeck where he was quartered, and I made the best of my way to the lower deck, and took my place at the gun. Lieutenant Broke drew his sword and told us not to fire till ordered. 'Point your guns sure, men,' said he, 'and make every shot tell—that's the way to show them British play!' He now threw away his hat on the deck, and told us to give the Turks three cheers, which we did with all our heart. Then crying out, 'Stand clear of the guns,' he gave the word 'FIRE!' and immediately the whole tier of guns was discharged, with terrific effect, into the side of the Turkish Admiral's ship that lay abreast of us. After this it was, 'Fire away, my boys, as hard as you can!' The first man that I saw killed in our vessel was a marine, and it was not till we had received five or six rounds from the enemy. He was close beside me. I had taken the sponge out of his hand, and on turning round saw him at my feet with his head fairly severed from his body, as if it had been done with a knife. My messmate Lee drew the corpse out from the trucks of the guns, and hauled it into midships, under the after ladder. The firing continued incessant, accompanied occasionally by loud cheers, which were not drowned even in the roar of the artillery, but distincter than these could be heard the dismal shrieks of the sufferers, that sounded like death knells in the ear, or like the cry of war-friends over their carnage.

About half an hour after the action had commenced, two boys, of the names of Fisher and Anderson, the one about 14 years of age, the other about 12, both servants to the officers in the wardroom, were standing on the after-hatchway gratings, nearly abreast of the gun I was quartered at, on the lower deck. They were both fine looking boys, and neatly dressed in jacket and trousers. Fisher indeed, was the most interesting boy I ever saw. His cheeks were blooming with health, and his large black eyes were shaded by long black curled hair. They were standing, as I said, on the gratings, hand-in-hand, and raising their tiny voices amidst the cheers of our men. I was loading the gun, and, not a moment before, had cried on Fisher to go to the fore magazine for some tubes, when a shrill shriek sounded in my ears, and turning round, I saw Fisher lying a lifeless corpse. Anderson had also fell wounded, but not mortally; his right legs was nearly cut across, and one of his arms was hurt in several places. But it was not himself he cared for. He crawled to the corpse of Fisher, and burying his head in his dead companion's bosom, uttered the most piercing cries I ever heard. Another and I were ordered to take him to the cockpit. We found Fisher had been struck by a shot on the back of the head. A smile was still on his lips, and his cheeks were as ruddy as ever. It was with great difficulty we could separate little Anderson from the body of his comrade. He implored us not to take his 'dear Ned' from him. Surrounded as we were with death and danger, it was impossible not to be affected at this scene; but we were obliged to use force and tear him away. The poor boy's sufferings were not complete; for as he was being taken to the cockpit, a splinter struck his right arm and broke it. Fisher was laid down among the common heap of slain, to await a watery grave.

The battle at this time was raging with the most relentless fury; vessel after vessel was catching fire; and when they blew up they shook our ship to its very kelson. We sustained a most galling fire from the two line-of-battle ships abreast of us, which kept playing upon us till they were totally disabled by having all their masts shot away, and whole planks tore out of their sides, by the enormous discharge of metal from our guns. We were ordered to only double-shot the guns, but, in this particular, we ventured to disobey orders; for after the first five or six rounds, I may venture to say that the gun I was at was regularly charged with two 32 lb. shot and a 32 lb. grape; and sometimes with a cannister crammed above all. On being checked by the officers for overcharging, one of the men replied, as he wiped the blood and dirt from his eyes, that he liked to give them a *specimen* of our *pills*. In the line-of-battle ship that was right abeam of us, there was a great stout fellow of a Turk in a red flannel shirt, working a gun in the port nearly opposite ours, and as he was very dexterous, he was doing us a deal of mischief. One of the marines, observing this, levelled his musket and shot our bulky antagonist through his head, who dropt back and hung out of the port head downwards, but was soon pitched overboard by the one that took his place.

From the effect every shot had on the finely-painted sides of the Moslem vessels, we expected them to strike speedily, and many were the inquiries whether they had 'doused the moon and stars yet', but the Turks were resolute, and not one of them struck colours during the engagement. 'Pelt away, my hearties,' cried the captain of our gun, a young Irish lad, and a capital marksman, 'if they don't strike, we'll strike for them. Oho', he continued, 'here's a glorious mark—look-out here; we'll load with grape entirely.' The gun was loaded nearly to the muzzle with grape. The Turkish Admiral's yacht, a fine frigate, that had been built for him at Trieste, drifted down (her cables being shot away) beside us. Her figure-head was a red lion bearing a shield, on which were the three half-moons or crescents, a broad gold stripe was above her port-holes all the way aft; her stern had large figures of angels, all gilt, supporting a balcony or stern-walk, which was also gilt; and when the sun pierced the dense cloud of smoke, which was only at intervals, the vessel glittered brilliantly. 'Stand clear there,' cried the captain of our gun, 'she's coming! she's coming! d——me, if I don't spoil her gingerbread work! Aha! I'm glad you have come this road at any rate. Now, let's see what I can do for you in a small way!' He pointed the gun, and, taking aim, fired; and when the smoke cleared away, I heard him above all the noise that assailed our ears, vociferating, 'I told ye! I told ye! I've done more than I bargained for; I've carried her spanker-boom as well as her gingerbread work away.' A few minutes after this she caught fire and blew up. As she was very near us, pieces of the burning wreck made their way through the ports, and nearly suffocated us with the fumes of some disagreeable substance that had been in the vessel when she blew up.

At an order from the quarter-deck, we were called away from our guns to clap on the larboard springs, so as to get our foremast guns to bear properly on the enemy. The men seemed unwilling to leave their guns, but on Captain Dickinson coming down on the lower deck, and speaking to them, the spring was hauled in, when all our guns were brought to bear, and that with an effect that was soon seen on the hulls and rigging of our opponents. I can say, with perfect certainty, that during the action, as the ship swung, the springs were repeatedly applied to, and used with alacrity.

As there is always a cask of water lashed to the stanchion on the deck in midships, called 'fighting water', one of the officers of the fore part of the deck, on his way to the cockpit, came aft, begging to get a drink. He had been wounded severely in the right arm with a piece of langridge shot, and the left was so bruised that he could not lift the jug to his head. De Squaw, who had been working the gun with an activity and smartness that surprised me for a man of his age, took the jug, and after skimming back the blood and dirt from the top of the cask, filled it, and offered it to the officer; but just as he was in the act of holding it to the wounded man's mouth, he dropt a mangled corpse, being cut nearly in pieces with grapeshot; the officer was knocked down, but not hurt. 'Poor fellow!' said he, 'He has died in performing an act of humanity—God rest his soul!' We assisted the officer down to the cockpit, where, illuminated by the dim light of a few pursers' dips, the surgeon and assistants were busily employed in amputating, binding up, and attending to the different cases as they were brought to them. The stifled groans, the figures of the surgeon and his mates, their bare arms and faces smeared with blood, the dead and dying all round, some in the last agonies of death, and others screaming under the amputating knife, formed a horrid scene of misery, and made a hideous contrast to the 'pomp, pride and circumstance of glorious war'.

During the heat of the action, only one instance of cowardliness came under observation. A big stout Manxman, who was stationed at one of the guns on the lower deck, and had showed signs of trepidity from the time the first broadside was given and received, finding an opportunity, slipped down the cockpit ladder, and did not make his appearance till the 'ball was finished'. When at length the thundering noise of the guns had ceased, their silence seemed to have a peculiar effect in reviving the exhausted spirits of the Manxman who, from lying on his face in the cockpit, gently turned on his side and eyed the surgeons, who were busy docking and refitting the shattered hulls of our shipmates. His motions were observed by the master-at-arms, who giving him a slight intimation of his presence by applying his foot to his seat of honour, asked him what was the matter with him? The poor Manxman looked up and said he had a very sore back, but it was better now. 'Go on deck, you rascal!' said the master-at-arms; 'here you've been all the time of the action, you skulking scoundrel, and the other poor fellows on deck getting themselves cut to pieces! Where the hell would the ship have been by this time if all the men had been like you. Go on deck directly, sir!' and seconding his command by another smart application to his breech, the Manxman bounded up the ladder and went to hide his face from the men. In a day or two after, the circumstances reached Captain Dickinson's ears, who turned the hands up and calling the Manxman out from the rest, the charge was proven against him, and he got three dozen with the thieves' cat under the shirt. The word COWARD was sewed on his jacket, and he was made to mess on the main deck by himself.

About half-past three o'clock, as near as I could guess, the bight of the main-sheet hung just down before our gun, and incommoded us in the pointing of it. I was ordered along with another to go on deck, and haul in the slack, to keep it out of the road of the muzzle. I can't say I liked this job, for during the action, a deep impression lay on my mind that I was safer at my gun than anywhere else; however, go I must. On gaining the main-deck, the scene of carnage and devastation far exceeded what was on the lower deck.

Shortly before this, I had heard a dreadful crash as if the whole ship's side had been stove in, and I now learned that it was occasioned by two marble-shot of 120 pound weight each, striking the main-deck abreast of the main hatchway. They had knocked two ports into one, and wounded five men, among whom was my dear messmate Morfiet, but this I did not know at the time. I saw Captain Bathurst coming down the poop ladder, when the tail of his cocked hat was carried away by a splinter from the bulwarks of the ship. He took off his hat, looked at it, and smiled, then coming down on the quarter-deck, which was the most eminently exposed part of the ship, issued his orders with the same calmness as if he had been exercising guns at sea. There was something at once noble and ludicrous in the appearance and situation of the old man, as he proudly walked the quarter-deck, with his drawn sword and shattered hat, amid showers of shot and splinters, insensible apparently to the danger that surrounded him. My companion and I essayed with all our might to haul in the clack of the mainsheet, but could not effect it, the rope being so heavy. The rigging of the ship was torn in pieces, her yards topped up and down, and some of them fore and aft, the lifts shot away, and the quarter-deck so bestrewed with splinters of wood, that it presented the appearance of a carpenter's shop. The Captain came forward to us, and looking up, exclaimed, 'By G——, the Union Jack's shot away! Go aft on the poop, and tell Davy, the signal man, to give me another Union Jack.' I went aft, and found Davy looking out with his glass at the *Asia*, which was about a cable's length astern of us. The Admiral was standing on the poop-netting, and with a speaking trumpet was hailing our ship with '*Genoa*, ahoy!' 'Sir Edward', was the reply of the signal man. 'Send a boat with a hawser to swing my ship's stern of a fireship that's drifting down upon us.' 'Ay, Ay, sir,' said Davy, and was going away when I told him what the Captain had sent me for. He said he had a Union Jack in his breast, where he had stowed it at the beginning of the action to be ready for any unlucky accident that might happen, and proceeded to the Captain.

When I came forward to the place I had left, I saw that the message I had been sent was the means of saving my life, for, during my absence, the hammock netting had been torn completely to pieces with shot, and the poor fellow, Holmes, who came up with me, was stretched on the deck. The Captain was at the gangway, looking into our opponent's vessel. 'Did you bring the Union Jack, Davy?' said he. 'Yes, sir,' replied Davy, and at the same time told him what the Admiral wanted. The Captain snatched the flag out of Davy's hand, and walking smartly forward, demanded, 'Who would go and nail the British Union Jack to the fore-royal-mast-head?'. A good-looking man, of the name of Neil, stept forward at once, and took it out of the Captain's hand, and without speaking, began to make the best of his way up the two or three tattered shrouds that were left in the fore-rigging. The Captain then ordered half-a-dozen of the nearest men (among whom I was one) to man a boat and take a hawser for the *Asia*. Having got over the side into the boat, we sat waiting, while two of the men were occupied in coiling it in. I had here a fine view of the contending fleets, and could see that we had a galling fire to sustain at this time from two line-of-battle ships, one of which, although on fire, still kept up a constant cannonading upon us. The *Asia*, which was astern of us, had at this time only one large vessel, a liner, and a double-bank frigate, playing upon her. I trembled for the fate of our ship, because I was sure that if the game continued to be played so unequally, we would stand a chance of coming off *second best*. I looked aloft to see how Neil had got up with the Union Jack. I saw him clinging with his feet to the royal-mast, and hammering away with a serving mallet. I watched till he got on deck in safety, and could not but admire the cool and determined manner in which he accomplished what he had undertook. The hawser being coiled in the stern sheets of the boat, we shoved off and proceeded to the *Asia*. The face of the water was covered with pieces of wreck; masts and yards drifted about on the surface, to which clung hundreds of poor wretches whose vessels had been blown up. Numbers of them imploringly cried upon us, in the Turkish language, a small

smattering of which the most of us had picked up at Smyrna.
We kept paying out the hawser as we pulled along but just as
we came within six fathoms of the *Asia*, our hawser terminated,
and we could not proceed any farther. The crew of the *Asia*, at
the gunroom port, seeing our dilemma, hailed us, and hove a
rope's end to make fast to our hawser; but this we could not
manage. A man, then, of the name of George Finney, Captain
of our main-top, seeing there could be no other way of getting
it done, jumped into the water and swam the distance between
the boat and the flag-ship; the end of the hawser was then put
out of the port, and Finney, catching hold of it, swam back to
the boat, bearing the end of the heavy rope in one hand and
swimming with the other. We soon made what sailors call a
Carrick Bend of the two ends, and began to pull back for the
Genoa. The Admiral appeared on the poop, in a plain surtout,
and signed, with a handkerchief, for us to make all speed.
Scarcely had we gained half-way between the *Asia* and our own
ship, when the former ship's mizen went over the quarter with a
crash. We thought the Admiral was involved in the wreck, as
we saw him standing at the place not a minute before the mast
went over, but we were relieved from this apprehension by his
reappearance on a conspicuous situation. We picked up, on our
way back, ten of the poor drowning wretches who were drifting
about during the storm of fire and thunder, that made the
ancient Island of Sphalactria tremble again. Several of them
were Arabs, quite black, but all were Mohometans, as we saw
by the lock of hair left on the crown of their heads, by which
Mahomet, according to their own beliefs, lifts them to Paradise.

Not a shot had struck the boat since we left our own ship,
although several pieces of burning wood and showers of burned
rice and olives from the Turkish ships rained down upon us in
plentiful profusion; but as one of our men, called Buckley, was
hauling a tall stout young Moslem out of the water, a shot blew
the head of the Turk to pieces, upon which Buckley, turning
coolly about, said 'D—— me, did you ever see the like of that?'

Cool, however, as a British sailor is in danger, nothing can
approach the Turk in this respect. George Finney had hauled
one into the boat, a fine-looking fellow, and elegantly dressed.
He was no sooner seated in the bow of the boat, than taking out
a portable apparatus, he began to fill his pipe, which having
done, he struck a light from the same conveniency, and com-

menced sending forth, with inconceivable apathy, volumes of smoke from his mouth. 'Do you see that Turkish rascal,' said Finney, who was provoked at this singular instance of indifference. 'Well, since he cares so little for being hauled out of his *Britannic Majesty's* clutches, we'll soon send him where he came from.' So saying, he made a spring forward, seizing the Turk, who could not understand how he had offended, tumbled him overboard before anyone could prevent him. The Turk soon recovered, and got upon a piece of the wreck of one of his own ships, where he was picked up by the *Albion's* boat. Another instance of Turkish coolness I may mention, which, although it did not happen in our ship, was told me under well authenticated circumstances. Some of the crew of the French frigate *Alcyone* had picked up a Turk, who by his dress appeared to be a person of rank in their navy. When he was brought aboard, he found his arm so shattered that it would need to undergo amputation; so he made his way down the cockpit ladder with as much ease as if he had not been hurt, and as much dignity as if he had made a prize of the frigate. He pointed to his shattered arm, and made signs to the surgeon that he wanted it off. The surgeon obliged him so far, and having bound up the stump and bandaged it properly, the Turk made his way to the deck, and plunging into the water, swam to his own vessel that was opposed along with another to the very frigate he had been aboard of. He was seen climbing the side with his one arm, but had not been aboard many minutes, when it blew up, and he, among others of the crew, in all probability perished in the explosion.

We reached the *Genoa* in safety, and I got into the lower-deck port, just abaft the gun I was stationed at in the fore part of the action.

In about half an hour after this, Captain Bathurst was carried down to the cockpit by four men, having received a mortal wound in the groin by a grapeshot of about four pounds' weight. The report flew about the decks like lightning, that the Captain was mortally wounded, and all firing ceased for the space of about two minutes, every one looking at another as if he himself had received his final blow. Then the whole crew, as if activated by one impulse, set up a cry of dire revenge, and the words 'OUR CAPTAIN KILLED! OUR CAPTAIN KIL-LED!' were heard above the roar of the guns. Dreadful as the conflict was before it now raged with triple violence. A single forty two pound shot came through one of our ports, and killed four men and wounded two. Some were wounded in so shocking a manner that it seemed to me as if death would have been a mercy to them. The line-of-battle ships that I mentioned as having been on fire when we were in the boat at the *Asia*, now burst forth in a blaze, but still her lower deck, and some of her main deck guns kept up a hot fire upon our bow that galled us severely, until she blew us with a terrible explosion, and pieces of iron, wood, and nail flew thick in at our ports.

The shot mentioned above that took such fatal effect was the most murderous that struck our ship; but another heavy shot took her on the main deck, right on the quarter, and knocked away the whole side of a port, clearing the gun. Of a father and son, stationed at this gun, the father was killed and the son knocked down, but not hurt otherwise.

Nine of our Petty Officers had wives aboard, who were occupied, with the doctor and his mates, in the cockpit, assisting in dressing the wounds of the men as they were brought down, or in serving such as were thirsty with a drink of clean water.

Some of them pretended, or were really so much affected by the shocking sight around them, that they were totally unable to render any assistance to the sufferers. Two of the number, I think it but justice to mention, acted with the greatest calmness and a self-possession. One of them was a Mrs. Buckley, and the other a Mrs. Clark, the latter a Marine's wife.

Many were of the opinion that the Turks would strike their colours after our first round, but this proved a gross miscalculation; for nothing could exceed the bravery of these devoted men.

It was now six o'clock, and dark, when we could observe that the heavy fire of the enemy began to slack, which made us the more anxious to bring the action to a close, and after three hearty cheers were given and a tremendous broadside we heard the speaking trumpet of Captain Dickinson who had taken command when Captain Bathurst was carried below, giving orders at the main hatchway to cease firing . . . (though the men were not anxious to do so.)

We had now time to look at the dreadful scene of carnage on our own decks; the gory heap under the after-ladder was the first thing my eyes met. Already had a few of the men begun to perform the last sad duty to their comrades.

I went down the cockpit ladder, and the scene here was more horrible than before. The heavy smell of the place, and the stifled groans of my suffering shipmates brought a cold sweat over me: and I found myself turn so sick that I was obliged to sit down for a little on one of the steps of the ladder. On recovering, I snatched up a lantern, and proceeded to look at those who were lying stretched on their backs. . . A voice (singing a sea song) came from a remote corner of the cockpit and on going forward I saw sitting upon the Doctor's medicine chest, a marine of the name of Hill. I held up the lantern, and saw the poor fellow wanted both arms, the one a little above the elbow, and the other a little below the shoulder. . . I turned round, and looking at the lid of a midshipman's chest, I saw my poor messmate (Tom Morfiet, for whom he had been searching) lying on his back, with his face quite discoloured. I took him by the hand; his lips moved, but he was quite unable to speak. 'Tom! Tom! can't you speak to me?' He pressed my hand feebly, and moved his lips again, but was denied the power of utterance. Wishing to alleviate his suffering if possible, I lifted his head up to put a bag under it, when I found to my horror a large wound just above the neck. The master-at-arms at this moment came down, and seeing me, he ordered me instantly on deck; for the Doctor had given strict instructions to let no one speak to the wounded, or stop in the cockpit. I was therefore obliged to go on deck, after taking a last look of my dying friend.

When I came to my berth I was welcomed by the whole mess more like a brother than a shipmate, but this day made us all brothers: feuds and animosities were buried in forgetfulness; and many who had entertained bitter hatred at one another, would be seen shaking the hand of friendship together. I took my seat and commenced looking about to see if any of the old familiar faces were missing: but it was difficult to recognise my messmates in the curious group of ferocious looking banditti that surrounded me. I found on inquiry that two of my messmates beside Morfiet were killed. . . We drank to the memory of our good old Captain, and all who fell on this glorious day. I found the wine revive me greatly and I soon went on deck to have a view of the scene of battle, by the light of the Turkish fleet that was blazing in all quarters.

I naturally turned my attention to our own ship first. We were in a wretched state, especially our masts and rigging. If it had come on the least breeze of wind, both our mizzen and main masts would have gone over the side. . . I mounted one of the forecastle guns, and took a view of the whole harbour. We saw I may say, thousands of poor wretches floating on pieces of the wreck of their own vessels. Out of the large and majestic Turkish fleet that had that day been stretched in the form of a crescent round the bay, only 15 small vessels were to be seen close to the shore; the remainder being either sunk, burnt, or mere wrecks. . . I then made my way down and I went forward to see how my messmates were holding out. I found a number of them stretched on the deck, sleeping as soundly as if they had been on a feather bed, with a pillow of down under their head, instead of a box of canister. I sat down on the range of the best bower cable and the past events of the day thronged into my mind, interwoven with hopes and fears of how the night was to be spent.

Soon after, the hands were turned up by the cry of 'all hands to work'. The mizzen was nearly cut through, and the main so terribly shattered that neither was expected to stand till morning. Not a shroud was left on the mizzen, while our main had but one, and that one was stranded. We proceeded to clear wreck, but so excessively fatigued were we all that we gave it up one after another, and went below. We were utterly unable to repair the rigging that night, even if it would have saved the mizzen-mast, and our officers had humanity enough not to force us from the little rest we stood so much in need of.

Even so the night was not a peaceful one, for a frigate in flames drifted down onto the *Genoa* and all the hands were sent to quarters, but a Russian ship blew her up before she got within reach.

As soon as daylight appeared the hands were turned up to clear wreck. In the midst of knotting, splicing, cutting, getting up new rope, storing away the remainder of old rigging, etc., we heard a pipe summoning all hands to muster on the quarter deck. We found Captain Dickinson, the Purser, the Doctor and the Captain, clerk, with other officers, waiting to score off the names of the killed. Captain Dickinson, after a short address, in which he informed us that our good old Captain was no more, and told us how pleased he was with the manly way we had behaved during the action, particularizing some of the instances of coolness and courage that had occurred under his observation, and complimenting Mr. Miller, the master of the ship, highly, for the gallant manner he placed the ship alongside the enemy, concluded by telling us to listen with attention, as Mr. Andrews called over our names, and to answer when any one's name was called that we knew was dead. The Purser then began to call the names; a dead silence reigned over the deck; only interrupted by the Midshipman of the watch reporting 'Another of the enemy blowing up, sir', followed by the explosion of the vessel of which he spoke.

The names had been called for a little, and the answer was 'Here', till one didn't answer. 'He's killed, sir,' said one; 'Mark him off, Mr. Andrews,' said the Captain. Thus it went on, every two or three names that were called being answered by 'killed' or 'wounded'. I, having answered my own, listened with anxiety to hear poor Tom's. At last his name was called. 'Thomas Morfiet', cried the Purser. 'Mortally wounded, but not yet dead,' said a voice on the other side. With joy I saw that the mark of red ink was not put down against his name, and I hoped I would yet have a chance to see him before he died. We found out the extent of our loss to be 26 killed and 33 wounded. The Captain said, that as there was no cocoa provided the day before, we should have tea for breakfast and ordered the boatswain to pipe down to get our breakfast as quick as we could, for we would be wanted in a very little time. Down we went, and while the cook was getting breakfast ready, I made my way to the cockpit, determined to see Morfiet. When I came under the half deck, a scene of carnage now presented itself to my view that had been hid during the darkness of the night. All the upper part of the deck was splashed with blood and brain; lumps of human flesh sticking to it; and in the eyebolts of the deck several of the same disgusting reminders of mortality met my view.

I was making my way down the after ladder, when I met two of the men bearing a purser's bread bag, which I knew would contain the body of one of my shipmates. I asked who it was. 'Why,' said one, 'it's just your own messmate, Tom Morfiet— dead at last.' At this I could not contain myself, but burst into tears. 'Lay him down here,' I said, 'and I'll wrap him in his spare hammock, and bury him myself, for you know he was my companion.' 'You're welcome to the job,' they said, as they deposited the body between two guns, and left me.

I went forward to the mess, where they were all at breakfast, to get a spare hammock. 'What's the matter?' said one, 'where are you going with that 'ere hammock, and the tear in your eye like a travelling rat?' I made no answer; but having borrowed a sail-needle and some twine, I went off to wrap the lifeless body of my messmate into his characteristic shroud. I undid the mouth of the bag, and cut it down with my knife, for I could not bear my fingers about the body, and I had nobody at this time to help me. The wound on the back of his head seemed to be the only one, but the neat white frock that he had on was sticking to his back with clotted blood. He had his knife with the lanyard round his waist, to which was attached the very thimble with which he had mended his jacket, sitting in the streets of Malta. The thimble I took to keep for his sake; and having stretched the knots out on the hammock, I proceeded to sew it up, beginning at the feet. While thus engaged, I was accosted by some one behind. I did not look up for I was still crying, but I knew the voice to be my messmate's Tom Croaker. When I told him whose body I was enshrouding Croaker offered to get the Prayer Book and read the service for the dead; 'For', said he 'Tom was always a yonker that I was fond of, and we sailed round Cape Horn and back again in the old *Tartar* together for three years eight months, and it will go very hard though I am no parson, if my peepers won't do him as he goes to Davy.' Croaker procured the Prayer Book while I finished my work, and having slung two 32 lb. shot to the feet, we bore it to the gunroom port. My assistant read the service with a sober steady voice, and when he came to the words, 'We commit his body to the deep' I let go my hold and with a gentle push, the body of poor Tom was launched into the water. We looked out, and saw it gradually sinking under the wave; and the hands being lined up, we went on deck to do our duty.

There is little more to add. The battle was a complete victory for the allies. The *Genoa* had in fact lost more men killed than any other allied ship and the total allied casualties were only 174, and 475 wounded, of these 75 and 197 respectively were British. No allied ship was lost, while at least 60 enemy ships were totally destroyed.

Codrington, however, was to be treated somewhat cavalierly. Though he was presented with the G.C.B. following the battle, he was recalled eight months later for having 'misinterpreted his instructions', and the government referred to the battle as an 'untoward event'. This was hardly surprising, as whatever individual members of the government might have thought, they were bound to object in principle to the use of force against the Turks. Indeed, the paradox of the battle was that Codrington himself was not particularly kindly disposed towards the Greeks. Cochrane and the other British irregulars caused him considerable problems and the Greeks themselves were constantly perpetrating acts of piracy which were equally objectionable. Yet, the Battle of Navarino determined that Greek independence was finally secure. Though the governments, and even Codrington, might pretend otherwise, the destruction of the Turkish and Egyptian fleet meant that the revolt of the Greeks could no longer be suppressed.

Codrington himself was not helped by the dispute that arose between him and Dickinson who had taken over the command of the *Genoa* on the death of Bathurst. Dickinson was extremely popular with the crew of the *Genoa* which is clear from the speech he made some days after the battle to the ship's company, as recorded by M'Pherson:

> If, said he, I have ever given you an angry word without cause, I generously beg your pardon, for after your noble behaviour, I must always hold you in respect, and shall be grieved if any of you shall ever forfeit the honourable estimation of you which you have established in my breast.

And M'Pherson goes on to relate that

> Jack Burgess who had survived this as well as many other actions, drew the slave of his Guernsey frock across his brow, and said 'Damn me, when I was aboard the *Tremendous*, our old shark of a Captain would never have axed pardon though he had seen all our back-bones!'

A 'Round Robin' was then signed by the crew petitioning the Admiral to allow 'Captain' Dickinson to retain command of the ship on its voyage home. This did not please Codrington at all, and the petition was disregarded, a new Captain appointed and a severe reprimand administered to Dickinson. M'Pherson however wrote:

M

That the crew of a man-of-war should express a wish regarding the government of their vessel was considered presumptious and a Captain Irbey was commissioned to take the place of the Commodore instead of Captain Dickinson—so little is mutual attachment and goodwill between master and man studied in the Naval Service.

Dickinson was later court-martialled on charges arising from his conduct in the battle and afterwards. The principal charges were that he had mishandled his ship in such a way as to endanger the *Asia* and the *Albion*. He was also accused of falsifying the ship's log as to the time of Bathurst's death and of submitting a Round Robin from the crew. The outcome was that Dickinson was honourably acquitted of all charges except that of submitting the Round Robin, and the reproof already administered by Codrington was considered to be an adequate punishment for this. More important still, Dickinson was given an independent command.

The return to England was uneventful but, emphasising how little the navy had changed, the new captain of the *Genoa* acted with considerable harshness. Following the funeral of Commodore Bathurst, who was taken ashore at Plymouth by his old barge's crew,

Several of them took the liberty of stopping ashore all night to see their friends, and next day they were brought up and underwent the thieves' cat most severely, to the apparent satisfaction of our Captain.

We had no liberty ashore whatever, notwithstanding the length of time we had been away and the action in which we had been engaged. Our Captain, however, was himself regularly ashore all day, only visiting us in the forenoon to *serve out slops* to those who had by stealth followed his example. Scarcely a day passed but some one underwent the barberous and disgusting operation of the lash.

All that has been said so far seems to emphasise the point that this was very much the navy of the French wars. The ships were similar—in some cases even the same; the discipline was almost as severe and leave, though occasionally granted, was still severely restricted.

However, there were changes, although the tradition of the Old

Navy lingered on. Some remarks made by a shipmate of M'Pherson's shortly before the Battle of Navarino should possibly not be taken too seriously and clearly M'Pherson himself somewhat discounts them, yet they do represent a tradition of the Old Navy:

'I say, Fitzpatrick; if you have any debts to pay, this will be the day, my boy, for rubbing out chalks.' 'What do you mean, Jew', said the man, 'I didn't understand you.' 'Don't understand me, you greenhorn! What man! Don't you know that in the heat of action a poor fellow has a chance of squaring yards with some of his tyrants. I saw the Captain of a ship I was of in the shooting season pinned to the gangway, where he was standing, with a crow-bar; it made him think the devil killed him, and he deserved it, for he was a Tartar!' I shuddered at this account of a deliberate murder, but I believe it is a very uncommon method of revenge, either in the British Navy or army.

Another incident which took place shortly before the battle though, emphasises the better side,

The Drum beat retreat, and several went and fell fast asleep between the guns. While lying there, a whisper arose of 'The Captain! The Captain!' Some started up and endeavoured to rouse others, but the Captain said, 'Let them lie, let them lie, poor fellows; they have enough to do before night!' and walking forward, he stepped over them with good care. By such small kindnesses did Captain Bathurst gain the affection of his crew.

One great and permanent change, however, had already taken place. Charles M'Pherson, with all his other shipmates, was a volunteer. The Press Gang remained legal—and in certain respects it possibly still is—but after 1815 it never went out again, and though the argument raged fiercely over how the navy could be manned in times of national emergency, more and more came to reject the Press Gang as a possibility. As the problem never arose for the rest of the century, it remained a matter for academic debate. Recruits for the navy might at times be scarce, but in general there were enough of them to meet the demands.

Still, in most other respects, Charles M'Pherson's experiences were far nearer to those of a seaman of the French Wars than to any of his successors. Like many before him, Charles M'Pherson at the age of seventeen, against his parents' wishes, ran away from his Scottish home to go to sea. His life from then on was very similar to that of his predecessors. He spent three months in a receiving ship, *H.M.S. Bittern*. During his first day he had a fight with a Petty Officer and knocked him out. He was cheated by the Purser, scrubbed the decks with holystone, he got drunk, thought of running away and was angered by the arbitrariness of the officers. He does claim that after the first day he never again thought of running away, but equally he did not re-enlist when he had the opportunity. He served for a time in the *Brittannia* and from there joined the *Genoa*. In that ship, he served for fourteen months of Lisbon, anchored in the Tagus with—shades of the Old Navy—virtually no shore leave. Then, after a brief Mediterranean cruise they arrived of Navarino with the results that have already been told.

The return to England marked the end of Charles M'Pherson's service. He gives no reason for his 'retirement'. It may have been the flogging meted out to the boat's crew, and others; it may have been the absence of shore leave, or even simply because it was the end of the *Genoa's* commission. All M'Pherson adds is that

> Captain Dickinson passed the word round the ship that he was going to take command of the *Wasp*, sloop-of-war, and would be happy if any of the young men would volunteer for her. A good number joined her but I thought it better notwithstanding our respect for Captain Dickinson to steer north as I had just got and seen enough of the service.

The last night on board was spent with some vigour:

> That night we slept none. The men were all merry and mischevious. If any one endeavoured to lie down he was sure to get a bucket of water dashed over him. We gathered round the galley fire, and with singing, roaring, drinking and playing all manner of practical jokes, we ushered in the morning which was to be our last together.

And on the following day:

> The Commissioner's yacht having hauled up alongside, we were ordered to go down as we stood by the ship's books and get our pay. It was pretty late in the day when we got ashore, and on slipping over the side, I cast a long last look at the old ship which had carried us faithfully through so many a danger. I left my baggage in the cash office, after taking my place for Liverpool, and next morning started for the Land of Cakes.

9

H.M.S. 'EXCELLENT'

(1830)

*The changes in naval gunnery and
the beginning of a scientific navy*

THE PICTURE OF THE NAVY that the seamen have given so far has not
been a particularly attractive one, but conditions on the lower deck
were deplorable and they continued for at least forty years after
the end of the Napoleonic Wars as later writers testify, though
Jack Nastyface writing in 1835 recalled punishments that had long
been abolished. The situation was improving, partly at least because after 1815 it was a smaller navy and also as a result of the
efforts of the Evangelicals to improve the 'moral tone' of the Navy.
In addition, after Navarino, one of the most important elements in
this change was the naval gunnery school at Portsmouth—H.M.S.
Excellent. In the first place the establishment of the *Excellent* was
the first step in the creation of a 'scientific' navy, with all that this
implies. As previous writers have shown, the personnel available
for the navy was not very promising material for the creation of
scientifically trained gun crews, and indeed no attempt was made,
as the following extract shows:

> With such materials to work with, it was Nelson's plain bull-dog
> policy, as well as practice, to run straight at his inexperienced
> enemy, without evolutions or circumlocutions. A considerable
> proportion of the old-fashioned long cannon were exchanged
> for cannonades of about two-thirds their length and weight.
> This was done because for yard arm practice, short guns are as
> good as long ones, indeed infinitely better, being more easily
> worked and consequently requiring fewer men. Thus manned
> and armed, as our Fleet bore down upon its antagonist, the
> scene on board was strongly characteristic of the British people.

In many instances, especially in hot latitudes, the ship's company were naked to the waist. They stood as from stem to stern silent at their quarters, clustered on each side of their respective guns, the centre of each deck remaining unoccupied.

Their calm, noble, manly countenances, and the tranquility of their powerful muscles, soon to be strained to their very utmost, were indicative of repose or even of peace. Yet they stood, without metaphor, in the very chamber of death. A short prayer was offered up in every well regulated ship, large tubs of water stood in the gratings of the main hatchway to allay the thirst invariably created by the smoke of gunpowder. The precaution was commonly taken of preparing sand for the deck, to enable the men to keep their feet when the deck should become clotted with blood. The narrow structure between decks soon would become in all probability the temple of victory: nevertheless, to those destined during the action to be thrown by their comrades as corpses out of the very portholes through which they had fired, it was indeed the temple of death. To those who have never witnessed the wholesale destruction of their fellow creatures, it would be impossible to describe the scene of excitement that existed during an action between the two vessels pouring broadsides into each other. The long wooden spounges which on being withdrawn from the gun necessarily protruded many feet through the ports were often snatched out of the hands of our men by the crew of the enemy. It was the custom then to serve out to each gun a spare rope sponge. This detail gives some idea of the short distance at which actions were occasionally fought.

Nelson's system of 'close quarters' resulted in the neglect of the science of gunnery. No Midshipman or Commissioned Officer was taught the principles of gunnery and it did not figure in the lists of subjects for examination. Manoeuvring of the ship after contact had been made with the enemy or prudence of any sort was 'unworthy of the British Flag', and decried. This was the direct consequence of Nelson's famous adage, 'No captain can do very wrong if he places his ship alongside that of an enemy.' To do less was to act in an unmanly fashion.

The idea of aiming the guns at the enemy seemed almost superfluous. No sights were fitted to the guns, and the captain of the guns looked along the top of the barrel and roughly pointed the gun at anything he could see through the smoke. The guns, however, were short and considerably tapered towards the mouth, so that the line along which the aimer looked was at a definite angle to the actual direction in which the bore of the barrel was pointing, and along which the shot was actually fired. As a consequence it was generally assumed in the fleet that the shot always rose as it left a gun.

The accuracy of the shooting was never seriously questioned, for everyone believed that, in any engagement with French or Spaniard, there was only one possible result. Down would come the enemy flag, to be followed by three glorious British cheers. As John Nicol wrote in his description of the battle of Cape St. Vincent, already quoted, 'For us to strike was out of the question.'

The aiming of the guns, though, was not the only problem of gunnery that was not considered. The guns themselves were grossly misused— it was not even a question of double shotting the guns—a doubtful expedient at any but the closest quarters. The guns were sometimes treble-shotted and the more foolhardy even loaded the guns with anything they could lay their hands on, as is shown in the following extract from the naval cooper, John Nicol's account of the action between the *Surprise* and the American frigate *Jason*, already quoted.

> I was serving powder as busy as I could, the shot and splinters flying in all directions when I heard the Irishman call from one of the guns (they fought like devils and the captain was fond of them on that account) 'Halloo bungs, where are you ?'.
>
> I looked to their gun and saw the two horns of my study (his anvil) across its mouth; the next moment it was through the *Jason's* side. The rogues thus disposed of my study which I had been using just before the action commenced and had placed in a secure place, as I thought, out of their reach. 'Bungs for ever!' they shouted when they saw the dreadful hole it made in the Jason's side. Bungs is the name they always gave the cooper.'

Successful though the shot may have been in this case, it seems rather an expensive projectile. However, so long as the British ships were successful there seemed no reason to change the system of gunnery.

There seems little doubt that the main reason for the successes against the French and the Spaniards was the outstanding courage of the British seamen, both officers and men. In many respects the

Captain was in a more dangerous situation than the crew, since it required great personal courage to walk the upper deck amidst the enemy's shot and shell, having knowingly placed your ship as close as possible alongside the enemy.

The old established prejudice that the French fired at the rigging in order to disable the enemy ships and to escape the fight while the British ships aimed at the hulk to sink them, has little basis in fact. In general, the French fought gallantly and had every intention of firing at the guns which were causing so much havoc among them. The only trouble was that too often they missed, and also they did not fire fast enough.

It is conceivable that the overshotting of the British guns on the one hand, and the over-aiming on the other, cancelled each other out, and resulted in surprisingly accurate shooting. Another factor that may have affected the issue is that more often than not the English obtained the 'wind gage', that is to say the wind blew them *onto* the enemy. Given the angle of the ships in the wind, the British guns therefore pointed down at the French, while the French guns pointed up over the British.

However, the success of the British and the failure of the French lay more in the superiority of the seamanship, training and morals of British seamen. To a certain extent it was simply a matter of 'sea-time'. In Mahan's phrase, 'The world has never seen a more impressive demonstration of the influence of sea power upon its history. Those far distant, storm-beaten ships, upon which the Grand Army never looked, stood between it and the dominion of the world.' And it was simply because those ships were storm beaten that they were successful. As previous extracts have shown, there was little fun to be had patrolling off Brest or Toulon in all weather, and the occasional action was a wonderful relief, but in the good ships this monotonous time was profitably spent so that the standard of seamanship was very high. The French, in harbour, nestling beneath the cannon of their forts, could gain no such experience.

The British seamen themselves were always keen to be at their enemies because this meant not merely prize money if they were successful, but a change from the deadly monotony of beating into the wind off a foreign coast and also the chance of a return to harbour and the pleasures that that entailed. For the French seamen, snug and comfortable in port, there was little to be gained. A victory might, conceivably, be won but it would probably mean an extension of hardship. They fought bravely, but too often merely with the courage of desperation.

If the war against Napoleon had been the only operation of the British fleet, it seems probable that the necessary revolution in gunnery and tactics would have been even slower to mature, but in 1812 war developed between England and the United States of America. In this, the British were by no means overwhelmingly successful. The capture of the *Macedonia* by the American frigate *United States* has already been described by Samuel Leech, and this was by no means the only defeat inflicted on the British Navy by the Americans. Indeed, except for the one notable exception, the engagement between the *Shannon* and the *Chesapeake*, in single ship action the American frigates were overwhelmingly successful. Also, in engagements in the Great Lakes, American warships won several notable victories. Part of the reason for the American success was that their frigates were, on average, a third larger than their British counter-parts and carried a similarly larger proportion of men. There is no doubt, for example, that the *Macedonian* was inferior in fire power to the *United States*. This was generally considered at the time to be a sufficient reason for British failures and only very few pointed to the inadequacies of the British gunnery. There is little doubt, though, that the inaccuracy of the British shooting was a major factor in the American victories. This is borne out by the fact that the captain of the *Shannon*, Philip Broke, was noted for his enthusiasm for gunnery and the ship itself was famed for its efficiency in this respect. The *Shannon* was inferior to the American in fire power and men, but Broke had the 'Great Guns' sighted and regularly exercised by the crew, firing generally twice a week at targets—an unheard of practice at that time. The prowess of the *Shannon's* gunnery was, however, somewhat forgotten because of the dramatic quality of the engagement itself. Before the *Chesapeake* left Boston, Captain Broke sent a challenge to the American Captain Lawrence:

> Sir,—As the *Chesapeake* appears now ready for sea, I request you will do me the favour to meet the *Shannon* with her, ship to ship, to try the fortune of our respective flags. . . .

The knightly element of the challenge, together with five previous British failures, gave the duel an almost homeric fame really more applicable to the legendary struggle between St. George and the Dragon than to a battle between two men-of-war.

Broke himself was badly wounded and never again able to go into active service, furthering the legend still more. For Tom Brown at Rugby nearly fifty years later, the glory of the *Shannon* and her Commander was a favourite theme for songs among British schoolboys. In the process the real reason for the victory tended to be forgotten. The victory was won largely because on the one hand the American ship had only recently been commissioned, and on the other because of the accuracy of the British gunnery.

In the long run, in spite of later American successes, especially on Lake Erie, the American coast, like the French, was blockaded and their trade brought to a virtual standstill. This was achieved by the sheer weight of power of the British Navy, especially when, after the defeat of Napoleon, further ships could be transferred to the other side of the Atlantic. In 1811 American exports totalled $45 million. In 1813 $25 million, and in 1814 they had been reduced to seven million dollars. The Americans had no ships of the line so that no Fleet action could take place to demonstrate their superior gunnery. As a result of the successful blockade, the lessons of the early part of the war tended to be forgotten and, given the enormous reduction in the fleet after 1815, for the next fifteen years little was actually done about improving the gunnery of the navy.

Philip Broke himself and several other eminent officers made repeated attempts to introduce improvements into the practice of naval gunnery, but with little success. Probably the only real achievement was to get half the guns fitted with sights. This still meant that the other half were pointed in the old manner and remained as inaccurate as ever. This practice was justified by the Admiralty on grounds of economy.

This is not the place to go into the details of the long battle fought with the Admiralty by a number of eminent naval officers to establish some form of gunnery school for the navy. However, in 1830, chiefly due to an appeal by General Sir Howard Douglas to the Admiralty, a school was started in H.M.S. *Excellent* and two years later it was permanently established as the home of naval gunnery under Captain Thomas Hastings. An extract from the *United Services Journal* of 1832 describes the school in its infancy.

Their Lordships have directed that a certain number of active and carefully chosen seamen, not above 30 years of age shall be engaged for 5 years at an advanced rate of pay; and at the expiration of this period, the term may be renewed, at a further advance of pay. From this body of men, duly instructed, it is proposed that, in future, the gunners, gunners'-mates and yeomen of the powder-room, will be selected, in order that they may communicate to the whole crew of the ships to which they may be appointed, the knowledge which they have acquired at the depot.

This in itself was revolutionary enough, but the actual instruction given was even more so.

. . . In the 1st place you will learn, I am sure, with particular satisfaction, that not merely the seamen are instructed in their various duties at the gun, but also the midshipmen, of whom there are a considerable number on board—very fine and intelligent young men—and likewise the Commissioned Officers. Every person, in short, without exception, on board the *Excellent* is required not only to make himself thoroughly—I may say familiarly, acquainted with the names of every part of the gun and carriage, to the smallest bolt, rope, or ring, but he must understand, and prove that he does understand, their several uses. For example, he must explain what is meant by the term 'dispart', in terms of lineal magnitude and also in degrees how it is taken, what are its purposes, and what the consequences of error; what is meant by 'line of metal range', what constitutes 'point blank', and, in a word, what is the effect on the range of a shot by elevating or depressing the gun. He must become acquainted with all the details relating to proportions of powder in the different charges, the effect of double shotting and so on. He must also prove that he is perfectly master, in his own person, of every part of the manual exercise; and, by repeated drilling, both in working with his own hands at each of the stations into which the crew of the gun is divided, and in giving the word of command, render himself fully competent to take any station at any gun and under any circumstances. . .

. . . Neither officer nor man is admitted to the actual firing practice till he satisfies the commanding officer that he is completely versed in the manual exercise and in giving the word of command; and it is amusing to see the eagerness with which they desire to step up the humdrum routine of mere drilling without shot—a sort of playing at the movements—to the more exciting process of actual firing. . . The staff take the utmost pains to explain the purpose of every operation, even to the very minutest, to the seamen, as well as to the officers, who show, in the most satisfactory manner, the importance of this constant system of explanatory discipline. I was amused one day by Captain Hastings endeavouring—but for some time quite ineffectually—to explain to a sailor how to use his handspike to the greatest purpose in training his gun. The honest fellow had got into a habit, in some other ship, of using this lever to great disadvantage. Captain Hastings, however, instead of merely ordering the man to relinquish his own method, and adopt that of the system established on board the *Excellent* contented himself at first by requiring the man to move the gun about for some time, according to the method which he evidently considered the best. 'Now', said the judicious commanding officer, 'take notice how I use the handspike, and you shall try the difference yourself.' The sailor watched the process with great attention, then resumed the handspike, and found, to his great surprise, that the gun now moved about with as much comparative ease as if from a 32-pounder, it has been changed to a 12-pounder. 'What think you know?' asked the Commander. 'I'll never use the other way as long as I live Sir', came the pithy reply.

. . . The seamen are also encouraged to improve themselves in reading, writing, and to a certain small extent in cyphering. The men themselves appear to be fully sensible that an ignorant man cannot be a good gunner; as even the simplest problem—that for instance of disparting a gun—requires some knowledge of figures; those who cannot read soon discover the advantage which their better informed companions possess over them and they become eager to learn. It is found to be very useful, also to have the means of studying at leisure the instructions for the manual and other exercises. Pride likewise enters into this matter; so that from one motive to another these incipient seamen gunners appear to consider ignorance as a degradation, and having themselves become sincerely anxious to learn, they have been met more than half way: and one of their own number, formerly mate of an Indiaman, acts as teacher to the rest, with so much success, that in time an express rating will probably be added to the establishment for this petty officer.

. . . The *Excellent* has been moored head and stern within 50 yds of the upper end of the Dockyard, so that her starboard side fronts the long extent of mud banks, nearly in the direction of Fareham; and no guns are fired with shot except when the banks are covered with water. A red flag is hoisted on board the *Excellent* during such periods of practice and also on board another ship, lying about a mile further up. The signal is well understood by all the watermen who take care to keep out of the line of fire. It will, however, not infrequently happen, that boats do cross, in spite of this warning, and in spite of the still more ominous notice of shot grazing or spinning along in what is called 'duck and drake' fashion. Whence this foolhardiness or stupidity arises, it is needless to inquire but as it becomes the duty of the officers on board the *Excellent* to intermit firing when any boat is in the way, the signal flag at the distant ship is 'dipped' as it is called, or lowered half-mast, when any boat is passing so near as to render it unsafe to fire. It may be asked, why not fire when the tide is out? But it appears the eagerness of the people to pick up the shot is so great, that the risk would be greater. The shot so recovered by these 'mud-larks' are carried over to Gosport and sold for a mere trifle to the iron founders. Surely it would be good economy in Government to receive back these shot, and to pay for them, not the full original value, of course, but something, probably much higher than the iron founders can afford to give. (This suggestion was later carried into practice and it was possible for a 'mud-lark' to earn up to 11s. a day by returning shot to the *Excellent*.)

. . . It is extremely interesting to observe the generous spirit which pervades the whole of this interesting establishment. Everything is conducted with a degree of order, regularity, and good humour, which point out to those who have attended to such things that one uniform and temperate system of discipline pervades the whole.

One of the main changes instituted in the *Excellent* was the first stage of a complete revolution in the relationship between the officers and men. One can scarcely imagine the Hon. Sir Charles Paget competing against the ratings in gun drill, yet this was the practice in the *Excellent* at an early stage. Admiral Moresby, who qualified as a Gunnery Lieutenant in 1849, describing the course wrote:

The rest of the day was occupied in various classes, interrupted once a week by first quarters, when officers and men competed in great gun drill. The guns were secured for sea, the decks cleared. Then, as the stirring drums beat to quarters, with a rush that made the old ship tremble, each crew took up its station, and proud was the one which, after loading and running out, first stood to attention. Generally, but not by any means always, this would be the officers' gun, and so also in the following evolutions.

It was a fine struggle, and the big guns flew from one end of the ship to another like playthings. A crushed finger still reminds me how severely a bit of clumsiness could be punished at such times.

Not that all the exercises were quite so serious, but in most of them officers and men competed on equal terms.

The one other exercise, especially devised by the Captain, was known as 'toggle and mount', and this always evoked much mirth, though the purpose was serious. After this manner did we toggle: all hands were massed on one side of the quarter deck, variously armed, in the motley manner of the period with boarding pikes, tomahawks, cutlasses, pistols, and muskets, a party carrying scaling ladders. The poop represented the enemy's fortress, to be captured by bold assault over the poop rail.

When all was ready, we were marched round the forecastle, and on reaching the opposite gangway the order was given 'toggle and mount'—and that was the supreme moment, and with a frantic rush and suppressed laughter, the ladders were toggled and upreared, and over the poop rail we surged in impetuous attack, to be brought up by the taffrail as we cut and thrust wildly in the air. It was all exceedingly absurd and delightful.

Important though the technical innovations were, and they certainly had an effect on the outlook and attitude of the seamen, they would not alone account for the crucial part that the *Excellent* played in the changing pattern of life on the lower deck. It was the need to acquire these techniques that resulted in the changes. Initially, for the seamen, it was only being able to read and write and 'cypher a little' that was necessary. Yet this in itself was an important step forward. Some of Nelson's seamen, as we have seen, certainly could write, but as seamen all that was required of them was agility in climbing in and out of the rigging like monkeys, manual dexterity in being able to handle ropes and sails in all conditions, and physical stamina to withstand the hardships imposed by the conditions of service. It was little short of complete heresy to suggest that intellectual ability of any sort was a qualification for a lower deck rating, or even for an officer, for that matter. But more significant still, H.M.S. *Excellent* demanded, and on the whole got, a different sort of recruit. The Captains of Nelson's time looked for prime seamen. If they had never served a day in the navy—no matter. Indeed, in many respects merchant seamen might be preferred since frequently those who had served only in the Navy had but little chance to learn much seamanship as these tasks generally fell to trained seamen and few attempts were made to instruct them in the art.

As for gunnery, the Irishmen, who as John Nicol records were much liked by his Captain, made the best fighting men. But the wild Irishman was not the best person to learn the new drills on board H.M.S. *Excellent*. A new sort of recruit had to be attracted and hence the terms of engagement: five or seven years at an increased rate of pay with the option of a further period of five years. This was at a time when the normal term was only for the commission of the ship, generally between three and four years, though sometimes it could be merely a few months. Thus, one of the most important elements introduced from the very beginning of the *Excellent* was the idea of continuous service. It was indeed to be another 25 years before this was introduced into the Navy as a whole, and longer still before it became the general rule. Nevertheless, this was a most important beginning. For a number of years the system on H.M.S. *Excellent* was held up by pamphleteers as the solution of the navy's manning problem so that, in spite of opposition from a number of naval officers who regarded the introduction of continuous service as a restriction of the sailor's age-old right to choose his ship, the system was finally introduced and was a most important element in the transformation of the navy.

The other crucial change as has already been noted was in the relationships between officers and men. From the examples written by the seamen quoted earlier in the book, it is clear that, though in some cases the officers were respected and at times even revered, they were regarded as existing on a totally different level. Some sailors, like Jack Nastyface, obviously resented this, though probably not as markedly as a later sailor, John Tilling, since few egalitarian ideas had penetrated the lower deck in the early part of the century. What Jack Nastyface really resented was ill usage by the officers. This certainly was conspicuously absent in the *Excellent*, but the fact that the officers under training had to drill against the men was even more revolutionary and was in line with the new attitude towards class divisions. It was obviously, at this point, only in a very elementary stage, but the idea that officers should prove their superiority to the men in practical exercises was something almost unheard of in the Old Navy. The midshipmen described by Jack Nastyface and Samuel Leech were detested by the men because of the way in which they misused their power. In the *Excellent* the officers under training did not have that power.

The revolution brought about in the *Excellent* was not complete or immediate. Each of the three changes already mentioned—the growing scientific approach, the introduction of continuous service and the altering relationship between officers and men—made much immediate impact, but the men themselves were different as the following letter, written by a young seamen under training to his father in Worcestershire, shows:

Dec. 15th 1838

My Dear Father,
I suppose by this time you have received my last letter. I shall endeavour to give you an idea in this of my different duties. They pipe up hammocks at 6 o'clock in the morning, we then clean ourselves and the mess tables till 7 o'clock. We are then piped to breakfast, which consists of Cocoa; at half past 7 o'clock, I go to the rigging loft in the dockyard till 12 o'clock; which is very good of Captain Hastings to put me there, being the only one in the ship that goes there. At 12 o'clock on board again and piped to dinner. At 1 o'clock the drum beats to quarters where we are instructed in the great gun exercise; after that the sword and musket exercises, the boats are hoisted up and our days work is nearly done. At half past four o'clock, tea, and the liberty men are piped away.

I am a mizzentop man. No. 86 at instructions. I shall have to buy a set of instruments before long, as soon as ever I get out of the second instructions, because I shall be put in the school room and shall not be able to do without them. I have had to buy several things already; a set of cards of instruction I have also bought, 3/6 the set, and a few clothes as we must dress all alike, when we are mustered which is every morning and must not dress in white in the winter. I pay 2/– per month for washing, subscribe twopence per month to an excellent library and 1/– entrance money. I shall have to buy a fresh monkey jacket as mine is so very shabby and you *must be clean and neat* and if you are always so, you are sure to be taken notice of. I am afraid I shall not be able to do without that money that Uncle John Jukes was so kind to give me. I do not like to draw any money here, at all events not for this five or six months; if you send it be sure to pay a penny with it and direct to me as J. Burnett Seaman-Gunner on board H.M.S. *Excellent* Portsmouth. I am very comfortable and happy here and quite well; what time I have to spare is fully taken up in learning my cards of instruction. Let me know when Sam comes home that I may write, and let me know how you all are and how everything goes on. I must now conclude for they are piping for Hammocks to be slung; give my best love to all dear friends and my grandmother, (and let me know particularly how she is) and dear Aunt Mary, and Mary, and if anyone should come near here to be sure to come and see me; there is a good deal to see, and now my dear father believe me, I remain your ever affectionate son.

John Alexander Burnett.

It is possibly unfair on other aspects of the naval service to end this part of the story with a description of the improvements in naval gunnery. Other factors were playing a considerable part in changing the conditions of the Royal Navy. Arctic exploration drew officers and men closer together. The Navy's role of policeman also helped in this way though often, when the role was the prevention of African slavery, the unity lay in death rather than life.

> Beware and take care of the bights of Benin,
> There's forty goes out for one that comes in.

Even so, H.M.S. *Excellent* did pave the way for the great changes that were shortly to overwhelm the 'Old' Navy. In the matter of material there was, to begin with, little enough change. The gun they aimed was still the 'great' gun, fired broadside, not the turret gun of later generations. The ships for which they trained their gunners were the old wooden walls of Nelson's or even Blake's Navy. Armour plating to protect the ships' sides was a problem that naval gunnery had not yet had to face. The new naval gunnery school though, did introduce 'scientific' ideas into the Navy for almost the first time. It did demand something more of the sailors than simple manly courage, and the public image of the sailor was thereby improved.

As we have seen, major changes were essential in three fields if the sailor's life was to be made tolerable—recruiting, the brutal treatment meted out to the men by the officers and the drunken and licentious behaviour of the men themselves.

For the changes over recruitment and the abolition of the Press Gang, public opinion was probably more responsible than H.M.S. *Excellent*. By the 1830's impressment was, for most people, unthinkable. Liberty had become a prized possession of all Englishmen and though they had long cried 'Britons never will be slaves', by the time Queen Victoria came to the throne in 1837 most people really believed that this should be so, even if in practice it was not. H.M.S. *Excellent* was important in that it provided an alternative system whereby men were drafted to the service by a better rate of pay and a secure term of employment, not compelled to serve at the rope's end. Jack Nastyface, writing in 1835, found an appreciative audience. It is doubtful whether he would have done in 1815.

Again, over the question of relationships between officers and men, H.M.S. *Excellent* led the way. Of course as we have seen there were plenty of good officers before 1830. Collingwood in H.M.S. *Culloden*, instructing the boys and making certain that they were put under the care of the best seamen, was doing just what the officers in the gunnery school were later to do. But all this depended on the Admiral or Captain concerned. H.M.S. *Excellent* could not change this—a generation of naval officers had to pass away and a new class of officers had to arise before this could become the rule. Above all the Admiralty had to lay down rules and regulations which all officers had to obey and not allow individual Captains' dictatorial authority over every aspect of their men's lives.

In the improvement of the sailors' behaviour the gunnery school produced the least effect, though by giving the men a technical pride in their work and a secure position it did help. What was really effective was the conscience of English society in general. The fact that every man-of-war in port was virtually a floating brothel was hardly significant to Nelson and his contemporaries; after all he himself was not above reproach over the question of sexual morality. It was still possible for Charles M'Pherson to indulge his appetites in this respect fairly freely, and it was not until the 1830's that any serious attempt was made to control this aspect of life on the lower deck. Then, groups of Evangelicals attempted to improve the moral tone of the Navy by persuading sailors of the sinfulness of their lives. This culminated in the work of Aggie Weston, who, among other achievements founded 'Sailors Rests' in the seaports so that the men had somewhere besides pubs and brothels to go ashore. This, though, was not achieved for another thirty years.

The change was not sudden, nor by 1830 was it complete. An able seaman, John Tilling, could write in the 1860's the same sort of criticism about officers as Jack Nastyface, and if women by then no longer played so prominent a part on board ship as they had, even as late as Navarino, drunkenness was even more rife.

In the long run these changes amounted to a revolution, and not least significant was the three-fold change in material—the sails were replaced by steam, the wooden walls by iron or steel, and the broadside guns by turrets; but this was the work of another generation, and there is another generation of sailors to tell the tale—or possibly to spin the yarn, and I hope to deal with these matters in another volume.

APPENDIX 1

NOTES ON ILLUSTRATIONS

Between pages 100 and 101

Sailors on a Cruise The *Arethusa* under the command of Edward Pellew had taken a French squadron off Ireland and all were well provided with Prize Money. Five of the sailors bought a coach, horses and all, and then hired a coachman to drive them about for three days—but all hands kept on deck; for what was the use of sculking under hatches in fine weather? So they stored the craft well with grog and 'bacca—got all snug, with a fiddler forward and an organ grinder abaft, and carried on between Plymouth and Dock during the whole time they stopped on shore.

The Point of Honour The Captain had heard one of the sailors talking out of turn and had ordered him to be punished. In fact it was another seaman who had been talking and though the other seaman said nothing at first, when he saw his mate about to be given two dozen lashes, he tore off his jacket and proclaimed his guilt. The Captain let them both off.

Between pages 140 and 141

H.M.S. *Hastings* After the death of her husband, William IV, Queen Adelaide went on a cruise to Malta in H.M.S. *Hastings*. This is an artist's impression of the quarter-deck and poop of the ship.

With the exception of the caricatures by Cruikshank, which are from the book *Greenwich Hospital*, published in 1826, all the other illustrations come from the National Maritime Museum, Greenwich, to whom grateful acknowledgement is made for permission to reproduce them.

APPENDIX 2

THE FULL-RIGGED SHIP

'Everyone who has looked upon a full-rigged ship must have noticed some distance up the main mast a framework or platform like a little scaffold. A similar construction may be observed on the fore- and mizen-mast, if the ship be a large one. This platform is called the "top", and its principal object is to extend the ladder-like ropes called shrouds that reach from the outer edge to the head of the mast next above, which latter is the topmast. It must be observed that the "masts" of a ship, as understood by "landsmen" are each divided into a number of pieces in the reckoning of a sailor. For instance, in a ship or barque, there are three, which are called respectively the main, fore-, and mizzen-masts—the main-mast being near the middle of the ship, the foremast forward, towards the bows, and the mizen-mast "aft", near the stern or poop. But each one of these is divided into several pieces, which pieces have distinct names in the sailors' vocabulary. Thus, the "mainmast" to a sailor is not the whole of that long straight stick which rises up out of the middle of a ship's deck and points like a spire to the sky. On the contrary, the mainmast terminates a little above the platform just mentioned, and is therefore designated the "maintop". Another mast, quite distinct from this and made up out of a separate piece of timber there begins, and runs up for nearly an equal length, but of course more slender than the mainmast itself, which latter supports it. This second is called the "maintop-mast". Above that a third is elevated, supported upon the topmast head by checks, treasles and crosstrees. This is shorter and more slender than the maintop-mast, and is named the "maintop-gallant-mast", and above this again, the "main-royal-mast" is similarly raised—though it is only in the largest and best rigged vessels that a royal mast is used. The "main-royal-mast" terminates the structure and its top, or head is usually crowned with a flat circular piece of wood called the main-truck, which is the most elevated point in the ship. The fore- and mizen-masts are similarly divided, though the latter is much shorter than either of the others, and rarely the latter is much shorter than either of the others, and rarely has topgallant sails, and still more rarely "royals".'

THE FULL-RIGGED SHIP

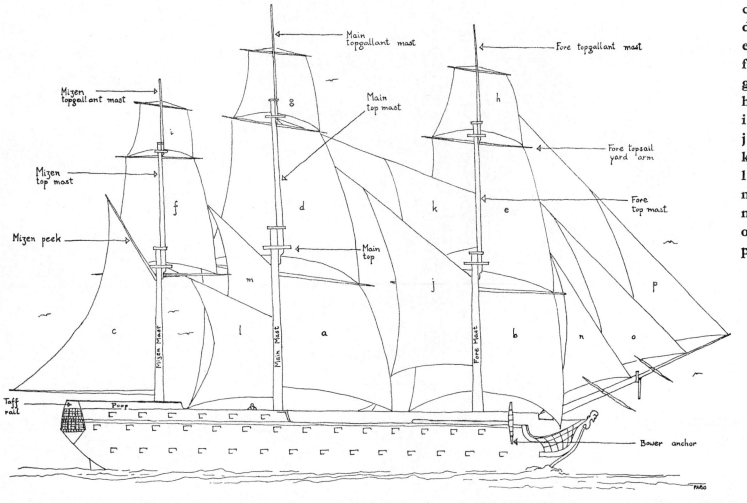

Main topgallant mast

Fore topgallant mast

Mizen topgallant mast

Main top mast

Mizen top mast

Fore topsail yard 'arm

Mizen peek

Fore top mast

Main top

Taff rail

Poop

Bower anchor

Mizen Mast

Main Mast

Fore Mast

LIST OF NAUTICAL TERMS

Athwart (p. 112). Across. (See also *Hawse*.)

Bashaw (p. 61). A Turkish title of honour and command; more properly Pasha.

Beach-master (p. 29). The officer appointed to take command of a landing party. 'His acts when in the heat of action if he summarily shoots a coward are unquestioned.'

Bight (p. 156). A loop in the middle of the rope as opposed to the ends.

Birds of passage (p. 48). Those not staying on board long.

Bower cable (p. 162). The cable attached to one of the anchors in the bows.

Braces (p. 38). The ropes belonging to the yards of a ship.

Brig (p. 122). A two-masted, square-rigged vessel.

Brûlot (p. 150). A fire-ship.

Bunting (p. 149). The material of which signalling flags are made— hence the flags themselves.

Canister (p. 38). Short for Canister Shot, also called Case Shot. Consists of a number of small iron balls packed into a cylindrical case which bursts on impact. (See also *Grape Shot*.)

Carrick bend (p. 158). A kind of knot used for joining two hawsers (special heavy ropes) together.

Carronades (p. 11). A short gun capable of carrying a large ball and generally carried on the upper deck; particularly useful at close quarters. Named after the foundry in Scotland where they were first made.

Caulkers (p. 8). Those who 'Caulk' or fill the seams between the 'planks' of a ship to keep it watertight.

Close reefing (p. 135). Taking in the last reefs in the sail.

Combings (p. 147). Raised ridges about the edges of hatches or openings to prevent the water on deck from running down below.

Cooper (p. 18). A man who repairs casks and barrels. In the navy generally a Petty Officer.

Copper (p. 140). The copper with which the bottom of a wooden ship was covered to protect it.

Coppers (p. 142). The ship's boilers, for cooking.

Cut them out (p. 17). To sail into an enemy harbour and capture a vessel using only the ship's boats.

Davy (p. 147). ie: Davy Jones' locker—the bottom of the sea.

Dispart (p. 175). The extent to which a gun tapers towards the muzzle, resulting in the line of sight along the gun differing from the line of the shot itself.

Dog Watches (p. 47). The 'half' watches of two hours each, from 4 pm. to 6 pm. and from 6 pm. to 8 pm. thus making seven watches in the 24 hours and allowing men to automatically change their hours of work each day.

Earing (p. 114). Certain small ropes employed to fasten the upper corners of a sail to its yard.

Eyebolts (p. 164). Bolts which have an eye or opening in one end for hooking tackles ('pulleys') to, or fastening ropes.

Fetch off the land (p. 135). Fetch means to reach or arrive at—hence sail away from the land and not go aground.

Fifer (p. 46). One who plays the fife—a shrill pipe.

Fifer and fiddler. 'Two very important aids in eliciting exact discipline for hoisting, warping and heaving at the capstan in proper time.'

Gaff. Spar attached to the top of sail, as opposed to the boom which is attached to the bottom.

Gineva (p. 127). A name for gin. (See also *Hollands*.)

Gingerbread work (p. 154). Profusely carved decoration on a ship.

Going-about (p. 135). Altering course through the wind so that at one point the wind is dead ahead. (See also *Tacking*.)

Grape shot (p. 40). A missile, between Case Shot and Solid or Round Shot, consisting of a number of small shot, not normally placed in a canister. (See also *Canister*.)

Grog; Three-water or *Five-water* (p. 22). Rum mixed with water in the ratio of one of rum to three or five of water.

Guinea man (p. 122). A negro slave ship.

Half deck (p. 156). The area of deck immediately forward of the Quarter Deck.

Hawse (p. 112). A general term, strictly that part of a vessel's bow where holes are cut for her cables to pass through but sometimes used to mean simply the bows. Hence, 'Arthwart the enemy's hawse' means to get across his bows where he cannot bring his guns to bear and your broadside can fire at him.

Hawser (p. 157). A large heavy rope used for hauling, warping or mooring.

Head braces (p. 79). Ropes used for squaring or traversing horizontally the upper yards of the ship.

Heavy press of sail (p. 140). Carrying all the sails that can possibly be used safely.

Hollands (p. 56). Another name for Gin. (See also *Gineva*.)

Holy-stones (p. 45). Blocks of sandstone that were used for scrubbing decks, so-called because their use entailed kneeling down. Medium-sized holy-stones were called bibles, and small ones, prayer books.

Iron hoops (p. 138). Here means the hoops holding the mast together.

Jury masts (p. 23). A temporary mast erected in a ship in place of one carried away in a gale, battle etc.

Jury-rigged (p. 39). Having rigged Jury masts.

Kelson (p. 153). An internal keel, laid upon the middle of the floor timbers, immediately over the keel and serving to bind all together.

Landsman (p. 129). The rating of those on board who had never been at sea.

Langridge shot (p. 154) (or *Langrel*). 'A villanous kind of shot consisting of various fragments of iron bound together.'

Lanyard (p. 164). A short piece of rope or line made fast to anything to secure it, or as a handle.

Lanyard of the lock (p. 150). The lanyard attached to the lock or firing mechanism of the gun and used to fire it.

Larboard (p. 154). The left side of a ship when looking towards the bows. Now commonly known as Port.

Larking (p. 44). 'Frolicsome merriment.'

Lateen-rigged (p. 106). A ship that has lateen sails—triangular sails attached to a lateen yard which is slung obliquely to the mast.

Lifts (p. 156). Ropes which reach from each masthead to their respective yard-arms to steady and suspend the ends.

Liner (p. 157). Line-of-battle ship. A large ship that can fight with others in the Line-of-battle.

Line of metal range (p. 175). The line of axis of the gun.

Loblolly men (p. 37). Men who helped the surgeon and his assistants—now Sick Berth Attendants.

Log line (p. 45). A small line about 100 fathoms long which is let out as the ship is under way and used to find the ship's speed.

Lubberly (p. 98). Awkward or unseamanlike behaviour.

Main chain (p. 151). Planks to which the main-mast shrouds were attached.

Master-at-Arms (p. 133). The senior rating responsible for the discipline on board ship.

Monkey (p. 149). Powder Monkey. Boy who was detailed to supply the gun with powder.

Pinnace (p. 132). A small vessel propelled with oars and sails. As a ship's boat, in size smaller than the barge.

Pointing the ropes (p. 47). The operation of unlaying and tapering the end of a rope so that it will pass easily through a block.

Poop (p. 178). The highest and aftmost deck of a ship.

Protection (p. 6). A paper giving 'protection' against impressment.

Purser (p. 163). An officer responsible for provisions and 'slops', but not primarily for pay.

Purser's dips (p. 155). A small candle.

Quarter deck (p. 154). The deck immediately forward of the poop, but on a lower level.

Quarter-watches (p. 107). A division of the crew into four instead of the usual two watches. This is sufficient in light winds in a well conducted ship. 'The officers are in three and must not be found nodding.'

Rattan (p. 9). A Malacca cane used for wicker work, seats of chairs etc.

Reef (p. 114). A certain portion of a sail. The intention of each reef is to reduce the size of the sail in proportion to the increase of the wind.

Round Robin (p. 165). An illegal petition got up by a group of seamen.

Sail halliards (p. 115). The ropes or tackles usually employed to hoist or lower any sail.

Schooner (p. 157). Strictly a small craft with two masts and no tops but the name is also applied to fore-and-aft vessels of various classes (i.e. Vessels with their sails fore-and-aft like a modern yacht, as opposed to square-rigged where the sails are generally at right angles to the centre line of the ship.

Serving Mallet (p. 157). A mallet, grooved on the under side with which spun-yarn, or other small thread is wrapped tightly round a rope.

Sheet (p. 89). A rope fastened to one or both the lower corners of a sail to hold the bottom of the sail in a required position. Hence, with 'three sheets blowing in the wind,' the sail is out of control.

Shrouds (p. 40). The permanent or standing rigging holding up the masts etc.

Sloop (p. 129). A type of vessel. In the navy the name came to be dependant on the rank of the officer in command, i.e. if a junior officer was in command of a ship it would be called a sloop.

Slops; serve out slops (p. 166). A name given to ready-made clothes and other articles provided by the service. Hence, what is provided in this case is punishment, especially the Cat.

Spanker boom (p. 154). The boom attached to the Driver. (See diagram on p. 186.)

Springs (p. 154). A hawser laid out to some fixed object to slew a vessel proceeding to sea.

Squaring yards (p. 167). To bring the yards in 'square' by the marks on the braces.

Stanchion (p. 154). Any fixed upright support.

Stood (p. 312). The movement by which a ship advances towards a certain object or departs from it. So, stand before the wind means having the wind behind the ship.

Stern sheets (p. 162). The part of a boat between the stern and the aftmost thwart or seat, furnished with seats for passengers.

Studding sails (p. 112). Certain light sails extended in moderate breezes, on either side of the main sails, i.e. the main top studding sail is a sail attached beside the main topsail.

Sweeps (p. 105). Large oars used on board ships of war in a calm.

Tacking (p. 48). Making headway into the wind by altering course from side to side. (See also *Going About*.)

Ticket (p. 6). An official warrant of discharge.

Wearing (p. 48). Going from one tack to another by putting the ship's *stern* through the wind. Opposite of Going About.

Wind and water, between (p. 38). When sailing a ship heals over away from the wind exposing a section of the ship normally under water. This area is said to be between wind and water.

Yard (p. 10). The horizontal beam to which the sails are attached.

Yonker (p. 164). Cabin-boy, or ship-boy.

INDEX

Date Due